CONSTRUCTION TECHNOLOGY AND MANAGEMENT

A series published in association with the Chartered Institute of Building.

This series will, when complete, cover every important aspect of construction. It will be of particular relevance to the needs of students taking the CIOB Member Examinations, Parts 1 and 2, but will also be suitable for degree courses, other professional examinations, and practitioners in building, architecture, surveying and related fields.

Project Evaluation and Development
Alexander Rougvie

Law for Building Practitioners
Keith Manson

Building Technology (3 volumes)
Ian Chandler
    Vol. 1 Site Organisation and Method
    Vol. 2 Performance
    Vol. 3 Design, Production and Maintenance

The Economics of the Construction Industry
Geoffrey Briscoe

Construction Management (2 volumes)
Robert Newcombe, David Langford and Richard Fellows
    Vol. 1 Organisation Systems
    Vol. 2 Management Systems

Construction Tendering
Andrew Cook

Administration of Building Contracts
James Franks

LAW FOR BUILDING PRACTITIONERS

Keith Manson

B.T. Batsford Ltd · London

in association with the Chartered Institute of Building

© Keith Manson 1994

First published 1994

Typeset by Deltatype Ltd, Ellesmere Port, Cheshire
Printed by Redwood Books, Trowbridge, Wilts

Published by B T Batsford Limited
4 Fitzhardinge Street, London W1H 0AH

A CIP catalogue record for this book is available from the British Library

ISBN 0 7134 7259 6

CONTENTS

PREFACE

The principal purpose of this book is to meet the needs of students studying for the Member Part 1 examination in Building Law of the Chartered Institute of Building. To that end the layout of the book takes into account the topics in the syllabus and the depth of study required with those topics. I have considered what I believe to be the relevant case law, particularly with regard to torts, and explained the general principles of law.

I have included some other material which I believe will be of interest to the student and I hope will make the book helpful to others in the construction industry. Their need for a knowledge of construction law, whether as a student for other examinations or as a practising builder or other professional, may well be met by this book.

As with any book of this nature, there is a need to supplement it by reference to articles in journals and reports in newspapers of decisions in cases which deal with construction law. In this way the reader will keep up to date with the subject and be aware of developments in construction law.

I would like to express my thanks and appreciation to Sheila Williamson for her excellence, as always, in producing a typescript from my handwriting.

TABLE OF STATUTES

Note that all page references in the Table of Statutes and the Table of Cases are set in **bold**.

TABLE OF CASES

ABBREVIATIONS

A.C.	Appeal Cases (Law Reports)
All E.R.	All England Law Reports
A. and E.	Adolphus and Ellis 1834–42
Build.L.R.	Building Law Reports
Ch.	Chancery (Law Reports)
Ch.D.	Chancery Division from 1876 to 1891
Const.L.J.	Construction Law Journal
Crim.L.R.	Criminal Law Review
E.G.	Estates Gazette
E.G.C.S.	Estates Gazette Case Summaries
Ex.	Exchequer Reports
H and C	Hurlston and Coltman
H.L.Cas.	House of Lords Cases 1847–1866
I.C.R.	Industrial Courts Reports
I.R.L.R.	Industrial Relations Law Reports
K.I.R.	Knight's Industrial Reports
K.B.	Kings Bench
L.R.H.L.	Law Report, House of Lords
L.J.Q.B.	Law Journal, Queens Bench
New L.J.	New Law Journal
Ph.	Philipps
Q.B.	Queens Bench
R.T.R.	Road Traffic Reports
S.J.	Solicitors' Journal
T.L.R.	Times Law Report

1 TORTS: AN INTRODUCTION

WHAT IS A TORT

An exact definition of a tort is difficult to find. Many learned authors have made the attempt but their efforts have not resulted in one simple definition which is acceptable to everyone. One which has received possibly the greatest recognition is that of the late Professor Winfield. This is: 'Tortious liability arises from the breach of a duty primarily fixed by law; this duty is towards persons generally and its breach is redressible by an action for unliquidated damages'.

From this it can be seen that a tort is a breach of a duty fixed by law. It is a duty owed to people generally and a breach of that duty allows the person injured by the breach to sue for a sum of money to redress that injury.

A further consideration is that a tort is a civil wrong committed on a person. That person then has a right in law to sue the wrongdoer to recover damages for the wrong he has suffered.

It is important to note that a tort is a civil wrong. It is therefore a private law matter. The injured person has the right to sue but need not do so if he does not wish to. Because it is a private right the state will not intervene to assist the injured person.

In order to bring an action in tort it has to be shown that there is a right to do so recognised by law. There are circumstances where a person suffers some injury but the law does not provide a remedy for what has happened to him.

The law of torts is based mainly in the common law, in the form of judgments by the courts. In this way the body of law has been built up. At different times the common law has been found to be deficient in circumstances where the courts ought to be able to grant a remedy. Where this has occurred Parliament has intervened and passed an Act of Parliament to correct the deficiency. An example of this is the Occupiers' Liability Act 1984 which was passed in order to clarify the duty an occupier owes to trespassers. This was necessary because of the uncertainty created by the House of Lords decision in the case of *British Railways Board v Herrington* 1972.

A person suing for a breach of tort, the plaintiff, will usually seek an award by the court of unliquidated damages. That is a sum of money, fixed by the court, which is considered appropriate for the wrong done to the plaintiff. In the case of a claim where the loss can be calculated, liquidated damages, such as loss of wages following an accident the court may make an award for that amount. There may also be circumstances where an award of money is not an appropriate remedy. Here the plaintiff may seek an injunction, such as to restrain an act of trespass, or an order that some goods be returned to their owner.

THE DISTINCTION BETWEEN A TORT AND A CRIME, CONTRACT AND A BREACH OF TRUST

As we have seen, a tort is a civil wrong actionable only by the person who has suffered as a result of the breach of law. A crime, however, is a breach of public law for which the appropriate authority will bring a prosecution in the criminal court. An example of this is a breach of safety law under the Health and Safety at Work etc Act 1974, where the Health and Safety Executive will prosecute the offender. Most criminal offences are dealt with by the police.

In the case of a contract the liability under the contract only arises because the parties have entered into that relationship. In that relationship the parties agree the terms. Only the parties to the contract have rights and obligations under the contract. No duties are therefore owed to persons generally and the state is not involved. It is possible that obligations under both contract and tort may arise from the same occurrence. This would be the case if a structural engineer failed to produce a proper design of a building, when that was perfectly possible, with the result the building collapsed. Here the structural engineer would be in breach of contract to his client for the failure to produce a proper design, and liable in tort to anyone injured as a result of the collapse.

A breach of trust differs from a tort in that a special relationship which has been created is infringed. A breach of trust arises when the trustees, who have been entrusted with property for the benefit of others, are in breach of that trust to those beneficiaries. The duty therefore is owed to these people only and they only may sue for the breach of trust.

LIABILITY IN TORT

In order to succeed in an action for tort it is not generally necessary to show that the defendant acted in some particular way. Liability may arise simply because a certain thing happened for which the law recognises that the award of damages is appropriate. In some circumstances, however, a person may suffer injury for which the law does not provide a remedy.

In an action for trespass to land the occupier does not have to show that the tresspasser had an intention to trespass. The act of entering on the land without any right to do so constitutes the tort. A person will therefore be a trespasser even if he strayed innocently on the land or even when he has a reasonable belief that he had the right to be on the land. Similarly in the rule in *Rylands v Fletcher* 1868 the fact that a certain event occurred means that liability arises. It is no defence to prove that all reasonable measures were taken to prevent that occurrence. The fact that a person had a bad motive when he committed an act does not make that act a tort provided that that act was lawful. This may be seen in the House of Lords decision in *Bradford Corporation v Pickles* 1985. Here the Corporation had been buying land for a water scheme. The Corporation did not buy Pickles' land which caused him disappointment. He therefore dug a shaft in his land with the intention of interfering with the flow of ground water through his land; this then went through the Corporation's land. His action did interfere with the flow of ground water. This action however was held not to be a tort. Digging a shaft on his own land was a lawful act. The fact that he had a bad motive did not convert a lawful act into an unlawful act.

In the case of *Fowler v Lanning* 1959 a member of a shooting party who was injured by the discharge of a gun by another member of the party was unsuccessful in his claim since he was not able to show any intention or negligence. The fact that he was injured by someone did not in itself mean that he could claim damages for his injury.

Accidents for which the law provides no remedy have caused public disquiet. For this reason suggestions have been made that there should be, as exists in some other countries, a 'no fault' insurance scheme. That is, a person should be properly compensated if he has an accident, whether at work or not, without having to prove that some person had committed a tort. The Report of the Royal Commission on Civil Liability and Compensation for Personal Injury made recommendations on these lines but so far no action has been taken to put these recommendations into effect.

WHO CAN SUE AND BE SUED

The general rule in the law of tort is that the injured person can sue the person who committed that tort on him. A simple example of this is that of a pedestrian who is knocked down and injured by a negligently driven car. The injured pedestrian can sue the driver for the tort of negligence and recover damages for his injuries.

There are some exceptions to this general rule in that a person who is not directly involved may have a right to sue. This is to be found in the torts of trespass and private nuisance. Normally the occupier of the land would be the one who was affected by the torts and could therefore sue. If, however, the occupier was a tenant only of the land the landlord would also be able to sue because his rights in the land have been or are likely to be infringed. This would arise when a building was to be erected on adjoining land and the foundations of that building would trespass into the landlord's land. The effect on the tenant would probably be minimal so that he would not wish to sue. The landlord however would see the matter as a serious infringement to his land. He could therefore sue. The same position would arise if a building on adjoining land was to cut off a right enjoyed by the landlord's property.

VICARIOUS LIABILITY

In certain circumstances a person may have the right to sue not only the person who actually committed the tort but also some other person. This is known as vicarious liability. This arises from the existence of a relationship whereby one person is liable for a tort committed by another. Where this situation exists the injured person may sue both the wrongdoer and the person who has liability for that person's wrongful acts. The advantages of this is that one of the two may be in a stronger financial position and so more able to pay damages by a court.

The most important example of vicarious liability is the liability of an employer for the wrongful actions committed by his employees in the course of employment which cause injury to someone. A simple example of this would be a pedestrian, X, knocked down and injured by the negligent driving of a bus driver, Y. The bus company as employer of Y would be vicariously liable for its employee's negligent driving. X could sue both the company and Y, but in practice he would sue the company since the company would have insurance to meet claims of this nature. Y could also be sued but since he would not have the financial resources to meet a claim taking this action would achieve nothing.

For a claim to be made successfully for vicarious liability in employment it must be proved that the wrongdoer is an employee and that when the tort was committed by him it was in the course of his employment. If these requirements do not exist then the employer is not vicariously liable.

Employee or independent contractor
It is not easy, particularly in the construction industry, to decide whether a person is working as an employee under a contract of service or working under a contract for services as an independant contractor. An independent contractor is not an employee but a

person, such as a self-employed bricklayer, who contracts to perform a given task. The distinction is important since the general rule with the use of independent contractors is that the person using their services is not liable for their torts. With an employee the employer is vicariously liable.

The approach of the courts in deciding whether a person worked as an employee under a contract of service or as an independent contractor under a contract for services has changed over the years. Originally the courts used the 'control' test. This was followed by the use of the 'integrated' test and now the 'multiple facts' test.

The 'control' test was based on the relationship which formerly existed of 'master and servant'. This is, that the master could not only tell the servant what to do but how to do it. The test still has relevance but is difficult to use on its own in the more complex employment relationships which now exist. The use of the test on its own is to be found in the House of Lords decision in *Mersey Docks and Harbour Board v Coggins and Griffith (Liverpool) Ltd* 1947. Here Mersey Docks and Harbour Board hired a crane and driver to Coggins and Griffith. The contract of hire contained a term that the crane driver was to be the servant of the hirers. In the course of his work the crane driver negligently drove the crane into an employee of Coggins and Griffith. In the subsequent court case the decision was that the driver was an employee of the board. The Board paid the driver's wages and national insurance and this was held to be sufficient to show that the Board still retained a sufficient degree of control to make the driver the Board's employee.

The courts have found the control test to be not wholly suitable in the case of highly educated and skilled workers, such as airline pilots and surgeons. In order to overcome this difficulty the courts introduced the 'integrated' test. This was explained in the Court of Appeal case of *Stevenson, Jordan and Harrison Ltd v Macdonald* 1952 as being where a man is employed as part of a business and his work is done as an integral part of the business, then he is working under a contract of service. In the case of a contract for services the work, although done for the business, is not integrated into it but is only accessory to it. The application of the test may be seen with a qualified accountant who is responsible for the financial affairs of a public company. His work would be an integral part of the business. On the other hand a qualified accountant who carries out the annual audit of the company would be doing something which was only accessory to the business. The company accountant is an employee working under a contract of service whereas the accountant carrying out the audit is an independent contractor working under a contract for services.

What is now accepted as the most appropriate test is the multiple facts test. The test was laid down in the case of *Ready Mixed Concrete (South East) Ltd v Minister of Pensions and National*

Insurance 1968. The case arose from the company setting up a comprehensive scheme for the delivery vehicle drivers to work as self-employed drivers. If the scheme was properly established the drivers would be responsible for payment of their own national insurance as self-employed workers. The Minister of Pensions and National Insurance, however, took the view that the drivers were still employees and so Ready Mixed, as employers, were also liable to pay national insurance contributions. The case was fought on this point and was decided in favour of Ready Mixed. The judge decided that for a contract of service to exist three conditions must be satisfied. These are: (1) the servant agrees that, in consideration of a wage or other remuneration, he will provide his own work and skill in the performance of some service for his master; (2) he agrees, expressly or impliedly, that in the performance of that service he will be subject to the other's control in a sufficient degree to make the other master; (3) the other provisions in the contract are consistent with its being a contract of service.

A case which shows clearly the importance of the distinction of a person working under a contract of service and under a contract for services is *Ferguson v John Dawson and Partners (Contractors) Ltd* 1976. Here Ferguson, a general labourer, sought work at one of the sites of Dawson and Partners. The site agent told Ferguson that it was a 'labour only' site and that he would be self-employed and responsible himself for paying income tax, national insurance and making his own provision for holiday pay. He would be told to do particular tasks and would be required to complete a time sheet. Ferguson started work but used a false name. One day he was told to go on a flat roof and throw down some scaffold boards which were required elsewhere on the site. In doing this he tripped on some rubbish which had been left on the roof and fell 15 feet suffering serious injury.

Ferguson sued claiming that he was an employee and so entitled to the protection afforded by the Construction (Working Places) Regulations 1961. The regulations only apply to employees. If Ferguson was a self-employed worker he was not entitled to the protection of the regulations and so could not sue for breach of statutory duty. The Court of Appeal decided, by a majority of two to one, that he was working as an employee under a contract of service. The dissenting judge was of the opinion that Ferguson's use of a false name was to defraud the Inland Revenue and this made his contract illegal, so that the court could not deal with the claim.

The reason for the court deciding that Ferguson was an employee, and so entitled to an award of damages, was that the site agent in evidence said that he had the power to 'hire and fire' people and to order them to go and work at other sites. This showed a degree of control which meant that Ferguson was an employee under a contract of service.

Although in this case the agreement made by Ferguson and his employers was by word of mouth only, an agreement in writing that a person will work as a self-employed worker does not bind the courts. The courts take account of any written agreement but also examine the true facts of the situation. They have in the past been prepared to set aside a written agreement as a sham. If the facts show, as in Ferguson's case, that despite an agreement to the contrary, a person is working as an employee under a contract of service then the court will so rule.

Another point to consider with vicarious liability is the practice of a person hiring out plant with an employee to operate the plant. It is usual practice to have a clause in the plant hire contract that the employee shall be treated as the employee of the hirer during the hire period. The effect of this, if it is effective, is to make the hirer of the plant liable for any torts committed by the plant operative during the hire period. The effectiveness of such a clause depends on its wording and the circumstances.

The Court of Appeal in *McConkey v AMEC PLC and Others* 1990 decided that when a crawler crane was hired, together with the driver, using the Contractors' Plant Association form of contract, the clause which sought to make the driver a servant of the hirer was ineffective. The reason for this decision was that the clause in the contract stated that the person supplied would be a competent operative. When McConkey was injured by the driver's negligent operation of the crane, his claim was allowed on the ground that the owner had failed to provide a competent driver. This meant that the driver remained an employee of the owner of the crane and they were vicariously liable for his negligent work.

Tort in the course of employment

The employer is only liable for a tort of his employee if that tort is committed in the course of the employee's employment. That is, if the employee does some wrongful act when he is not in his employment, known as being on 'a frolic of his own', the employee only is liable.

What is committed within the course of an employee's employment depends on the individual facts of an occurrence. As a general rule it may be said that if what the employee is doing is something he has been authorised to do by his employer then he is acting within his employment. The simple example of this is the bus driver who is employed by a bus company. When he drives the bus he is acting entirely within his employment provided he keeps to the authorised routes. The bus company is liable for his negligent driving even if before driving the bus he was warned not to drive negligently. An example of an employer's liability for his employee's negligence is the House of Lords decision in *Century Insurance Co v Northern*

Ireland Road Transport Board 1942. A driver of the Board was delivering petrol from a tanker he had driven to a garage. Whilst the petrol was being pumped into the storage tank the driver lit a cigarette and threw away the match. The match set fire to some material on the ground and the fire spread to the storage tank manhole. The petrol tanker was driven away but the delivery valve was not turned off properly. The result was the petrol tanker exploded and the garage was extensively damaged. The Board, as the driver's employers, were held to be liable. The driver's duty was to see that the petrol from his tanker was properly delivered into the storage tank. To light a cigarette and throw down a lighted match at that time was a negligent discharge of his duties and so his employers were liable.

It may be that even though the employer specifically instructs his employee not to do a certain thing if that instruction is disobeyed the employer will be liable. This is dependent on the employee being engaged on something to further the employer's business. The application of this rule was examined in *Rose v Plenty* 1976. Here a milk roundsman was expressly warned, by notices in the depot, that he was not to take children on his milk float. Despite this warning he allowed Rose, a 13 year old boy, to help him. Rose was on the float when Plenty, the driver, drove it negligently so that Rose was injured. Rose sued Plenty and the employer. His claim was successful on the basis that what Plenty had done, despite it being a prohibited act, was done within the course of his employment. This made the employer of Rose vicariously liable.

Where however the thing done is not part of the employee's duties the decision is different. This is to be seen in the case of *Conway v George Wimpey and Co Ltd* 1951. Here a lorry driver employed by Wimpey on a site where other contractors were employed was given express instructions not to give lifts to anyone who was not an employee of Wimpey. He ignored this instruction and gave a lift to another contractor's employee. This employee was injured whilst he was a passenger. His claim against Wimpey was unsuccessful. The Court of Appeal decided that Conway's claim failed. The reason for this was that the court believed that what the lorry driver had done had not been in the course of his employment. He had given a lift to a person not employed by his employers and this was not merely a wrongful way of performing the work he was employed to do but was an act of a class he was not employed to perform at all.

The use of transport in employment was considered by the House of Lords in the case of *Smith v Stages and Another* 1989. This action was brought by Mrs Smith who had remarried after the death of Mr Machin, her husband. Both Machin and Stages were employees of insulating contractors who carried out work at power stations. They were working at a power station at Burton-on-Trent when their employers sent them to do an urgent job at a power station in South Wales. The job was to be completed by working long hours from Tuesday finishing by working straight through the weekend to 8.30 a.m. on Monday. They drove to South Wales in Mr Stages' car on the day before the work started. Shortly after finishing work they drove back in Mr Stages' car to the Midlands. On the way back Mr Stages drove the car off the road and through a brick wall. Mr Machin was seriously injured and started an action but later died from lung cancer. When it was discovered that Mr Stages was not insured the employers were brought into the action. It was claimed that the employers were vicariously liable. The arrangements for the travel to and from South Wales were that the employees were paid eight hours pay each way, for the travelling time. In addition they were paid a sum of money equivalent to the rail fare for the journeys. There was not however any stipulation as to how the employees should travel.

The claim was successful. The Law Lords decided that the fact that the employees had been paid wages and not just a travelling allowance whilst travelling back from South Wales meant that they were acting in the course of their employment. This was so even though the time and method of travel was not stipulated. Consequently the employers were vicariously liable for Mr Stages' negligent driving.

In the course of their judgment the Law Lords explained the legal position of an employee travelling to and from and in connection with his work. Lord Lowry said:

> The paramount rule is that an employee travelling on a highway will be acting in the course of his employment if, and only if, he is at the material time going about his employer's business. One must not confuse the duty to turn up for one's work with the concept of being 'on duty' whilst travelling to it.

It was then suggested that certain propositions could be made. These include:

1) An employee travelling from his ordinary residence to his regular place of work, whatever the form of transport and even if provided by his employer, is not on duty and is not acting in the course of his employment. If he is obliged to use the employer's transport by his contract of service he will normally, unless there is an express condition to the contrary, be regarded as acting in the course of his employment.
2) Travelling in the employer's time between work places, whether accompanied by goods or tools, would be in the course of employment.
3) Receipt of wages, but not travelling allowance, will indicate that the employee is travelling in the employer's time and for his benefit and is acting in the course of his employment.

4 An employee travelling in the employer's time from his ordinary residence to a work place other than his regular work place or in the course of peripatetic occupation or an emergency, such as a breakdown, will be acting in the course of his employment.

5) A deviation from or an interruption of a journey taken in the course of employment, unless merely incidental to the journey, will for the time being, which may include an overnight interruption, take the employee out of the course of his employment.

'A frolic of his own'

As we have seen, an employer is not liable for his employee's wrongful acts if they are not within the course of his employment. What is and what is not within an employee's course of employment depends on individual facts. A clear example would be a lorry driver who deviated some distance from his route in order to fulfil a private purpose, such as moving some goods for a relative. The driver in *Conway v George Wimpey and Co Ltd* 1951 was on a 'frolic of his own' when in complete disregard of specific instructions he gave a lift to another contractors' employees. In the case of *Coddington v International Harvester Company of Great Britain* 1969 the employer was held not to be vicariously liable when one employee kicked a tin of paint thinners which was burning and giving warmth to other employees sitting near it. Coddington was severely burnt and sued his employer. There was not reason to believer that the employee would act in a foolish way and consequently the action was outside his course of employment.

Criminal activity in the course of employment

There are circumstances where an employer will be liable for the criminal activity of one of his employees. In the case of *Morris v C. W. Martin and Sons Ltd* 1966, where an employee of Martin stole a fur coat which had been given for cleaning, the Court of Appeal decided that the employers were liable for their employee's dishonesty. Similarly in the case of *Nahhas v Pier House Management (Cheyne Walk) Ltd* 1984 the landlords of a block of flats were held liable for the dishonesty of the porter, an employee of theirs. He had used his keys to enter Nahhas' flat and stolen his goods.

The fact that an employee has been, by reason of his employment, put into a position where he could be dishonest does not in itself make the employer liable. In the case of *Heassmans (A Firm) v Clarity Cleaning Co Ltd* 1987 an employee of the cleaning company whilst in the offices of Heassmans carrying out her duties improperly made use of the telephone. This use increased the bill by some £1,499. Her duties included cleaning and disinfecting the telephone. The Court of Appeal decided that the employer had no reason to believe that the employee was likely to act in this way so the company was not negligent in employing her in this work. The fact that her employment had given her the opportunity was not sufficient to make the employer liable.

LIABILITY FOR THE TORTS OF INDEPENDENT CONTRACTORS

The importance of the distinction between an employer having an employee work for him and having work done, under a contract for services, by an independent contractor is, as we have seen, the employer's liability for the wrongful acts of those working for him. The general rule is that a person is not liable for the torts of his independent contractors.

Before considering the rule it is important to note that the use of an independent contractor does not release an employer from his common law obligations to his employees. This is so even if he selected the independent contractor with all reasonable care. The House of Lords considered this matter in the case of *McDermid v Nash Dredging and Reclamation Co Ltd* 1987. McDermid was a deckhand on a barge owned by a Dutch company which was the parent company of Nash Dredging. At the time McDermid suffered a serious injury the barge was under the control of a Dutch captain. Because of the negligent handling of the barge by the captain McDermid suffered his injury. McDermid sued his employers and as part of their defence they pleaded that they had delegated their common law duties to the Dutch captain. The Law Lords rejected this attempt to transfer the employers' common law duties. The employers' common law duties were ones which could not be delegated to a third party even if the employers reasonably believed that they had made delegation to someone competent to perform those duties.

The general rule of not being liable for the torts of an independent contractor is subject to a number of exceptions. The first requirement to note is that the employer must use reasonable care in selecting the independent contractor. To engage a contractor to undertake work which is not work normally done by that contractor would mean that the exception would apply. If an independent contractor's work is such that an ordinary individual would be competent to check that it has been completed satisfactorily, then the work must be checked. The case of *Haseldine v Daw and Sons Ltd* 1941 demonstrates this point. Daw owned a block of flats which had a lift. Daw called in a firm of engineers to repair the lift. Haseldine went to visit an occupier of one of the flats and made use of the lift. Owing to the negligent way in which the engineers had done their work the lift fell to the bottom injuring Haseldine. The court decided that Daw was not liable. In the opinion of the court it could not be right to hold the landlord liable when he had no electrical or mechanical knowledge which would enable him to judge the standard of work carried out. He had appointed a competent firm of engineers and this was sufficient to discharge Daw's duty at law.

The case of *Woodward v Mayor of Hastings* 1945 dealt with a situation where it was obvious that some work had been done negligently. For this reason the dangerous condition which resulted from that negligence ought to have been dealt with. The case arose from a failure to clear snow properly from the steps of a public building which created a dangerous state. Woodward fell on the steps and suffered injury. The court decided that the occupier was liable since the work undertaken was so obvious and simple no skill was needed to see its dangerous condition.

The exceptions of greatest importance to builders are those circumstances where there is strict liability at law. That is, the matter is of such importance that the common law will not permit the use of an independent contractor to be used as a defence.

Operations affecting the highway which are not part of normal use in passage come within the exceptions. The case of *Tarry v Ashton* 1876 is a good example of this. Here Ashton used an independent contractor to repair a lamp which was attached to the wall of his house and projected over the pavement. The independent contractor failed to note that the securing bolts were rusted and unsafe. The lamp fell on Tarry who was lawfully using the pavement. He sued and Ashton was held to be liable. He was under a duty not to create a danger to users of the highway.

Operations which the courts treat as 'extra hazardous' are ones where there is liability for the torts of an independent contractor. The term 'extra hazardous' has been given a wide interpretation by the courts. The use of explosives is an obvious example, added to which are operations which give rise to fire damage and extensive building operations. The case of *Honeywill and Stein Ltd v Larkin Bros Ltd* 1934 dealt with fire damage. Here Honeywill and Stein hired a cinema in order to make use of its interior for a photographer, Larkin Bros Ltd, to take photographs for advertising purposes. The photographer used a magnesium flare which set fire to the curtains. The resulting fire damaged the cinema. Honeywill and Stein were held liable to compensate the owners of the cinema for the act of their photographer, even though they were independent contractors. They then, in turn, could recover the compensation from the photographer.

Extensive building operations can be something which affects a large area or something more confined. In the case of *Mantania v*

National Provincial Bank Ltd 1936 the bank as landlords were held liable for nuisance caused to another tenant by building alterations carried out for them by independent contractors.

Another matter which comes within the exceptions is where a person has work done by independent contractors which withdraws support to his neighbour's land. The duty not to do this lies on the landowner and if there is an infringement the owner is liable. This was considered by the court in *Bower v Peate* 1876, where an independent contractor was engaged by Peate to demolish his house. The builder undertook to do all that was necessary to provide support to the adjoining house whilst the demolition was being carried out. This however was not done and Bower, the owner of the adjoining house, was successful in his claim against Peate.

A recent development is the Court of Appeal decision in *Alcock v Wraith and Others* 1992. A Mr and Mrs Swinhoe obtained a local authority improvement grant to re-roof their terraced house. The terraced houses had a continuous roof of slates which was not interrupted by the party walls between neighbouring houses. Because of the expense concreted interlocking tiles were used instead of slates. Some months after the work was done Mr Alcock in an adjoining house, noticed dampness in a bedroom. A survey showed that this was caused by water penetration through the joint made between the tiles and the slates on Mr Alcock's roof. The court was told that it was notoriously difficult to make such joints satisfactorily. Mr Wraith went bankrupt and the claim proceeded against Mr and Mrs Swinhoe.

The Court of Appeal decided that they were liable for the tort of nuisance and negligence committed by their independent contractor. The court observed that it was not possible to provide a list of activities which could be regarded as 'extra hazardous' so as to fall within the exception of liability where an independent contractor was employed to carry out a task which was 'extra hazardous'. The court suggested that where a person had a right to interfere with an adjoining property, as with a party-wall, then that person was under a duty to see that reasonable skill and care was used and that duty could not be delegated to an independent contractor.

Finally, as will be seen later, there are certain duties under Acts of Parliament which cannot be delegated, and at common law under the rule in *Ryland v Fletcher*.

2 TORT: DEFENCES AND REMEDIES

INTRODUCTION

Some torts have defences and remedies which are applicable to those torts only. For example, an occupier of land may use reasonable force to remove a trespasser who has refused a request to leave. This right is a defence to any claim the trespasser may make that the forcible removal constitutes assault. There are, however, a number of defences and remedies which apply to a wide range of torts. An examination of these will be helpful for the later consideration of torts.

DEFENCES

Volenti non fit injuria

This Latin term means that a person who has volunteered to run a risk cannot complain of an injury which results from the running of that risk. The application of the maxim depends on the person freely consenting to run the risk and to have consented to that particular risk.

The defence has been used in cases where individuals have made claims for damages following injuries suffered in sports. Persons taking part in sporting events thereby agree to run the risks which are inherent in those events. The boxer who suffers a serious head injury and the football player who breaks a leg have no claims for these injuries provided the injuries did not result from a breach of the rules of the sport. The fact that a person has undertaken to take part in a sport does not thereby mean that he has agreed to be injured by a breach of the rules. The defence is also used in the case of a spectator at an event when the mere presence as a spectator carries with it a known risk of injury.

Two cases show the application of the defence in these circumstances. In the case of *Simms v Leigh Rugby Football Club* 1969 a rugby player received a broken leg following a tackle by an opponent. The tackle was within the rules of the game and the injured player's claim failed. He had volunteered to run the risk of that injury in playing the game. In contrast, the Court of Appeal in *Condon v Basi* 1985 upheld an award of substantial damages to an amateur football player who was injured by a tackle made in a reckless and dangerous manner without malicious intent but in an excitable manner without thought of the consequences. Here the player had not consented to run that kind of risk which was not within the rules of the game.

The situation of the spectator is to be seen from the decision in *Hall v Brooklands Auto Racing Club* 1993 where a spectator at a motor race was injured when a racing car left the track and ploughed into the crowd of spectators. Hall's claim failed. Motor racing was a dangerous sport for both participants and spectators. They all volunteered to run the risk of injury.

Volenti non fit injuria may arise when a person has by agreement accepted that risk. For instance, a person may be allowed to enter property subject to a condition to exempt the occupier from liability. This common law rule is subject to provisions in the Unfair Contract Terms Act 1977. These prevent the occupier of business premises or a person who undertakes business activities from relying on such a clause to exempt liability for negligence which results in death or personal injury.

For the principle to apply it is necessary to show that the consent was freely given and that the person had knowledge of the risk undertaken. Both these matters are of importance in the employment of workers. The courts have recognised that workers might be in the position that if they refused to undertake a task they would lose their jobs. Added to this was the fact that the worker, unlike the employer, might not have knowledge of the risk. The leading case on this is the House of Lords decision in *Smith v Baker* 1891. Here a man worked in a quarry with a crane swinging blocks on heavy stones over his head. He was not warned when the crane was to pass over him. Both he and his employer were aware of the risk of stones falling on him. A stone did fall and injure him. He sued and the question of his *volenti non fit injuria* was considered. The Law Lords decided that where a person undertakes work which is dangerous, even though reasonable care has been taken to make it as little dangerous as possible, then that person has undertaken to run the risk voluntarily and cannot complain if he suffers an injury. If, however, there is a risk to a worker, which might result in injury to him, which has been created or enhanced by the negligence of the employer, then the fact that the worker continued employment did not bring the principle into account. So the principle did not apply in this case.

A case where the principle applied was another House of Lords decision. This was *Imperial Chemical Industries Ltd v Shatwell* 1965. Shatwell was working with his brother in carrying out blasting operations. There were detailed safety regulations dealing with the blasting operations and both brothers were aware of these regulations. In addition, their employer had given a specific instruction that the work had to be done in compliance with the regulations.

Despite their knowledge of the regulations and the instruction from the employer some blasting was done in contravention of the regulations. The claim by Shatwell for his injury was dismissed. He had volunteered to run the risk.

Rescue cases

English law accepts that where a person has by his negligence created a situation whereby another person is at risk of death or personal injury then a duty of care extends to the person who puts himself at risk in rescuing the person from the emergency or danger. Attempts have been made in various cases to avoid liability by claiming that the rescuer had volunteered to run the risk. The courts however have refused to accept that *volenti non fit injuria* applies when a person is at risk of death or personal injury. Depending on the circumstances, it may well be that this rule applies where a person is injured in rescuing property.

A case which dealt with the rescue rule was the Court of Appeal decision in *Baker v T.E. Hopkins and Sons Ltd* 1959. Hopkins and Sons Ltd was a company which constructed wells and carried out maintenance to them. On this occasion three employees were working on a pump in a well on a farm. Two were down the well when they were overcome by fumes from a petrol engine. Help was summoned and Baker, the local doctor, went down the well to assist the two affected employees. He too became affected and died. The claim by the widow was successful. The court refused to accept that he had volunteered to run the risk. Two reasons lead to this approach. The first is that the courts hold that a duty of care is owed directly by the wrongdoer to the rescuer. The second is that the rescuer acts under an impulse and is under a moral and social duty to act in that way. So consideration of acceptance of the risk does not arise.

Public policy

A matter closely linked to *volenti non fit injuria* is the application by the courts of striking down a claim on the ground of public policy when a person has been involved in a crime. In the case of *Pitts v Hunt* 1990 the Court of Appeal dismissed a claim by Pitts, who had been injured whilst riding pillion on a motor cycle driven by Hunt. Hunt was drunk, uninsured, untaxed and had driven the motor cycle in a reckless manner on the encouragement of Pitts. It was contrary to public policy to allow Pitts' claim.

Necessity

It is a defence to a claim in tort for a person to plead that what was done, which caused injury to a person or his property, was done in order to protect a person or his property. Although there are a number of cases where damage has been done to buildings in order to protect other buildings doubt has been cast on the application of the defence of necessity, in these circumstances, at the present time. Another doubt exists as to the obligation to pay compensation for the damage caused to another's property. In the case of *Burmah Oil Co v Lord Advocate* 1965 the House of Lords held the company to be entitled to compensation for damage caused to oil wells of the company by the armed forces in order to prevent them falling into enemy hands. This decision, however, was overturned by Parliament passing the War Damages Act 1965 which disallowed claims for compensation in similar circumstances.

The leading case on the defence of necessity, which shows the different approach of the court when lives are at risk, is the House of Lords decision in *Esso Petroleum Co v Southport Corporation* 1956. Here a tanker ran aground in a river estuary and in order to save the lives of those on board the tanker oil was discharged. This lightened the ship and allowed it to be brought under control. The oil flowed down the estuary and was deposited on the corporation's beach causing serious pollution. The corporation incurred heavy expense in cleaning the beach and sued for negligence. The claim failed. The judge at the trial, Mr Justice Devlin, stated that the safety of lives was different to the safety of property. The two cannot be compared and the necessity of saving life had always been a proper ground for inflicting damage on another's property if that was necessary.

What is accepted with the defence is that it is only applicable if an emergency has arisen, as was the situation in *Esso Petroleum Co v Southport Corporation* 1956. In the case of *John Trenberth Ltd v National Westminster Bank Ltd* 1979 a deliberate act of trespass to carry out essential repairs was held not to come within the defence of necessity, even though to trespass on the adjoining land was the only way to carry out the work. As a result of this case Parliament passed the Access to Neighbouring Land Act 1992, which allows a right of access to adjoining land for maintenance works in certain circumstances.

Statutory authority

This form of defence exists because Parliament has passed an Act which authorises the doing of something which, without that authorisation, would be a tort. The extent to which the defence may be available depends on the exact wording in the Act. The approach of the courts is that Parliament is taken not to have removed the private rights of citizens unless that is evident from the Act. For instance, if the activity authorised by Parliament gives rise to a nuisance, but reasonable care was exercised, then the defence will be available. This is the case if Parliament authorised the activity to one particular place. If this is not so, as where an activity may be carried out anywhere, then the defence is not available.

The leading case on this form of defence is the House of Lords decision in *Manchester Corporation v Farnworth* 1930. Farnworth was a farmer who owned land on the outskirts of Manchester. Nearby was a power station built and operated by the Corporation. Fumes from the chimneys of the power station poisoned Farnworth's land. When Farnworth sued the defence of the Corporation was that the Manchester Corporation Act 1914 empowered them to set up the power station. The House of Lords awarded damages to Farnworth and an injunction, which was suspended for a year in order to permit work to be carried out to minimise the nuisance. In the House of Lords Viscount Dunedin said:

> When Parliament has authorised a certain thing to be made or done in a certain place, there can be no action for nuisance caused by the making or doing of that thing if the nuisance is the inevitable result, of the making or doing so authorised.

Limitation of actions

English law requires that a person bringing a legal action, whether for a tort or a breach of contract, must bring the action within a specified period of time. Failure to do so means that the action is 'statute barred'. That is, despite the justice of the claim, the claim is barred because of the failure to bring the claim within the specified time. The periods of time and the associated provisions are contained in the Limitation Act 1980. These are six years for a tort which does not give rise to personal injury, and in the case of personal injury the period is three years. A further point with personal injury is that the three year period starts to run from when the person has knowledge of the injury. This covers the situation where a person suffers injury, such as asbestosis, but does not discover that injury until some time later.

The reason for Parliament making these requirements are the belief that if a person has a right to bring a legal action that person should bring the action within a reasonable time and that a person should not be at risk of being sued many years after some event. In addition it would clearly be difficult to trace witnesses and collect evidence of what happened some years earlier. The witnesses in any case are likely, after the passage of some years, to be unable to recall accurately what happened years earlier. This in turn means that the courts have great difficulty in coming to a proper decision.

The date from which the limitation period starts to run is the date on which the right of action accrues. In the case of torts where it is not necessary to prove damage, for example trespass to land, the date is the date on which the tort was committed. In the case of a tort where proof of damage is required, such as negligence, then the date is the date on which the damage occurred. This is so even though the damage is not discovered at the time it occurred, subject to a possible extension in the case of the concealed defect.

At one time it was the view of the courts that time started to run from the time the damage was discovered or ought with reasonable diligence to have been discovered. The House of Lords in the case of *Pirelli General Cable Works Ltd v Oscar Faber and Partners Ltd* 1983 however decided that time started to run from when the damage occurred whether it was discovered then or not. The case arose from Pirelli deciding to have a new factory built, which included a chimney. Pirelli obtained a design for the chimney from a specialist sub-contractor who undertook to construct the chimney to that design. Pirelli instructed Oscar Faber and Partners Ltd, consulting engineers, to examine and report on the design and proposed construction of the chimney. This was done and the work proceeded. The chimney was built in July 1969. Damage in the form of cracks occurred not later than April 1970. The damage however was not discovered until November 1977. Pirelli in 1978 issued a writ claiming damages for negligence from Oscar Faber and Partners Ltd.

The House of Lords decided that the date when the right to bring an action occurred was in 1970. Under the Limitation Act 1939, now 1980, the limitation period was six years. They also decided that the right to bring an action started on the day the damage occurred. The fact that it was not discovered on that day did not make any difference. This ruling meant that Pirelli had issued the writ more than six years since the right of action arose and so the claim was statute barred.

Latent damage

Construction operations have been the subject of many legal actions in recent years with the special problem of latent defects in buildings not being discovered until some years after the work was done. Most of these claims have been based on the foundations of buildings not being to building regulation standard. That is, foundations not being deep enough or the concrete mix not being to standard.

The obvious difficulty with these latent defects is that it may be a number of years after the building is erected that walls begin to crack and other signs indicate the foundations are defective. If the damage is not discovered until more than six years after the foundations were laid then a claim in the usual way is statute barred.

In order to overcome this difficulty Section 32 of the Limitation

Act 1980 provides that where there has been fraud or the plaintiff's cause of action has been deliberately concealed, then time does not begin to run against the plaintiff until the plaintiff has discovered the fraud or concealment or could with reasonable diligence have discovered it. The meaning and application of these terms have presented difficulties to the courts in cases involving construction operations.

In the case of *Archer v Moss* 1971, where a house was built with strip foundations instead of a raft foundation and the concrete was 15 to 1 instead of 8 to 1, the Court of Appeal applied the provisions in Section 26 of the Limitation Act 1939, the predecessor of Section 32 of the Limitation Act 1980. This allowed Archer to succeed in his claim against the builder more than six years after the foundations were installed. In the course of the case Lord Denning, the Master of the Rolls, said:

> The section applies whenever the conduct of the defendant or his agent has been such as to hide from the plaintiff the existence of his right of action, in such circumstances that it would be inequitable to allow the defendant to rely on the lapse of time as a bar to the claim. Applied to a building contract, it means that if a builder does his work badly, so that it is likely to give rise to trouble thereafter, and then covers up his bad work so that it is not discovered for some years, then he cannot rely on that statute as the bar to the claim.

This approach, however, was not applied by the Court of Appeal in *William Hill Organisation v Bernard Sunley and Son* 1983. Here the contractors put stone cladding on to a building. The work was done in 1960. Cracks appeared in 1971 with movement in 1974. Examination then revealed that the fixings which had been used had been defective. The claim for damages for negligence sought to overcome the claim being made more than six years after the work was done by alleging that there had been 'fraudulent concealment'. This however was not accepted. The court was of the opinion that the fact that the contractors got on with the work did not amount to fraudulent concealment.

It appears from these decisions that each case will be decided on its own circumstances. Some cases will obviously come within the scope of the section, whilst others will be less clear-cut.

Latent Damage Act 1986

During the 1970s and 1980s serious problems arose for all those concerned in the erection of buildings, including local authorities who carried out building control under the Building Act 1984. The problems were that builders, architects and local authorities were being sued for negligence in the construction of buildings where the damage had not become apparent for some time. The owners of buildings were frequently unable to sue for breach of contract and so sued for negligence. In many cases architects, builders and others were being sued many years after the work was done, and in some cases where the person had retired from work.

In order to try and strike a balance between the need for a building owner to sue for damages because of defective work to his property and that of the professional man who is at risk of being sued many years after he did his work, the Law Reform Committee in its 24th Report recommended changes to the limitation periods for negligence. The Latent Damage Act 1986 was the result of the committee's report.

The Act changed the law by inserting new sections in the Limitation Act 1980. The Act, which does not apply to personal injuries, states that an action shall not be brought after six years from the date the action accrued or three years from the 'starting date' if that period expires later than the six year period. The starting date therefore comes into consideration only when the six year period has expired. The starting date is the earliest date on which the claimant or his predecessor first had both the knowledge required to bring an action and the right to bring the action.

The knowledge required to bring an action means knowledge of both the material facts about the damage and of other facts relevant to the action. Material facts are such facts about the damage as would lead a reasonable person who had suffered such damage to consider it sufficiently serious to justify instituting proceedings for damages against a person who did not dispute liability and was able to satisfy a judgment.

What this means is that if the six year period has expired, say the ninth year after the work was done, the owner has three years from the date he had knowledge, the starting date, within which he can bring an action for damages. If the owner ignores those signs which a reasonable person would have noted and acted on, then the starting date still becomes operative. A person can therefore lose the right to sue after the six year period has expired by failure to act promptly and properly.

The Act protects the professional man by providing what has been termed the 'long stop'. That is, that no action shall be brought claiming damages for negligence after 15 years have expired from the date on which there occurred the act or omission which it is claimed constituted negligence. This applies even though damage has not yet occurred. So if damage first becomes apparent 17 years after a building was erected the long stop operates and prevents a claim being made.

The Act also provides that the provisions in Section 32 of the Limitation Act 1980, concealment of facts relevant to a claim, shall apply despite the new limitation periods. This means that even if the

15 year long stop has expired a claim based on concealment may still be made.

Defective Premises Act 1972

This Act was passed by Parliament to provide a remedy for a house owner whose property is constructed in such a way as to fail to meet the standard prescribed by the Act. The Act has its own limitation period. This is six years from when the dwelling was completed. This is subject, in the case of any remedial work, to the period running from the date of completion of the remedial work.

REMEDIES

In actions for torts the courts have power to award two remedies: the common law remedy of damages and the equitable remedy of an injunction. The common law remedy of damages is awarded as of right, that is a person is to be awarded damages which are consistent with the claim. The equitable remedy of an injunction is, as are all equitable remedies, granted at the court's discretion. In this case a person who proves his case cannot demand an injunction. The court can and will take his own conduct into account and might therefore decide not to agree to the request.

Damages

The award of damages, with one exception, is compensatory for the injury. There is no intention that a person shall make a 'profit' out of his claim. Added to this is the obligation on a plaintiff to take reasonable steps to mitigate his loss in respect of his claim.

Types of damages

Damages claimed in actions for torts fall into different categories according to the kind of claim made. The court may, however, having heard the evidence and decided the case in favour of the plaintiff, award damages lower than those claimed.

Special damages are claimed as specified sums of money. They are calculated as losses the plaintiff has suffered because of the tort and are claimed up to the date of the court hearing. Included in this type of damages are claims for loss of earnings, damage to clothing and travel costs to hospital.

General damages are those that cannot be quantified as special damages. The amount awarded by the court is that that the court thinks appropriate in the circumstances. In a claim for nuisance caused by building operations the court has to assess the appropriate award of damages for loss of sleep because of the noise from the operations. Similarly, the court assesses the amount of damages for pain and suffering in accident cases. Where there is an injury such as the loss of an eye, courts tend to award amounts which are roughly the same. It is not in the interests of justice that amounts awarded by courts should vary greatly.

Exemplary damages are the exception to the general rule that damages should be compensatory in nature. This type of award is intended to punish the wrongdoer and to deter him and others from acting in a similar way in the future. The circumstances in which such an award may be made are limited. The House of Lords in the case of *Rooks v Barnard* 1964 decided that exemplary damages could only be awarded in two circumstances. The first is where there is oppressive, arbitrary or unconstitutional action by servants of the Government. The second circumstance is where the defendant's conduct has been such that it would allow him to make a profit. That profit may exceed the amount of compensation payable to the plaintiff. Exemplary damages have been awarded where a landlord wrongfully and in some cases physically, evicted a tenant. The landlord would if unchallenged obtain vacant possession of the property and so secure a financial advantage.

Contemptuous and nominal damages are awarded by the court in circumstances where compensation is not considered to be appropriate. If a person brings a claim and succeeds with it, but in the opinion of the court the claim ought never to have been brought, then the award will be the smallest coin of the realm. Where, however, the claim is one which seeks to establish a legal right and no real damage has been suffered, then the award will be a nominal amount. This is usually a sum not exceeding £5. Actions where nominal damages are awarded are often trespass cases. The real issue here is usually that the landowner is seeking to establish his legal right to the land and damages are incidental to the claim.

A matter closely linked with damages is that of the costs of the case. The general rule is that costs are at the court's discretion but this is subject to the judge following the practice of awarding costs to the successful party unless some good reason exists for not doing so. In cases such as where contemptuous or nominal damages are awarded the successful party may well not be awarded costs.

Injunctions
An injunction is a court order requiring someone to do something or, more usually, to stop doing something. Injunctions are equitable remedies and so granted at the court's discretion. Added to this is the rule that an injunction will not be granted if an award of damages would be a sufficient remedy. As will be seen later, injunctions are often sought in connection with the torts of trespass and nuisance.

Injunctions may be prohibitory or mandatory. A prohibitory injunction restrains a person from doing something. A mandatory injunction requires a person to do something. Both forms of injunction may be granted by the courts as either interlocutory or perpetual. An interlocutory injunction is granted by the court before the court hearing to determine the claim. It remains in force until the court hearing which determines the dispute. A perpetual injunction is one which is granted at the court hearing and is permanent in its effect. The power of both forms of injunction is that they are court orders and a failure to observe an injunction is contempt of court. Courts have extensive powers of punishment for contempt of court.

An interlocutory injunction may be granted by the court to give the plaintiff relief until the court hearing of his claim. So a person who suffers a nuisance from construction operations may make a claim, which will take some time to come before the court for determination. In the meantime, in order to control the nuisance temporarily, the plaintiff may ask the court to grant an interlocutory injunction. In deciding whether to grant the interlocutory injunction the court will require the plaintiff to give an undertaking to pay damages for the loss suffered from the operation of the interlocutory injunction if the claim is lost in the court hearing. In addition, in exercising its discretion the court will be guided by the House of Lords decision in *American Cyanamid Co v Ethicon* 1975. That is, does the plaintiff have a serious issue to be tried and does the balance of convenience lie in favour of granting or refusing the application.

A mandatory injunction is one which requires the taking of some positive action. For this reason it is more difficult to obtain from the court than a prohibitory injunction. An example of the court granting both forms of injunction is in the case of *John Trenberth Ltd v National Westminster Bank Ltd* 1980. Here the bank's builder went on Trenberth's land in order to carry out urgent repairs to that bank's building. This was done without permission and was a clear act of trespass. Trenberth obtained interlocutory injunctions to remove the scaffold and other builder's material on the land, a mandatory injunction, and to forbid further acts of trespass, a prohibitory injunction. In the case of *Redland Bricks Ltd v Morris* 1969 the House of Lords laid down three principles to be applied in granting mandatory injunctions. These are:

1) an award of damages must not be an adequate remedy for the plaintiff;
2) if the defendant has acted wantonly or tried to steal a march on the plaintiff or the court the expense caused by a mandatory injunction to the defendant is immaterial, but if the defendant has acted reasonably, even though wrongly, the cost of remedying the earlier activities is an important consideration;

3) if a mandatory injunction is issued the court must be careful to see that the defendant knows exactly what he has to do, so that proper instructions can be given to contractors for the carrying out of the work.

A *quia timet* is a form of injunction which is not often issued. It is an injunction which is issued where damage has not yet occurred but serious damage is almost certain to occur. Sufficient evidence must be available to show that substantial damage will occur and that it is imminent. An example of the issuing of this form of injunction is found in the case of *Hooper v Rogers* 1975. In this case Rogers had used a bulldozer to deepen a track which was next to Hooper's house. This exposed the land to erosion which in a matter of time would lead to support being withdrawn to the house with eventual collapse. The court accepted that the danger was serious and imminent and therefore issued a *quia timet* injunction.

Extra-judicial remedies

These remedies, which are also referred to as self-help, are reasonable actions taken by persons in certain circumstances without having assistance from the courts. In all circumstances the person must act in a reasonable way. Not to do so may mean that that person becomes the wrongdoer.

With the occupation of land the occupier has the right to remove trespassers who have refused to leave the land after being asked to leave. Reasonable force may be used in the removal. It is also permissible to use reasonable force to prevent trespassers entering the land.

In the case of nuisance it is permissible to take action to abate a nuisance. If appropriate, notice should be given before the action is taken. Where there is some urgency then action may be taken without notice. In the case of *Lemmon v Webb* 1895 it was held that it was possible to abate a nuisance from branches of an overhanging tree by cutting them off back to the boundary. Where this is done the branches must be returned to the owner of the tree. In the case of *Davey v Harrow Corporation* 1958 the Court of Appeal decided that the roots of a tree which spread into adjoining land constituted a nuisance and that the landowner could dig down on his land and cut off the intruding roots.

A person is allowed to defend himself against any force used or threatened to him. This might also extend to the protection of a person's family. It is also possible to use reasonable force to prevent a crime being committed.

In the case of goods, the owner may retake those goods from the person who has wrongfully taken them. It is also permissible to enter the land of that person in order to recover the goods.

3 TORTS AFFECTING LAND

TRESPASS TO LAND

Trespass to land arises when there has been a direct interference with the possession of land. This means that there has to be an intrusion into the land. It is this which differentiates trespass from nuisance. Nuisance arises without there being any direct intrusion. In the case of *Lemmon v Webb* 1895 branches of a tree which grew over the boundary of a property were held not to constitute trespass. They did however form the tort of private nuisance.

Trepass is a tort which is actionable *per se*, that is actionable without the proof of damage. The reason for this is the recognition that the occupier of the land has had his legal right to exclusive possession infringed. If however the trespass caused physical damage then the court would take this into account in awarding damages. It should also be noted that the tort of trespass has been committed even if there had not been any intention to trespass. So a person who innocently goes on another person's land is committing the tort of trespass, just as does the person who deliberately sets out to trespass.

Except in a limited number of circumstances trespass is a tort and the occupier of the land has the right to sue for damages and an injunction. Parliament has however made trespass into a criminal offence where it has recognised the need to deal with trespassers in the criminal courts by prosecution rather than by making a claim in the civil courts. A number of authorities, including British Rail, have this power and trespass on their land is a criminal offence.

Trespass to land can occur in three ways. There is the usual form of trespass to the surface of the land, and the other less usual forms of trespass to the land beneath the surface and to the air space above the land.

Trespass to the surface of land
It is under this heading that most acts of trespass occur. The commonest example is that of a person going on the land of another without the occupier's permission. It is also trespass if a person has been given permission to go on land but then acts in such a way as to abuse that permission, such as stealing. Where this occurs the trespass relates back to when entry was first made. This is known as

trespass *ab initio*. A person who is on land lawfully can be asked to leave and if he fails to do so, having been given a reasonable time to leave, then he becomes a trespasser.

Trespass to the surface of land also occurs when objects are placed on the land without permission. So the dumping of building materials or rubbish or the positioning of scaffolds on another person's land without permission is trespass. A point to note here is that for each day a trespass occurs there is a fresh cause of action. The importance of this is to be seen in the case of *Holmes v Wilson* 1839 where buttresses were built on Holmes' land to provide support to a road. This was done without permission. Holmes was compensated for this. The buttresses however were not removed and Holmes sued on the ground that they constituted a further act of trespass. Holmes was successful in his claim.

Many acts of trespass have occurred when an occupier went on adjoining land, without permission, in order to carry out maintenance work to his own property. A number of people believed that they had the right in law to enter another's land so as to carry out maintenance work. This however was incorrect. The position was examined by the High Court in the case of *John Trenberth Ltd v National Westminster Bank Ltd* 1980. Here the bank had a branch office which adjoined Trenberth's land. The branch office had cladding to the walls, some of which became loose and unsafe. In order to carry out the necessary remedial work entry on Trenberth's land was necessary. The bank asked for permission to enter the land but this was refused. Trenberth maintained this refusal even though offered a full indemnity and insurance. The bank then decided that in the circumstances they had no alternative but to go on Trenberth's land. This was done with materials being deposited and scaffolding erected.

Trenberth immediately sued claiming an injunction prohibiting further acts of trespass and a mandatory injunction requiring the removal of the materials and scaffolding. The court refused the bank's suggestion that they should be allowed to continue with the work and pay damages. Similarly a suggestion that an injunction, if granted, should be suspended for a period of time sufficient to allow the work to be completed. The injunctions were therefore granted.

This case demonstrated the difficulty an occupier of land faced if entry to adjoining land was refused, even though essential maintenance work was needed. The position was examined by the Law Commission and in 1985 a report, Rights of Access to Neighbouring Land, was published. Parliament has now passed the Access to Neighbouring Land Act 1992, which came into force on 31 January 1993. The provisions in the Act are considered later.

Trespass beneath the surface of the land

This form of trespass occurs less frequently than the other forms. In construction operations it occurs when piles are driven at an angle into adjoining land and when foundations extend into adjoining land. In the case of *Willcox v Kettell* 1937 Kettell had a building demolished and rebuilt. The foundations for the new building extended 20 inches into Willcox's land. Willcox sued claiming trespass to the subsoil of his land. His claim was accepted and he was awarded damages.

Trespass to air space

It was not until the Court of Appeal decision in *Kelsen v Imperial Tobacco Co Ltd* 1957 that it was accepted that there could be trespass to air space. The case arose from Imperial Tobacco erecting an advertising sign on a building. The sign projected eight inches into the air space of Kelsen. Kelsen asked for its removal but this was refused. Kelsen therefore sued claiming an injunction that the sign be removed. The Court of Appeal accepted that the intrusion of the sign was a trespass and that Kelsen was entitled to an injunction that the sign be removed.

What this case did not decide was whether there could be trespass to air space when there was a temporary intrusion only. This question was considered by the High Court in *Woollerton and Wilson Ltd v Richard Costain Ltd* 1970. Here Costain tendered for the construction of a building in the centre of Leicester. The site was congested and the use of a crane was necessary. The crane had to be positioned in one corner of the site. On this basis Costain tendered and got the contract. The use of the crane meant that the jib swung some 50 feet above the roof of the premises of Woollerton and Wilson. To this they objected. There was no nuisance or damage from the use of the crane. The assurances of Costain that the company had never had a claim for damage caused by the use of a crane and that it had adequate insurance cover were not accepted. Costain then offered £250 to cover the acts of trespass that had already occurred and for any future acts. This was rejected. Woollerton and Wilson suggested a payment of £50 a week, which Costain refused to pay.

Woollerton and Wilson sued claiming trespass to air space and requesting an injunction to restrain further acts of trespass. The judge agreed that the swinging jib was trespass to air space. He observed that this was the first case of its kind; that Costain had had to place the crane in that position because of the difficulties of the site; and that Costain found itself in this position through mere inadvertence. The judge also took the opportunity to warn other contractors not to act in a similar way.

The judge then did something which has been the subject of

criticism by other judges and, now, appears to be of doubtful authority. He granted an injunction but suspended its operation until the date for the completion of the contract.

Despite the warning of the judge other contractors have operated cranes so that the jibs passed over adjoining premises and so trespassed to the air space. A case which showed the need to position cranes with great care was *Anchor Brewhouse Developments Ltd and Others v Berkley House (Docklands Developments) Ltd* 1987. This was a large development which had several tower cranes in use. These when in use or when left to swing free had their jibs passing over property belonging to Brewhouse. Brewhouse objected to this and sued claiming an injunction to restrain the acts of trespass.

Berkley by way of defence claimed that the height at which the jibs passed through the air space meant that there was no trespass. Even if there was trespass it was suggested that an injunction ought not to be granted or if granted suspended.

The judge decided that the use of the cranes was trespass to air space. This entitled Anchor Brewhouse to an injunction which would come into effect immediately. He refused to suspend it. He expressed an opinion, which has not been acted upon, that Parliament should legislate so as to allow the use of cranes in construction operations even if adjoining owners object.

The possibility that individuals exercising their private rights to sue for trespass might thereby interfere with public services caused Parliament to pass the Civil Aviation Act 1982. The Act prevents any action for trespass being brought for civil aircraft flying at a reasonable height above a person's land.

Defence to trespass

There are a number of circumstances where no right of action exists. These include:

1) Entry by authority of law, for instance a police officer entering premises by means of a search warrant.
2) By means of a licence. A licence is permission granted to a person to enter land.
3) Entry to abate a nuisance. For example if a person enters his neighbour's land in order to deal with an emergency which is creating a nuisance to him.
4) Entry to retake goods placed on that land by the occupier of that land.
5) Doubtful legal title to the land. If a person takes occupation of the land of another openly and without that person's permission then that, after the passage of 12 years, gives the occupier title to that land. The owner's title is extinguished under the Limitation Act 1980. This is known as adverse possession or 'squatter's title'.

Remedies for trespass to land

A plaintiff in an action for trespass to land has a number of remedies available depending on the circumstances. These include:

1) Claim for damages as compensation for the act of trespass. If no harm has been done by the trespasser then the award will be nominal. If, however, harm has been caused then the award of damages will be consistent with that harm.
2) Injunctions may be granted to restrain a person from continuing to trespass on the land. A mandatory injunction may be granted to require the removal of the object which constitutes the trespass. Unlike the award of damages, injunctions cannot be demanded as a right. Injunctions are at the court's discretion.
3) Legal actions may be brought to secure the removal of a trespasser.
4) Physical action is also permissible, if reasonable force only is used. Such action may be taken to prevent entry by a trespasser and to remove a trespasser.

Access To Neighbouring Land Act 1992

As we saw earlier, the decision in the case of *John Trenberth Ltd v National Westminster Bank Ltd* 1980 led the Law Commission to consider the legal difficulty in obtaining access to neighbouring land in order to carry out maintenance work. Parliament passed the above Act to deal with this difficulty. The Act came into force on 31 January 1993.

The Act allows either the High Court or the County Court to make an access order which permits a person to go on neighbouring land so as to carry out maintenance work. The land to which the maintenance works are to be carried out are referred to as the 'dominant land' and the land to which access is sought as the 'servient land'.

The court is to make an access order if, and only if, it is satisfied that the works are reasonably necessary for the preservation of the whole or any part of the dominant land; and that the works cannot be carried out, or would be substantially more difficult to carry out, without entry upon the servient land. All this, however, is subject to the court being restrained from making an access order if it is satisfied that the other person would suffer interference with or disturbance of his use or enjoyment of the servient land, or he would suffer hardship. If in these circumstances it would be unreasonable to make the access order then it is not to be made.

The Act, in order to assist the courts, defines the maintenance works which are to be considered reasonably necessary. These are referred to as 'basic preservation works'. Included are maintenance, repair or renewal of any part of a building; clearance, repair or renewal of any drain, sewer, pipe or cable; the execution of certain works to hedges, trees or shrubs which are or are likely to become dangerous because of disease or some other specified cause; and the filling in or clearance of a ditch.

The definition of these works as being reasonably necessary means that the court does not have to consider whether these works are reasonably necessary. All such works are because the Act states that they are. The court therefore grants an order for such works, subject to it being reasonable to make the order.

Other works may be considered as being reasonably necessary as prescribes circumstances indicate, even if they involve making some alteration, adjustment or improvement to the land or the demolition of the whole or part of a building or structure comprised in or situate upon the land. Power is also given to the court to make an access order for a person to inspect the dominant land and make maps or plans of drains, sewers, pipes or cable in preparation for the works to be carried out.

As will be apparent, the aim of the Act is to allow maintenance works to be carried out to existing buildings. The provisions in the Act do not extend to the erection of new buildings or to permit jibs of cranes used in new construction to swing over adjoining land.

The access order is to stipulate the period of time it is to apply and any terms and conditions. The terms and conditions are for the avoidance or restriction of loss, damage or injury which might otherwise be caused by the entry on the servient land. Inconvenience or loss of privacy caused to the occupier of the servient land must also be considered. In addition the terms and conditions may specify the manner of execution of the works, the days and hours of work, the persons who may enter the land and the precautions to be taken.

The occupier of the servient land has his interests protected by the court having the power to require the applicant for the access order to pay compensation for loss, damage or injury or for any substantial loss of privacy or other substantial inconvenience, which will or might be caused by the entry on the land. The applicant may also be required to be insured against specified risk. A record of the condition of the servient land may also be ordered, so that any damage may be properly assessed.

What is probably the main point of financial importance to the occupier of the servient land is the power of the court to require payment to be made for the privilege of entering the land. In assessing the appropriate sum regard is to be had to the financial advantage gained by the order and the inconvenience likely to be caused to the occupier. No payment however may be ordered where the application is made for works to residential property.

The effect of an access order is to make an entry lawful and permit materials, plant and equipment to be brought on the servient land. Waste may also be stored on the servient land. When the work is completed any damage is to be made good.

An access order, which binds a purchaser of the servient land as well as the original owner, may be varied. Failure to observe an access order or its terms or conditions means that damages may be awarded. In order to make it known to a possible purchaser that an access order has been made, it must be entered on the registers kept under the Land Charges Act 1972 and the Land Registration Act 1925.

NUISANCE

Nuisance may exist as public nuisance, private nuisance and statutory nuisance. Public nuisance is a criminal matter but an individual who suffers an injury over and above that suffered by others may sue for that injury. To that extent it is a tort. Private nuisance is a common law tort and, unlike public nuisance, only arises in connection with land. Statutory nuisance exists only in the prescribed circumstances in the Act which permits such to be dealt with as statutory nuisances. The Environment Protection Act 1990 specifies statutory nuisances and the procedure to be followed by local authorities, who enforce the provisions in the Act, in order to secure the abatement of the matters which give rise to the nuisances. In addition, the Control of Pollution Act 1974 empowers local authorities to control noise nuisance from construction operations by the service of notices. Failure to comply with the notices is punishable by fine, with the power of local authorities to take action to deal with the nuisance and recover the expenses incurred.

Public nuisance

A public nuisance is an unlawful interference with the rights of a section of Her Majesty's subjects. It is a criminal matter for which a prosecution may be brought. Actions for public nuisance may be brought by the Attorney General, the senior law officer, or by a local authority under powers in Section 222 of the Local Government Act 1972. Members of the public may ask the Attorney General to take action. When he agrees to do so this is known as a 'relator' action.

The question as to the number of the public who must be affected for a public nuisance to exist was answered by Lord Denning in the Court of Appeal case of *Attorney General v P.Y.A. Quarries Ltd* 1957. He said that a public nuisance existed when it is so widespread in its range or so indiscriminate in its effect that it would not be reasonable to expect one person to take proceedings to put a stop to it, but that it should be taken on the responsibility of the community at large. So there is no minimum number of people who must be affected for a public nuisance to exist.

Public nuisance can take various forms. Obstructions of highways or the creation of dangers on highways constitute public nuisance. Noise or vibration from construction operations have been held to be public nuisance.

An example of obstruction of a highway causing a public nuisance is the case of *Attorney General v Gastonia Coaches Ltd* 1977. The coach company started to park their coaches on a highway in such a manner as to obstruct the highway without blocking the highway completely. The parking did, however, cause the drivers of other vehicles to be forced on to the grass verge or to have to wait whilst other vehicles reversed. Even though the nuisance occurred at only certain parts of the day an injunction was granted on the ground of public nuisance.

In order for an individual to sue for damages or an injunction for public nuisance it must be shown that the damage is particular, direct and substantial. In the case of *Halsey v Esso Petroleum Co Ltd* 1961 Halsey occupied a house near to a depot of the company. Tankers entered and left the premises all hours of the day and acid smuts were emitted from a chimney of the depot. Halsey lost sleep with the noise from the tankers and the paintwork of his car was affected by the acid smuts. He was successful in his claim for damages and for an injunction to limit the hours when tankers could use the depot.

Private nuisance

A definition of a private nuisance, which has been widely accepted for many years, is that of Professor Winfield. This is that a private nuisance is an 'unlawful interference with a person's use or enjoyment of land, or some right over or in connection with it'.

An examination of this definition will show the application of the tort. The first point to note is that the interference must be unlawful. If the interference is such that it is not unlawful then the tort does not exist. The House of Lords in *Bradford Corporation v Pickles* 1895 decided that a landowner who dug a shaft on his land and extracted ground water which otherwise would have flowed to the land owned by the corporation was not acting unlawfully. The Law Lords decided that what Pickles did was a lawful activity on his own land. The fact that he had a bad motive in what he did did not change a lawful action into an unlawful action. The corporation's claim for private nuisance was therefore unsuccessful.

The next point is that private nuisance is concerned with the occupation of land. The right of occupation must be infringed if the tort is to arise. To this extent private nuisance differs from public nuisance and negligence where rights in land are not involved. The interference with the person's use or enjoyment of land may take various forms. The tort arises from nuisance from noise, smoke, smell, dust, fumes, damp and vibrations. Liability arises whether actual damage has been caused or not. Something which inconveniences, such a loss of sleep from noisy construction operations, can constitute private nuisance.

Although most actions for private nuisance are based on conduct which has extended over some time it is not impossible for private nuisance to arise from a single event. If a claim were based on a single event it would be necessary to show that it was an event of some substance. A case based on a single event was *Midwood and Co Ltd v Manchester Corporation* 1905. Here a fault in the corporation's electric cable caused the bitumen to vaporise and subsequently explode. The resulting fire damaged Midwood's property. The claim by Midwood that this was private nuisance was successful. This approach was followed in the later case of *Spicer v Smee* 1946 where the electric wiring to a bungalow was defective. A fire started and spread to the adjoining building. Again this was accepted as being private nuisance.

The definition of private nuisance refers to rights over or in connection with land. This part of the definition covers those matters known as easements. Easements include rights of support, rights of light and rights of way. When there is an infringement of such a right the landowner entitled to the right may sue for private nuisance.

Locality

Industrial areas have activities conducted within those areas which may be private nuisances. There is an understanding that those who live or work in such areas have to accept some inconvenience. This applies too, in a more limited form, in urban areas provided what is done is in all respects reasonable. In the case of *De Keyser's Royal Hotels Ltd v Spicer Bros Ltd and Minter* 1914 the court stated that people living in towns had to expect inconvenience from time to time. The case, which was a claim of private nuisance from pile-driving operations, was decided in favour of the plaintiff since the pile-driving was being carried out at unreasonable hours. An injunction was granted to restrain pile-driving between 10.00 p.m. and 6.30 a.m.

In the case of *Andreae v Selfridge and Co Ltd* 1938, which dealt with noise from an extensive building project, the court indicated that new methods of construction had to be accepted even if they gave rise to problems which would not have been present with old methods. This meant that an hotel owner in a built-up area of London was unsuccessful in his claim.

The fact that a person has moved close to an industrial plant does not mean that that person has to accept nuisance from that plant. The House of Lords case of *St Helen's Smelting Co v Tipping* 1865 decided that if an activity caused damage to another's property which constituted a nuisance the fact that the injured person had moved to the area after the industrial activity had started was no defence. In the case Tipping bought an estate in an area where St Helen's Smelting Co carried out copper smelting. The fumes from this process were discharged into the atmosphere. Less than two years after buying the estate Tipping found that trees on the estate were being damaged by these fumes. He sued claiming nuisance. He was successful; the fact that the process was in operation when he bought the estate was no defence. He had suffered nuisance and this entitled him to damages.

Sensitivity

The law regarding nuisance does not provide a remedy when a claim is made which is based on either the sensitivity of the plantiff or of his goods. If therefore a person had an extended hearing range, which meant that noise which those with ordinary hearing range would not find inconvenient, but he did, then that person cannot succeed in a claim for private nuisance from that noise.

The leading case on sensitivity is that of *Robinson v Kilvert* 1889 where Kilvert occupied the lower floor of a building and there carried out a process which required hot dry air. An upper floor was occupied by Robinson who had brown paper stored there. The hot dry air came up from the lower floor and caused damage to the brown paper. This would not have happened to ordinary paper. This fact led the court to decide that there was no nuisance. The goods were of a sensitive nature and this was the reason for the damage.

Malice

Private nuisance is based on reasonable conduct between people. Such conduct brings into consideration the intention of the person who by some means causes a nuisance to another. As we have seen, the House of Lords in the case of *Bradford Corporation v Pickles* 1895 decided that a lawful act is not turned into an unlawful act because the doer of the act did it with malice in his mind. In the case of *Christie v Davey* 1893 Christie was a music teacher who had pupils attend his home for lessons. The noise from these lessons annoyed Davey. Davey reacted by, when the music lessons started, banging metal trays together and blowing a whistle. This was done next to the party wall and disturbed the music lessons. Davey's actions were restrained by an injunction since the court was satisfied that the actions were deliberate and done maliciously.

The distinction between the two decisions has been explained as that where what has happened did not infringe any right or interest of a person then that person has no claim of infringement. So the matter of malice is not relevant. This was the approach in Pickles' case. In Davey's case however Christie had a recognised right not to be disturbed by noise. This right was infringed and so the claim was successful. It would also be an actionable matter if the noise was a nuisance whether it was done with malice or not.

Who can sue

As private nuisance is a tort concerning the occupation of land it follows, and is usually the case, that the occupier will be able to sue. With certain forms of private nuisance, such as infringement of rights of support, light or way, the landlord's interests are being infringed. In such circumstances the tenant of the property is hardly likely to bring a legal action to protect the landlord's interests. Landlords may therefore bring an action for private nuisance in order to protect their rights and interests. Where a person occupies land as a licensee, which is a lesser legal position than that of a tenant, there is no recognised right to bring a legal action.

Who can be sued

Action may be taken against the person whose actions had created the private nuisance. In most cases this will be the occupier of the land where the activity which has caused the nuisance has been conducted. An occupier will be vicariously liable for the actions of his employees which create a nuisance.

The general rule in tort is that a person is not liable for the action of his independent contractor. To this rule, as we have seen, there are a number of exceptions. Included is that of an occupier of land being liable for nuisance from hazardous operations conducted by an independent contractor. In the case of *Mantania v National Provincial Bank* 1936 the bank occupied one floor of a building. The bank had builders carry out extensive building work which caused nuisance from noise and dust to Mantania who occupied another floor. The bank was held to be liable for the action of the independent contractor. The same approach was used by the court in the earlier case of *Bower v Peate* 1876. Here builders were engaged by Peate to carry out work on his land. This work withdrew support to Bower's house. Peate was held liable.

An occupier of land is not liable for nuisance caused by a trespasser. This however is subject to the exception where the occupier knew or ought to have known of the existence of the nuisance and failed to deal with it. The House of Lords applied this exception in the case of *Sedleigh-Denfield v O'Callaghan* 1940 where a pipe and grating were, without the occupier's permission, installed so as project into a ditch. The ditch was owned by the occupier and he had a worker whose job included clearing and inspecting the ditch. The Law Lords took the view that this worker ought to have noticed the installation of this pipe and appreciated that it formed an obstruction in the ditch which could lead to flooding. This failure made the occupier liable when the ditch flooded on to adjoining land.

At one time it was believed that a person would not be liable for a nuisance if it was caused by natural forces. This belief was not supported by the Court of Appeal in *Leakey v National Trust for Places of Historic Interest and Natural Beauty* 1980. In this case Leakey occupied a house next to land of the National Trust. There was a large mound on the land of the National Trust and from time to time, after rain, soil was washed down into Leakey's back yard. On one occasion this happened and choked a drain in the back yard causing flooding to the house. The fact that what had occurred was solely the result of natural forces was no defence. Private nuisance had occurred and the National Trust was liable.

A landlord would not normally be liable for nuisance arising from the premises he had left. Where however it can be shown that he authorised the activity which caused the nuisance he will be liable. This made the landlord liable, together with his tenant, in the case of *Harris v James* 1876 when the landlord had leased land knowing it was to be used for the manufacture of lime. This process caused a nuisance and so both were liable

There are two Acts of Parliament which place liability on a landlord for repairs which might constitute nuisance. The Landlord and Tenant Act 1985 imposes obligations on landlords of houses or flats where the lease is for less than seven years. The obligations on the landlord are to keep in repair the structure and exterior of the dwelling-house and to keep in repair and proper working order the installations for the supply of water, gas and electricity and for sanitation, and space and water heating. The Defective Premises Act 1972 also places an obligation on landlords of any premises to ensure that all those who might reasonably be expected to be affected by defects in the premises are reasonably safe from personal injury and damage to their property.

Defences to nuisance

The defences considered earlier apply to a claim made for nuisance. There is also a defence that the nuisance has continued without interruption for a period of not less than 20 years. This defence is provided by the Prescription Act 1832. For the defence to succeed it must be proved that what constitutes the nuisance was done openly and without permission. The period of time does not start to run until the nuisance affects someone in the enjoyment of his property. This is to be seen from the decision in *Sturges v Bridgman* 1879 where a baker's premises adjoined the rear garden of a doctor. The baker used machinery in the part of the premises near to the garden. The doctor built a consulting room at the end of the garden. He then discovered that he could not use the room for his practice because of the noise and vibrations from the baker's premises. His claim for an injunction for nuisance was resisted by the baker on the ground that his work had gone on for more than 20 years. This defence was rejected. There was no actionable nuisance until the doctor built the consulting room and then found the noise and vibration to affect him.

It is no defence to show that what was being done was for the benefit of people generally, if what was done created a nuisance from the unreasonable way it was carried out. For example, the construction of a new hospital, which is urgently needed, cannot justify creating excessive noise which disturbs the sleep of the occupants of nearby houses. It is also no defence to plead that what was done formed a small part of the nuisance. So the driver of a vehicle, which together with other forms a nuisance, is liable for the nuisance.

Remedies For Nuisance

The remedies available to a court to deal with nuisance are damages and injunctions. Damages will be awarded by the court to compensate for the nuisance, for example for loss of sleep. Injunctions may be granted, either prohibitory or mandatory, as the circumstances require. Courts have power to grant injunctions at short notice on the evidence of one party only, known as *ex parte* applications.

The rule in Rylands v Fletcher

The tort in the rule in *Rylands v Fletcher* 1868 is generally considered to be an extension of the law of nuisance. Its main distinction is that it is a tort of strict liability. That is, the tort is committed if the requirements of the rule are satisfied. Reasonableness does not play any part in the matter, unlike nuisance.

The rule arose from a decision in the High Court which was approved by the House of Lords. The facts of the case were that Rylands wished to have a reservoir constructed for use with his mill. He engaged an apparently competent contractor, an independent contractor in law, to undertake this task. During the excavation work some old vertical shafts were discovered by the contractor. These were filled in but, as later events showed, in an inadequate and negligent manner. Unknown both to Rylands and the contractor these shafts connected with the shafts of Fletcher's mine on the adjoining land. When water was put in the reservoir it burst through the inadequately filled shafts and flooded Fletcher's mine. The mine was put out of commission resulting in a loss of profit to Fletcher. Fletcher sued Rylands for damages.

In the High Court Mr Justice Blackburn decided the case in Fletcher's favour. He said:

> a person who for his own purposes brings on his lands and collects and keeps there anything likely to do mischief if it escapes, must keep it at his peril, and if does not do so, is prima facie answerable for all the damage which is the natural consequence of its escape.

When Rylands appealed to the House of Lords against the decision, Mr Justice Blackburn's decision was upheld subject to a modification. The modification was that for the rule to apply the use of the land which gave rise to the liability had to be 'non-natural'. From this, the approach of the courts has been that there is no liability unless the use was 'unnatural' in the sense of abnormal or unusual use.

Before considering the application of the rule it is necessary to examine the elements which have to be satisfied for the tort to exist. The first of these is that the occupier must have brought something on to his land which is liable to do mischief if it escapes. Secondly there must be an escape. Thirdly the damage must be the natural consequence of the escape. Finally, as the result of the House of Lords modification, the question of non-natural use has to be determined.

The rule was for a number of years applied to a wide range of activities. It might well be that if similar cases came before the courts today the decision would be different. The attitude of the courts has changed and a person may well be successful if the claim for the wrong done to him was based on some other tort.

An example of the extent to which the rule was applied is seen in the case of *Attorney General v Corke* 1933 where a landowner was held liable for the damage done by gypsies he had allowed to come and stay on his land. Other cases have dealt with damage done by fire, explosions, electricity, oil and noxious fumes.

The need for there to be an escape for there to be liability was evident from the House of Lords decision in *Read v Lyons and Co Ltd* 1947. Mrs Read worked as an inspector in a munitions factory owned by Lyons. An explosion occurred in the shell-filling part of the factory and Mrs Read was injured. She sued basing her claim on the rule in *Rylands v Fletcher*. Her claim was unsuccessful. The principal ground for the decision was that there had not been an escape. The Law Lords said that an escape had to be from the land over which the defendant had control or occupation to a place which was outside this control or occupation. This had not happened with regard to Mrs Read; she had been in another part of the defendant's factory. The Law Lords expressed the opinion that the rule did not allow a claim to be made for personal injury. This opinion however has not been accepted as binding law by some judges. An example of this is the case of *Shiffman v Order of St John* 1936 where a flagpole of a tent belonging to the defendants fell because it had been negligently secured. Shiffman was injured by the fall of the flagpole. The court decided that the claim for personal injury succeeded under the tort of negligence. The court also expressed the opinion that there was also liability under the rule. This view is supported by a number of judges despite the opinion expressed in *Read v Lyons*. The Law Lords also were of the view that the use of the factory for the manufacture of munitions in war time was natural use of land.

The application of the rule with regard to natural use of land was examined in the case of *Mason v Levy Auto Parts of England Ltd* 1967. Here Levy stored in open land large quantities of oil, engine parts protected by grease and other combustible materials. A fire broke out in unknown circumstances and spread to Mason's land. Mason's claim under the rule was successful. In reaching this decision the judge indicated that he had taken into account the quantities of combustible materials stored; the way in which they were stored; and the character of the neighbourhood. All this constituted non-natural use of the land. This decision may be compared with that of *Giles v Walker* 1890 where a landowner ploughed up land which then became overgrown with thistles. These seeded and blew on to adjoining land. The claim was unsuccessful; what had happened was natural use of land.

Defences to the rule

If the plaintiff has consented, either expressly or impliedly to the presence of the risk on the land then this is a defence to a claim under the rule. Coupled with this is the presence of something which is of common benefit such as the presence of water pipes in a building shared by the plaintiff and the defendant. In the case of *Peters v Prince of Wales Theatres Ltd* 1943 the presence of a water sprinkler system was held to be of common benefit. Damage caused by its malfunction could not be claimed under the rule.

In the case of *Dunn v Birmingham Canal Co* 1872 where the plaintiff mined under the canal, with flooding from the canal to the mine, it was held that the plaintiff was entirely to blame and so could not recover damages.

Where the escape is the result of the action of a stranger this constitutes a defence. The leading case on this is *Rickards v Lothian* 1913 where both parties were occupiers of different floors in an office building. A stranger maliciously put the plug into a wash basin and left the taps running. A flood resulted and the plaintiff's claim was dismissed on the ground of the act being that of a stranger or trespasser.

Claims have been made against statutory authorities providing services to the public. It appears from the different decisions that whether there is liability or not depends on the words in the statute authorising the activity. Where there is a statutory duty to provide a service, rather than a permissive authority only, the courts have been unwilling to hold the statutory authority liable. This is evident from the case of *Smeaton v Ilford Corporation* 1954 where Smeaton suffered damage from sewage which overflowed from the corporation's sewer. The sewer was overloaded because of new housing development. The corporation could not refuse to allow new connections to be made to the sewer since the new house owners had a statutory right to make such connections. This provided a defence to the claim.

Act of God is a defence. In *Nichols v Marsland* 1876 a storm of exceptional severity caused three lakes constructed by Marsland to overflow and damage the property of Nichols. The court accepted the defence of Act of God.

LIABILITY FOR SPREAD OF FIRE

Liability for the spread of fire may arise under the torts of nuisance, *Rylands v Fletcher*, and negligence. There is also an Act of Parliament which is relevant to this matter. The Act is the Fires Prevention (Metropolis) Act 1774. Despite its title the provisions apply throughout the country and not just in the London area, and it is still fully in force. The Act provides that no action is maintainable against anyone in whose building or on whose land a fire accidentally begins. It is important to note that the word 'accidentally' has been strictly interpreted by the courts. If therefore a fire started because of nuisance or negligence the Act does not provide protection.

The operation of the provisions of the Act may be seen in the case of *Collingwood v Home and Colonial Stores Ltd* 1936 where a fire broke out on the premises of the defendants and spread to Collingwood's premises. The fire started from the defective electrical wiring on the premises of the defendants. Since there was no negligence on the part of the defendants and the rule in *Rylands v Fletcher* was held not to apply the provisions in the Act provided a defence. This case may be compared with *Musgrove v Pendelis* 1919 where a fire started accidentally in the engine of a car in a garage. The fire could have been stopped by simply closing down a control valve on the fuel pipe from the petrol tank to the carburettor. The chauffeur failed to do this and the fire spread to Musgrove's flat above the garage. Here the Act could not be used as a defence since the fire had started accidentally and had spread by the chauffeur's negligence. His employer was vicariously liable for his negligence.

The case of *Mason v Levy Auto Parts of England Ltd* 1967, considered earlier with regard to liability under the rule in *Rylands v Fletcher*, indicates the application of the rule in the liability for spread of fire.

Liability for the spread of fire is strict and so a person is liable for the actions of his independent contractor. In the case of *H. and N. Emanuel Ltd v Greater London Council* 1971 the council were held liable for the spread of fire from rubbish being burnt from the demolition of some prefabricated bungalows. The contractors engaged by the council were restrained in their contract from burning rubbish on the site. The council as occupiers of the land were held liable for the escape of fire caused by negligence. In a circumstance such as this, it would be possible for the council to sue the contractors for breach of contract and recover the amount they had had to pay. This assumes, of course, that the contractors have either the financial assets or insurance to meet that claim.

4 NEGLIGENCE AND BREACH OF STATUTORY DUTY

INTRODUCTION

Negligence is probably the most important common law tort of the whole range of torts. Its application extends over a wide range of circumstances and unlike trespass to land and private nuisance it is not related solely to land, although it may be in appropriate circumstances.

The word negligence is used in two senses. The first is in connection with the committing of various torts. So a defamatory statement may be made negligently which results in the tort of libel being committed. The second sense is to use the word in a limited way only; that is to refer to the common law tort of negligence.

The tort of negligence, in its modern form, is based on the House of Lords decision in the case of *Donoghue v Stevenson* 1932. Before this decision actions were decided by the courts on the ground that there was a duty not to act carelessly so as to cause damage to persons or property. This duty however was loosely expressed and it was not defined with precision. In addition there was a reluctance of the courts to apply this principle with any vigour and certainly to apply it to different circumstances.

As will be seen later, the courts in recent years have extended the law of negligence and, more recently, have retreated from that position. The reason for this is that the courts became alarmed by what had happened earlier and feared that it had resulted in people being able to sue in circumstances where, on reflection, there should not be a right to sue. In the words of one judge: 'It opened the floodgates to claims.' This advance and retreat by the courts has created difficulties in the interpretation of judicial reasoning. Some judges have had to retract their earlier decisions and publicly recognise that they were wrong.

The reverse in the application of the tort of negligence means that some earlier decisions, even of the House of Lords, have to be considered in the light of the changed judicial approach. With this different approach a number of earlier cases on the tort of negligence are no longer of judicial standing.

Before considering the tort of negligence in detail it will be helpful to distinguish the tort from those of trespass to land and nuisance. Trespass to land is a tort which relates solely to land whereas negligence does not. Private nuisance, too, relates solely to land. Unlike trespass the tort of negligence requires that damage shall have occurred. With private nuisance liability arises even if the interference was not reasonably foreseeable; this is not so with negligence. As will be seen later, the tort of negligence has three component parts each of which must exist if liability is to be established. Furthermore, the courts now refuse to award damages in the tort of negligence if the claim comes within the definition of economic loss.

Donoghue v Stevenson 1932

The decision of the House of Lords in this case is the starting point of the modern law of negligence. The facts of the case were that Mrs Donoghue and a friend went out for a walk and called in a café for a drink. The friend bought a bottle of ginger-beer. The owner of the café took the metal cap off the bottle, which was of dark opaque glass, and poured some of the liquid into a tumbler. Mrs Donoghue drank the contents. The friend then poured some more from the bottle into the tumbler. With this liquid there flowed out the decomposed body of a snail. The effect of seeing this sight, and realising that she had drunk liquid in which the remains of the snail had been, caused her shock and gave her gastro-enteritis from the impurities in the liquid. Mrs Donoghue claimed that Stevenson, the manufacturer of the ginger-beer, was responsible for the washing of the bottle, the filling of it with ginger-beer and its sealing with a metal cap. All this, she claimed, put a duty on Stevenson to ensure that his system of business would prevent snails entering his ginger-beer bottles and provide an efficient system of inspection of the bottles so as to prevent snails entering the bottles before being filled with ginger-beer. His failure to do these things, she claimed, had caused the accident.

It is important to note that Mrs Donoghue was not the purchaser of the ginger-beer; if she had been then the case would have been a straightforward claim for breach of contract for failure to supply a drink which was fit for human consumption. The absence of a contractual relationship meant that Mrs Donoghue, if she were to receive any compensation, had to show that there was some duty owed to her. It should also be noted that the shopkeeper could not be at fault since the manufacturing process was one where the metal cap was squeezed on the bottle. There was thus no opportunity for the café owner to have tampered with the bottle.

The House of Lords decided that Stevenson did, in these circumstances, owe a duty of care to Donoghue. In the course of coming to this conclusion one of the Law Lords, Lord Atkins, made a statement which has been accepted as showing the principle on which the tort of negligence is based. He said:

The rule that you are to love your neighbour becomes, in law, you must not injure your neighbour; and the lawyer's question, who is my neighbour? receives a restricted reply. You must take reasonable care to avoid acts or omissions which you can reasonably foresee would be likely to injure your neighbour. Who, then, in law is my neighbour? The answer seems to be – persons who are so closely and directly affected by my act that I ought reasonably to have them in contemplation as being so affected when I am directing my mind to the acts or omissions which are called in question.

An examination of this statement will show the essential features of the tort of negligence. The first point to note is that the tort covers both acts and omissions. So failure to do something can give rise to liability as well as the doing of an act. The next point is that reasonable care is to be used. The use of the word reasonable means that it is not a tort of strict liability. If, therefore, a person does exercise reasonable care he has done that that was required of him. It can also be noted that the term 'reasonably foresee' puts a limit on liability. If, therefore, something happens which could not be reasonably foreseen then there is no liability. Finally, the duty is owed to those persons who ought to be in the contemplation of a person when that person is directing his mind to the acts or omissions which are later questioned.

From this we can see that the tort of negligence is one where reasonableness is an essential element. The fact that a person is injured does not mean that that person automatically has a claim against the person responsible for the injury. The injured person must prove that there had been a lack of reasonable care and that what had happened was reasonably foreseeable.

The tort of negligence is defined as having three essential elements, each of which must be proved if a claim is to succeed. These are:

1) a duty of care must exist between the parties;
2) there must be a breach of that duty of care;
3) injury must result from that breach of duty of care.

DUTY OF CARE

The question as to whether a duty of care is owed in particular circumstances has presented difficulties to the courts. Furthermore the attitude of the courts has changed in recent years and some early decisions, even of the House of Lords, can no longer be relied upon. The change in approach has been the fear of the courts that a too liberal application of the principle of law could lead to a vast number of claims being made. This has been referred to as 'opening the floodgates'. When the courts thought that this might in fact be happening they felt obliged to revert to the earlier more restrictive approach.

There are circumstances where the courts have held that no duty of care exists even though the circumstances suggested to the ordinary man that a duty of care would exist. An example of this is the House of Lords decision in *Rondel v Worsley* 1967. In this case Rondel was charged with a serious criminal offence. He was represented by Worsley, a barrister. On conviction he was sentenced to six years imprisonment. Some years after this conviction he sued Worsley, claiming that he had been negligent in the presentation of the case on Rondel's behalf. The House of Lords decided that there was no duty of care owed by the barrister to his client. The reason for this was that of public policy. A barrister owes a duty to the court for the true administration of justice and this was one reason for giving barristers who appear in court immunity from being sued. This immunity also applies to solicitors when they are acting as advocates in court. Where, however, negligence occurs outside the courts in the preparation of a case then this immunity does not apply. Here a duty of care exists.

Another example is the House of Lords decision in *Hill v Chief Constable of West Yorkshire* 1988. Mrs Hill sued the Chief Constable for negligence following the murder of her daughter by a person who eventually confessed to the murder of 13 women and the attempted murder of eight others. When the murderer was caught he did not correspond to the identity of the person the police had been searching for and this, Mrs Hill believed, meant that they had been negligent in their duties. This she believed resulted in her daughter's murder. The House of Lords dismissed Mrs Hill's claim on two grounds. The first was that there was not a sufficient proximity of relationship between the daughter and the police and so no duty of care arose. The second ground was that public policy prevented a duty of care existing in such circumstances.

The reluctance of the courts to allow a duty of care to exist which could result in a large number of claims is seen in the Court of Appeal decision in *Electrochrome Ltd v Welsh Plastics Ltd* 1968 where the driver of a vehicle negligently drove it into a fire hydrant on an industrial estate. This interrupted the water supply to the estate and lost Electrochrome a day's production and profits. The claim made was dismissed on the ground that there was no duty of care owed. To allow the claim could well mean that many actions would be brought which, the court believed, ought not to be permitted.

The House of Lords, during the 1970s made a number of decisions which extended the application of negligence. It seemed at that time that a person had a right to sue unless there were special circumstances which indicated that that should not be so. In the

1980s there was a change of attitude and the approach was more restricted. The main ground for this change was that many claims were made where there was neither physical damage to property nor personal injury. This type of claim was for economic loss. The term economic loss means, for example, an article is found to have a defect in it. That defect however has not caused any personal injury or damage to property. Because of the defect the article cannot be used safely until it is repaired or replaced. In such a circumstance the loss to the owner is economic, that is, the value of the repair or the cost of its replacement. With one exception the position now is that economic loss on its own cannot be recovered.

Economic loss

The most prominent feature of the attitude of the courts has been to limit claims for economic loss. The exception where economic loss on its own may be claimed is where there has been a negligent misstatement. The authority for this is the House of Lords decision in the case of *Hedley Byrne and Co Ltd v Heller and Partners Ltd* 1964. The facts in the case were that Hedley Byrne were advertising agents who were approached by a customer, Easipower Ltd, to give advice as to a suitable form of advertising for Easipower's products. Their advice was that advertising on television was required. Hedley Byrne were instructed by Easipower to place this advertising. This they did which made them personally liable for the cost. As they had some doubts as to the financial strength of Easipower they asked their bankers to obtain from Easipower's bankers, Heller and Partners, a statement of Easipower's financial standing. The reply was satisfactory but the letter was headed 'For your own private use and without responsibility on the part of this bank or its officials'. Relying on this reply, which Hedley Byrne took to mean that there was no risk, they did not cancel the advertising contract. Shortly after this Easipower went into liquidation and Hedley Byrne lost over £17,000.

Hedley Byrne sued Heller and Partners claiming that they were in breach of a duty of care to them. This claim was rejected in the High Court on the ground that Heller and Partners had been careless but there was no duty of care. This view was supported by the Court of Appeal. The House of Lords, however, decided that there could be a duty of care in these circumstances, a person giving information, but in these particular circumstances there was no duty. This was so because Heller and Partners had expressly, by the disclaiming words, not undertaken any duty of care.

In the course of the judgments Lord Morris of Borth-y-Gest said:

> I consider that it follows and that it should now be regarded as settled that if someone possessed of a special skill undertakes, quite irrespective of contract, to apply that skill for the assistance

of another person who relies upon such skill, a duty of care will arise.

This decision, therefore, established the principle that a person could be liable for a statement made negligently, outside a contractual relationship, if the person to whom it was made suffers loss. The use, however, of words which disclaim liability will mean that no duty of care exists.

Since this decision the use of a disclaimer has been further examined by the House of Lords. This was in the case of *Smith v Bush* 1989 where Mrs Smith wished to buy a modestly priced house. She followed the usual practice of approaching a building society for a loan to purchase the house. She paid a fee to the building society for a valuation survey. The society then instructed Bush to make this survey. The surveyor failed to note that where a chimney breast had been removed in a bedroom the brickwork in the roof space was left unsupported. The survey report indicated that a loan was appropriate and the society acted upon this. The survey report however contained an extensive disclaimer of liability. Mrs Smith was given a copy of the report.

After bricks fell through the ceiling causing damage Mrs Smith sued Bush. The case came before the House of Lords where, first, they decided that the survey had been conducted negligently. They then examined the disclaimer and decided that the provisions in the Unfair Contract Terms Act 1977 applied. This meant that the disclaimer, if it was to stand and protect the surveyor, had to satisfy the test of reasonableness, under the Act. The decision was that the disclaimer did not do this and so was ineffective in protecting the surveyor. Mrs Smith was therefore successful in her claim.

The decision in *Hedley Byrne and Co V Heller and Partners Ltd* has been applied in a number of circumstances since then. It does seem as if the courts are determined to keep the principle of law confined and not to allow it to be used in very different circumstances. This seems to follow from the decision of the House of Lords in the case of *Caparo Industries PLC v Dickman* 1990. Here a firm of auditors prepared an annual report for a company, Fidelity PLC. Before this was issued the directors of Fidelity issued preliminary results which showed results much less than expected. Caparo held shares in Fidelity and bought more shares which had fallen substantially as a result of the published figures. They continued to buy after the auditors had agreed the accounts and eventually took over the company. They then discovered that instead of a £1.3 million profit, as the accounts showed, there was a loss of £400,000. Caparo then sued the auditors claiming that they had been negligent in certifying the accounts as showing a profit when there was in fact a loss. They claimed that a duty of care was owed to them as both existing and potential shareholders.

The House of Lords decided that Caparo were owed no duty of care. They said that in the absence of exceptional circumstances auditors owed no duty of care to third parties who rely on company accounts. Clearly, for the Law Lords to have held that auditors in agreeing company accounts owed a duty of care to existing and potential shareholders would have made them liable to innumerable persons.

As we saw earlier, the courts recognize the validity of a claim for economic loss which is associated with physical damage to property or with personal injury. An example of this is the decision of the Court of Appeal in *S.C.M. (UK) Ltd v W.J. Whittall and Son Ltd* 1971 where building contractors were working in a road in an industrial part of Birmingham. Whilst excavating in the road an employee cut a high voltage cable. This caused a power failure with the current cut off for several hours. S.C.M. (UK) Ltd had a factory in the area which manufactured office machinery. When the electric power was cut off molten plastic in extrusion machinery started to solidify. Machines had to be stripped down and the solidified material removed. This caused damage to certain machine parts which required replacing. There was therefore a loss of value of the parts and profits from failure to produce. S.C.M. made a claim for damages for negligence. The decision of the court was that the claim could succeed for the physical damage and for the economic loss associated with that physical damage. Part of the claim which related to loss of production from undamaged machinery which could not be operated simply because of the loss of electric power was refused. This was economic loss on its own and to allow the claim would be to go against policy.

This decision was followed by the Court of Appeal in the case of *Spartan Steel and Alloys Ltd v Martin and Co (Contractors) Ltd* 1972 where the facts were not dissimilar.

Application of negligence

The tort of negligence has been applied in circumstances where buildings were constructed with defects which became apparent at some later date. Claims were made by those who were not in a contractual relationship with the builder or, if a contract had been made, it was too late to sue having regard to the provisions in the Limitation Act 1980.

It was with these cases the courts first allowed the tort of negligence to apply and then, when it became apparent that this was leading to the opening of the floodgates, the thing the courts feared, a complete reversal of the courts' approach occurred.

The case which began the run of cases was *Dutton v Bognor Regis Urban District Council* 1972. Here Mrs Dutton bought a house from a Mrs Clarke who had bought it from the builder about two years earlier. Because the house was almost new Mrs Dutton felt she could rely on the valuation survey of the building society. When this was satisfactory she bought the house. Not many months later cracks appeared in the walls and a detailed survey revealed that the foundations were not built to building regulation standard. The house had however been subject to building control by the local authority in the usual way. She was not in any contractual relationship with the builder so to sue him for breach of contract was not open to her. She sued him and the local authority for negligence. In the Court of Appeal both were held to be liable to her. Damages were awarded to the value of the house, which was not capable of repair at reasonable cost, as if it were not damaged.

This decision was applied in a number of cases and the principle received the approval of the House of Lords in *Anns v London Borough of Merton* 1977. In this case one of the Law Lords said that there would be liability when there was a 'present or imminent danger to the health or safety of the occupants of the building'.

The application of this principle meant that many cases were brought by owners of buildings against local authorities where it could be shown that their building control officers had been negligent in approving work as being to the standard of the building regulations when this was not so. The local authorities were vicariously liable for the negligence of their employees. The position was reached whereby once liability could be seen to exist the local authority insurers would seek to settle the case in order to avoid the expense of litigation.

The case which indicated that the courts were unwilling to continue to apply the principle in Anns' case as liberally as had happened, was the House of Lords decision in *Peabody Donation Fund v Sir Lindsay Parkinson and Co Ltd* 1985. The case arose from a large residential development being carried out for Peabody on their own land. Because of the nature of the ground, London clay, there was a possibility of movement and so the drainage systems of the houses were designed for the use of flexible pipes. Despite plans being approved by the local authority for the construction of the drainage systems in this manner the council's drainage officer and the resident architect, without any authority from their employers, changed the plans. Rigid pipes were used in the systems and they soon fractured. The claim by Peabody was dismissed. The House of Lords were of the opinion that in these circumstances there was no duty of care owed by either the local authority or the main contractor. They were also of the opinion that where an owner used the services of an architect or engineer and some defect occurred in the building work the owner should sue the professional for negligence.

A further indication of a change of view of liability of builders and others for defects in building work was the decision of the House of

Lords in *D. and F. Estates Ltd v Church Commissioners for England and Others* 1988. The facts of the case, in brief, were that plastering work was done by a sub-contractor. It was done contrary to the manufacturer's instructions and so was not properly keyed to the walls. This became known when redecorating was required. No plaster however fell. The cost of replastering and redecorating was substantial. The House of Lords refused to award damages. The loss was economic loss only and recovery of such loss would go against policy on that matter.

The complete reversal of the principle laid down in Dutton's case and approved in Anns' case was the decision of the House of Lords in *Murphy v Brentwood District Council* 1990. In this case a construction company submitted for building regulation approval plans for a pair of semi-detached houses. The houses required a reinforced concrete raft and the plans and calculations for this were provided. The local authority did not have a structural engineer on the staff and so sent the plans and calculations to an outside consulting engineer for checking. He recommended approval and the local authority took his advice. The building control officer then made the usual inspections and gave final approval. Some 11 years later Murphy, who had bought the house from the builders, noticed cracking in the walls. Detailed investigation revealed that the raft was defective. The cost of the remedial works was estimated to be over £40,000. As Murphy could not afford this expense he sold the house for £35,000 less than its market value as a sound house free from defects. He then sued the local authority for negligence. When the case came before the House of Lords they took the opportunity to review the cases which had been decided on the principle in Dutton's case and that of Anns'. They decided that Dutton's and Anns' cases had been wrongly decided. There was no duty of care on a local authority to pay for the cost of remedying defects in a building which resulted from the failure of the local authority to ensure that the building was designed and erected in accordance with building regulations. If the defect became apparent before there was any physical damage the loss suffered by the owner was economic loss on its own. To allow a claim of this nature would be contrary to policy.

The Law Lords observed that there might still be a duty of care owed to an owner in certain limited circumstances. Examples given were where a separate contractor undertook work which caused damage to other parts of the building, such as a steel frame which fails to give support to floors or walls. Other examples quoted were electrical work, boilers or other ancillary equipment which if defective caused damage to other parts of the building. In addition the Lord Chancellor left open the matter of the liability of a local authority if the latent defect in the building led to personal injury. The Law Lords also observed that Parliament had passed the

Defective Premises Act 1972 which dealt specifically with the duty of care owed to the owner of a dwelling.

The explanation of this substantial reversal of a principle of law which had applied by the courts in numerous cases is that it was a new development in negligence which went too far. Earlier developments had been gradual, extending over a period of time. This development was too much in a short period of time. The creation of a new duty of care on a matter of this importance, in the light of experience, was too much to accept. Furthermore, there was the fact that all the claims had been for economic loss and to allow such claims was contrary to policy.

Junior Books Ltd v Veitchi Co Ltd 1982

When the Law Lords in *Murphy v Brentwood District Council* examined all the relevant case law there was a previous decision which they did not overrule. This was *Junior Books v Veitchi Co Ltd*. In this case Junior Books decided to have a factory built. An important feature of the construction of the factory was that the floor had to be laid to a high standard. For this reason they approached Veitchi who were specialist flooring contractors. Veitchi undertook to do all that was required and when the main contractor was appointed Veitchi were nominated as the flooring sub-contractors. The factory was built and Junior Books installed machinery and started production. A few months later cracks appeared in the floors. Junior Books had experts examine the cracks. They were told that the cracks could be repaired but that further cracking would occur. They were therefore faced with a continuous maintenance problem. Rather than have this difficulty they decided to have the floor relaid. This meant removing the machinery, laying off the staff, tearing up the defective floor, relaying it and then reinstalling the machinery. All this cost in the region of £200,000. Junior Books sued Veitchi for breach of duty of care. The House of Lords agreed that there was a duty of care and that it had been breached so Junior Books' claim was successful.

A number of reasons have been advanced as to why this case was not overruled and so remains good law. The main reason appears to be that the Law Lords were satisfied that the proximity of relationship between Junior Books and Veitchi was such as to be almost a contractual relationship. This meant that a duty of care existed. The fact that Veitchi knew that they had been selected to produce a floor to a high standard and had failed to do so constituted a breach of duty of care. A further reason advanced for the case not being overruled is that it is a case based on its own special facts. Some judges have, however, expressed doubt about relying on it when making any further claim.

Defective Premises Act 1972

The Act was passed by Parliament at the same time as the Court of Appeal in *Dutton v Bognor Regis Urban District Council* 1972 was creating the principle that a builder and a local authority owed a duty of care to the owner of a building which had a defect in it which did not become apparent for some time. Because of the decision in Dutton's case it was easier to sue for breach of duty of care for the common law tort of negligence than it was to bring an action under the provisions in the Act.

Now that the House of Lords in *Murphy v Brentwood District Council* 1990 have overruled Dutton's case and indicated that they would expect any claims to be brought under the provisions of the Act it will be used on an increasing scale. For this reason an examination of its main provisions is necessary.

Section 1, sub-section (1), of the Act states:

(1) A person taking on work for or in connection with the provision of a dwelling (whether the dwelling is provided by the erection or by the conversion or enlargement of a building) owes a duty
  (a) if the dwelling is provided to the order of any person, to that person; and
  (b) without prejudice to paragraph (a) above, to every person who acquires an interest (whether legal or equitable) in the dwelling;
  to see that the work he takes on is done in a workmanlike or, as the case may be, professional manner, with proper materials and so that as regards that work the dwelling will be fit for habitation when completed.

As can be seen, the duty is owed by anyone who takes on work. So the architect, builder and sub-contractor may be liable. The wording does not limit the duty. A most important point is that the duty only arises in connection with the provision of a dwelling. The provisions of the Act do not therefore apply to industrial or commercial buildings. The provision of the dwelling is not restricted to new construction. The duty owed is not just to the person who ordered the work to be carried out but also to every person who acquires an interest in the dwelling. This means that the duty is owed to those who buy from the original owner. The duty is specified as being to do the work in a workmanlike or professional manner, which is a clear indication that the duty is not just that of the builder. Proper materials are to be used. The Court of Appeal decision in *Hancock v B.W. Brazier (Anerley) Ltd* 1966, a breach of contract action, is relevant here. In this case the builder was held to be liable for the use of hardcore, which unknown to him contained harmful salts, for the solid floors of a house he was building. When the salts expanded the floor swelled and structural damage resulted to the house. The builder was held to be liable despite his ignorance of the quality of the hardcore. Finally, the house is to be fit for human habitation when completed.

The section also continues by providing that if a person takes on work under the section which is to the order of another person, then if he complies with those instructions properly he is to be treated as having discharged his duty. This, however, is subject to a duty to warn the other person of any defects in the instructions. So a person who wants to have a house built in a particular manner and instructs his builder to do this is owed no duty under the section other than to be warned of some defect in his instructions. A person who agrees to the work being done in a specified manner, with specified materials or to a specified design is not thereby to be treated as having given instructions. This particular provision covers the situation of a prospective purchaser of a dwelling on a new development requesting a house to be built according to one of the types available. Here the prospective purchaser has not given any instructions so as to deprive him of the protection of the Act. Any cause of action which arises from a breach of the duty of care imposed by Section 1 is deemed to have accrued at the time the dwelling was completed. If, however, work has been done to rectify work already done the cause of action in respect of that work is deemed to have accrued when the remedial works were finished. So the limitation period of six years starts to run from when the dwelling was completed subject to any remedial works being done, in which case for those particular works the period runs from their completion.

Section 2 of the Act allows an exception to the provisions of the Act where a scheme has been approved by the Secretary of State for the Environment. A scheme is an arrangement whereby rights of protection are given to the owners of dwellings. The Secretary of State did approve a scheme a short while after the Act came into force but since then has withdrawn approval. No approved scheme exists at the present time.

Section 3 of the Act provides that where work of construction, repair, maintenance, demolition or other work is done to premises the duty of care remains even if the premises are disposed of.

Nervous shock

An area of the tort of negligence where difficulty has arisen and does still arise is the liability for 'nervous shock'. The courts have been cautious in allowing claims to be made under this heading. This is partly because of the problem of assessing the depth of reaction to be accepted as being nervous shock, and also because of the difficulty of deciding on the circumstances where a duty should exist. As part of the wish to put this topic on a firmer basis the courts have recently referred to psychiatric illness rather than nervous shock. What the courts have been unwilling to accept as actionable is ordinary distress or grief.

The leading case on nervous shock is the House of Lords decision in *McLoughlin v O'Brian* 1983. Here Mrs McLoughlin was at home whilst her husband was out in the car with three of their children. The eldest child was the driver. An hour or so later a friend called at the house and told her that an hour earlier the car had been involved in a bad accident about two miles away. The friend then drove her to the hospital. On her arrival she found her husband and sons covered in blood, bemused and screaming. She was told that her eldest daughter was dead. O'Brian was the negligent person who it was claimed had been responsible for the events which caused Mrs McLoughlin severe shock, organic depression and a change of personality. She was assumed to be a person who was of normal fortitude.

In the High Court and the Court of Appeal Mrs McLoughlin was unsuccessful in her claim. The view was that as she was not on the road near the accident spot there was no duty of care. The House of Lords however allowed her appeal. They accepted that there was no necessity of showing direct impact or fear of immediate personal injuries; that the 'nervous shock' must result from injury or fear of injury to a near relative; that there could be liability where the plaintiff did not witness or hear what had happened but came on it immediately after it had happened.

Where a person suffers nervous shock as a result of assisting at an accident where the circumstances were particularly distressing there is liability even if those involved are not relatives but strangers. This was established in *Chadwick v British Railways Board* 1967 where Chadwick assisted at the scene of a train accident. As the result of what he saw there he later suffered severe nervous shock. The Board was liable.

Two recent developments have been the cases of *Attia v British Gas PLC* 1987 and *Alcock v Chief Constable of South Yorkshire* 1991. In the first case the Court of Appeal accepted that there was liability for nervous shock when a woman saw her house being burnt down even though there was no one in the house. British Gas were liable since their negligence had led to the fire. In the second case the Court of Appeal decided that liability for nervous shock from seeing pictures on television of a tragedy would only apply if the pictures were of relatives of the viewer.

As will be appreciated from this consideration of liability for nervous shock there is a lack of clearly defined rules.

BREACH OF DUTY OF CARE

For the tort of negligence to be committed there must not only be a duty of care but also a breach of that duty. Whether a person who owes a duty of care is in breach of that duty is decided by the application of the standard of 'the reasonable man'. Guidance on this standard is gained from the statement of Baron Alderson in the case of *Blyth v Birmingham Waterworks Co* 1856. He said: 'Negligence is the omission to do something which a reasonable man, guided upon those considerations which ordinarily regulate the conduct of human affairs, would do, or doing something which a prudent and reasonable man would not do.'

Of course, in real life such a person does not exist. Attempts have been made by the courts to define this person with some degree of accuracy. The reasonable man is, it was suggested in one case, the man who travels on the top deck of the Clapham omnibus. That is, the ordinary man who goes about his business and his life in an ordinary way. In another case the reasonable man was said not to be a perfectionist. Despite this the Court of Appeal in *Nettleship v Weston* 1971 decided that a learner driver had to come up to the standard of the ordinary, competent driver. This obligation even extended to his instructor.

In practice, the assessment of the standard of the reasonable man is that of the judge trying the case having regard to all the circumstances of the case. If a jury is used, which happens very infrequently, it is the responsibility of the jury to decide the facts of the case, including the reasonable man standard.

Where a person, such as a professional man, claims to have a particular skill then the standard expected from him is not that of a reasonable man but that of a reasonable member of his profession or calling. If a member of a profession or calling meets that standard then there is no negligence on his part even if someone has suffered a serious injury.

The standard for professional people was expressed by the judge in the case of *Bolam v Friern Hospital Management Committee* 1957. The case arose from a claim that a doctor in a hospital had been negligent in the treatment he gave to a patient. Mr Justice McNair said:

> In one case it has been said you judge it by the conduct of the man on the top of the Clapham omnibus. He is the ordinary man. But where you get a situation which involves the use of some special skill or competence, then the test as to whether there has been negligence or not is not the test of the man on the top of a Clapham omnibus, because he has not got that special skill. The test is the standard of the ordinary skilled man exercising and professing to have that special skill. A man need not possess the

highest expert skill; it is well established law that it is sufficient if he exercises the ordinary skill of an ordinary competent man exercising that particular art.

In the particular circumstances of the case the doctor had not been negligent. He had done what the ordinary doctor would have done in the same circumstances and this absolved him of liability.

If a person chooses to give a task which requires some skill to a person who does not profess to have that skill then he cannot be held to be negligent in the same way as the skilled man.

The approach of the courts is to balance the risk against the expense needed to guard against the risk. If, therefore, the risk is high or even if the risk of an event occurring is not high its consequences could be very severe, such as the discharge of toxic material, then adequate precautions have to be taken.

Two cases indicate the approach of the courts to this matter. The House of Lords in the case of *Bolton v Stone* 1951 decided that the likelihood of injury occurring was so slight a cricket club had not been negligent in not taking precautions additional to those taken. The case came before the court because Miss Stone, whilst standing on the highway outside her home, was hit on the head by a cricket ball struck out of the cricket ground on the opposite side of the highway. There was a seven foot high fence to the ground and the playing area of the ground was about ten foot below the level of the adjoining highway. Records showed that batsmen had hit the ball out of the ground in a similar manner on six occasions only in the last 30 years. The risk therefore of a person being injured, as Miss Stone was, was such that it was not reasonable to expect the cricket club to take additional precautions or to stop playing cricket at the ground. This case may be compared with the decision in *Hilder v Associated Portland Cement Manufacturers Ltd* 1961 where Hilder was riding his motor-cycle along a road which was by the side of land owned by Associated Portland and on which children were allowed to play football. A football was kicked into the road and caused Hilder to have an accident. In these circumstances there was a much greater risk of users of the highway being injured than was the case in *Bolton v Stone*. For this reason Associated Portland were held to be liable for having allowed football to be played on their land without taking additional precautions.

The importance of the need to guard adequately when the risk is one of serious injury was pointed out by the House of Lords in the case of *Paris v Stepney Borough Council* 1951. Paris was an employee of the council and they were aware that he had sight in one eye only. He was therefore a known risk of total blindness if he should lose the sight of his one good eye. He was engaged in a task where the possibility of injury was not such as to require protective goggles to be provided by the employers for a normal man with sight in both eyes. Paris lost the sight in his good eye from an accident in the work he had undertaken. He sued the council and was successful. He was a known risk of total blindness and this risk required that he be provided with protective goggles even though this was not necessary with an employee with two good eyes. If the accident had happened to such an employee he would still have had sight in one eye.

From this decision the rule is that a person with a known disability should be adequately protected from any risk which goes with that ability. This is so even if with other employees without that disability no precautions would be needed. This liability depends on the disability being known to the other person. If, therefore, an employee chose to conceal from his employer the fact that he suffered from fits or blackouts this would deprive him of the right to make a successful claim against his employer. This is subject to his employer not having any reasonable ground which would make him aware of the condition of his employee.

Another case involving special risk, and one which is of some importance to the construction industry, is the House of Lords decision in *Haley v London Electricity Board* 1965. In this case two employees of London Electricity Board attended to a breakdown in an electricity supply cable buried in the pavement of a road. They dug down to the cable and before completing the repair went off to have a meal. The excavation was left open but with a wood mallet laid across the pavement with the end of the shaft resting on the adjoining railings. To a sighted person this would be a reasonable warning. Haley, a blind person, was walking on the pavement using a white stick to assist him. Unfortunately he failed to detect the warning with the result he fell into the excavation. He suffered serious head injuries and sued London Electricity Board for damages.

In the High Court and the Court of Appeal Haley was unsuccessful. Both courts were of the opinion that no special duty of care was owed to a blind person unless the work was being done in the vicinity of a blind institute or blind school. Their approach was that what was adequate warning and protection for a sighted person satisfied the duty of care. When the case came before the House of Lords their approach was totally different to that of the lower courts. They decided that Haley could succeed in his claim. The Law Lords held that the presence of a blind person on the streets of London or other towns was not so unusual that they could be ignored. This being so the Board had not fulfilled its duty of care to users of the highway. What had been done was inadequate to protect blind users of the highway. The possible presence of blind persons had not been taken into account and that was a breach of duty of care by the Board. In order to assist contractors who have to excavate in highways one of the Law Lords said that it was not necessary to have an elaborate form of scaffolding around an excavation. The use of the three sided folding barriers telephone companies use would be sufficient in the circumstances of Haley's accident.

The element of reasonableness in discharging a duty of care is to be seen in not requiring the taking of unusual measures or precautions where the circumstances do not justify such measures or precautions. The balancing of the risk against the measures to guard against it was considered by the House of Lords in the case of *Latimer v A.E.C* 1953. Here a factory of A.E.C was flooded and when the flood went the floor was left in a slippery state. A.E.C. sought to remove the danger by spreading sawdust on the floor. When the supply of sawdust ran out some parts of the floor had not been treated. Further supplies of sawdust were sent for but in the meantime work was restarted. Latimer slipped on a part of the floor which had not been treated and suffered injury. Latimer made a claim that A.E.C. had been negligent in restarting work before the whole of the slippery floor had been treated. His claim however was dismissed. The Law Lords held that the risk created by the parts of the factory floor not treated was not so great as to keep the factory closed.

Res ipsa loquitur

In an action for the tort of negligence the general rule is that the person making the claim must prove his claim if he is to succeed. This is expressed as: 'He who alleges must prove.' This burden of proof, unlike a criminal trial, is discharged if on the balance of probabilities the plaintiff has proved his claim. To put this in arithmetic terms, if the plaintiff satisfies the court as to 51 per cent of his claim he succeeds. Unlike criminal cases, the question of reasonable doubt does not arise, the balance of probability is in his favour and the claim succeeds.

This burden of proof is shifted in two circumstances. The first is under the Civil Evidence Act 1968 and the other under the doctrine of *res ipsa loquitur.*

Section 11 of the Civil Evidence Act 1968 provides that if a person has been convicted of a criminal offence, and that can be proved, then that criminal conviction can be used in evidence in a civil case. This places the burden of proof on that person to show that, in a claim for negligence, he has not been negligent. For instance, if a car driver knocked down a pedestrian and was convicted of driving without due care and attention then that conviction could be used in the pedestrian's claim for damages. The car driver then has to prove that he was not negligent if the pedestrian's claim is to be defeated.

The doctrine *res ipsa loquitur*, 'the thing speaks for itself', may be pleaded by the plaintiff and in appropriate circumstances this reverses the burden of proof. The basis of the doctrine is found in the case of *Scott v London and St Katharine Docks Co* 1865. Here Chief Justice Erle said:

> where the thing is shown to be under the management of the defendant or his servants, and the accident is such as in the ordinary course of things does not happen if those who have the management use proper care, it affords reasonable evidence, in the absence of explanation by the defendants, that the accident arose from the want of care.

From this judgment it can be seen that the thing which causes the damage must be under the control of the defendant or his servants and that what happened would not have occurred in the ordinary course of events. In addition, there has to be no evidence as to how the accident occurred. An example of control is found in the High Court case of *Gee v Metropolitan Railway* 1873 where not long after a train left a station a door flew open and Gee fell out of the carriage. This was held to be evidence of negligence by the company. The matter of the accident not happening in the ordinary course of things without there being negligence is seen in the case of *Scott v London and St Katharine Docks Co* 1865. Here Scott a custom and excise officer was walking past a warehouse belonging to the defendants when bags of sugar fell from the warehouse injuring him. The defendants were held liable in negligence to Scott on the basis of *res ipsa loquitur*. Bags of sugar do not fall from buildings unless there is negligence.

The absence of explanation is necessary if the doctrine is to apply. If there is an explanation then the case proceeds on the usual burden of proof. In the case of *Barkway v South Wales Transport Co Ltd* 1950 the House of Lords considered a claim where Barkway was a passenger in an omnibus which left the road and fell over an embankment. Barkway was killed. Evidence was given that the accident happened because of a defect in a tyre. It was accepted that this defect could have been discovered if the defendants had had a reporting system whereby drivers would report if incidents had occurred where the tyres might have been damaged. This was held to exclude the doctrine since the cause of the accident was known and on the facts there was negligence by the defendants.

If a defendant can show that due care was exercised then he will not be liable. What constitutes due care depends on individual circumstances. In the case of *Henderson v Henry E. Jenkins and Sons* 1970 the House of Lords considered a claim by Henderson's widow. He had been killed when a heavy lorry went out of control down a hill as a result of a brake failure. The failure was because of corrosion in a brake pipe. Evidence was given to the effect that there had been regular inspection of the pipe. The corrosion however occurred at a point where it could only be seen if the pipe was removed. Neither the manufacturer nor the Department of Transport had recommended removal of the pipe for inspection. Despite this the House of Lords held the defendants to be liable. The reason for the decision was that there was a heavy burden of proof on a person who sent a heavy lorry on journeys involving descents of steep hills.

REMOTENESS OF DAMAGE

A tort such as negligence requires that damage has to have been suffered by the plaintiff which was in whole or in part the fault of the defendant. Coupled with this is a requirement that the damages should not be too remote. This requirement is based on the courts' unwillingness to accept that all injuries suffered by a plaintiff in an action for negligence are ones for which the plaintiff should receive damages. According to the circumstances of events occurring, some things happen which are readily understood and accepted, others however are not. From the cause of the action there is a link to the events which follow. The courts have decided that, as a matter of policy, not all the events which are linked are ones which will allow awards of damages to be made. At some point along this link or chain there has to be a point beyond which the courts ought not to accept that there should be liability. The point at which the link or chain is cut is decided on an individual basis according to the circumstances of each case. The broad principles which the courts use as guides are fairness, common sense and consistency with the policy the courts have created. It follows from this that courts have made some decisions which are not acceptable by everyone as being too remote. Each case has to stand on its own particular facts. From all these decisions of the courts a general pattern has emerged.

The foreseeable test
The general approach of the courts now is by the application of the foreseeable test. This however has not always been so. The Court of Appeal in *Re Polemis* 1921 decided that there was liability for all the damage which was the direct consequence of the negligence, even though what happened could not reasonably have been anticipated. In the case a ship, the Polemis, had in a hold a cargo of benzine in tins some of which had leaked. A stevedore negligently dropped a plank into the hold and the benzine fumes immediately caught fire. The ship was destroyed. The stevedore's employer was held to be vicariously liable for his negligent act. The fact that the dropping of a plank could cause some damage was foreseeable and this constituted a breach of duty of care. What was not foreseeable was that dropping the plank would lead to the total destruction of the

ship. The destruction of the ship was, however, a direct consequence of the stevedore negligently dropping the plank and so liability existed.

The decision in *Re Polemis* was considered by the Judicial Committee of the Privy Council. The committee is made up of the same Law Lords who sit in the House of Lords and deals with appeals brought to it from decisions in the colonies and former colonies of Great Britain. Its use now is very limited. The committee's consideration was in an appeal case from an Australian court. The name of the case is *Overseas Tankship (UK) Ltd v Morts Dock and Engineering Co Ltd* 1961. The case is usually referred to as The Wagon Mound, after the name of the ship involved in the incident. The facts of the case were that the ship was taking on fuel oil. A member of the crew negligently failed to connect a coupling so that fuel oil spilt on to the water. This oil floated to the wharf belonging to the plaintiff. Welding work was being carried out. The manager of Morts Dock and Engineering stopped this work and sought advice as to the fire hazard of sparks falling on the oil. He was informed that there was no risk and so allowed the welding to be resumed. A day or so later sparks fell on some cotton waste floating in the oil and this caught fire and set the oil burning. Extensive damage was caused to the wharf and the ship which was being repaired. The committee decided that as the damage caused from the fuel oil catching fire was not foreseeable there was no liability. In making this decision the decision of the Court of Appeal in *Re Polemis* was not followed. Since the members of the committee were the same Law Lords as sit in the House of Lords this decision has been accepted as a correct expression of what the law is on this matter. In strict fact, the decision of the Committee of the Privy Council does not bind English courts since the Privy Council is not part of the English court system.

Consideration of some judicial decisions on this topic will show how the principle is applied by the courts. In the case of *Hughes v Lord Advocate* 1963 the House of Lords had to deal with a claim where the injury was much worse than might have been expected. Here the Post Office opened a manhole in a street and when the workmen left at night a canvas shelter was erected over the manhole with paraffin warning lamps but no night watchman. Hughes, an eight year old boy, and a friend were playing with the lamps. Hughes went into the shelter with a lamp which fell into the manhole. The lamp exploded and Hughes fell into the manhole and was severely burnt. Hughes sued and the Post Office was held liable. It was foreseeable that if paraffin lamps were left unattended in a street young children might play with them and suffer burns as a result. The fact that Hughes had suffered extensive burns from the explosion of the lamp after it fell into the manhole did not affect the liability. Hughes' burns were more severe than might have been expected but the injury was of the same type as that which would be expected. In the case of *Bradford v Robinson Rentals Ltd* 1967 Bradford, an employee of Robinson Rentals, was sent on a long journey in an unheated van. At the time of the journey the weather was severely cold in the middle of a very bad winter. After this journey he was found to be suffering from frostbite. His claim for damages was successful. The court took the view that to require the employee to undertake a long journey in severe weather in an unheated van was to expose him to a foreseeable risk. A decision where the judge took the view that a personal injury was not foreseeable and so the employer was not liable to his injured employee was *Tremain v Pike* 1969. Tremain was a farmworker on Pike's farm. The farm was badly infested with rats. The measures to eradicate the infestation were inadequate and Tremain contracted Weil's disease (this disease is conveyed in the urine of rats). Tremain's claim was dismissed. The judge said that it was accepted that a person bitten by a rat could develop an infection and that rats could cause food poisoning but to contract Weil's disease from rat urine was not foreseeable. It was an event which was too remote and different in kind from the other possibilities.

As we have seen, if the damage suffered by a person is of the kind which might be expected there will still be liability even if it is more severe than might have been expected. To take this further, the courts accept that there is liability if the damage suffered is more severe simply because of the defendant's particular weakness. This principle is usually expressed as 'the defendant must take the victim as he finds him'. This is also known as the 'egg-shell skull' rule. That is if, say, a person is knocked down by someone's negligent driving and the injured person suffers a fractured skull because he has a thin skull and this would not have happened if he had had a skull of normal thickness, there is full liability. Liability cannot be avoided or reduced because of the injured person's weakness. In the case of *Robinson v Post Office* 1974 Robinson slipped on a ladder at work which was unsafe because of some contamination with oil. He went to hospital for treatment and was given the standard anti-tetanus injection. Unfortunately he was allergic to such treatment and consequently developed a severe reaction. The Post Office were held liable. Their failure to guard his safety at work had led to his injury and the fact that he had an unexpected reaction to his treatment did not diminish their liability.

The approach of the courts to claims for damages for financial loss is to limit the award to the direct consequential loss. Any additional loss which arises because of the plaintiff's own financial position is disregarded. This is based on the decision by the House of Lords in the case of *Liesbosch Dredger v S.S. Edison* 1933, where the dredger Liesbosch was sunk by the negligent navigation of the crew of the Edison. The owners of the dredger were contracted to carry out some work in a limited time. Because they were too poor to buy a replacement dredger to complete the contract they were put to greater expense in fulfilling their contract. The Law Lords refused to allow any additional loss which arose solely from the poverty of the plaintiffs. That factor was held to be an extraneous matter and so too remote. Although this decision of the House of Lords has not been overruled it is true to say that present-day judges find difficulty in accepting its correctness. A number of judges question the decision openly and seek to find ways round its application.

Novus actus interveniens

This term, 'a new act intervening', enshrines a principle that when a new act breaks the chain of causation, that break ends the liability of the plaintiff. This means that the intervening event is the reason for the damage which follows. The intervening act may be some natural event, an act of a third party or an act of the plaintiff. In the case of *Lamb v Camden London Borough Council* 1981 the Court of Appeal had to deal with a claim for damage. The events started with the council's contractors negligently breaking a water main in the road outside Mrs Lamb's house. The flow of water undermined the foundations of the house. Mrs Lamb moved out so that remedial works could be carried out. She went on holiday to the United States and on her return had her furniture moved out so that some building work could be carried out. Squatters then moved in. These were removed but some months later another lot of squatters moved in. They caused considerable damage by the time they were removed. Mrs Lamb sued the council. The decision of the court was that the entry of the squatters and the subsequent damage was not foreseeable and was an intervening event from the original negligent damage to the water main. In the case of *McKew v Holland and Hannen and Cubitts (Scotland) Ltd* 1969 the House of Lords considered a claim by a construction worker. He had been injured at work because of his employers' negligence. This left him with a left leg which on occasions unexpectedly gave way on him. He went to visit a tenement flat with members of his family. When leaving the flat he went down some steep stairs which were not provided with a handrail. He was holding his young daughter by her hand at the time. He felt that his left leg was about to give way and that he was about to fall. He pushed his daughter to safety and in an attempt to avoid falling jumped. He landed heavily on his right foot and broke his right ankle and a bone in his left leg. The House of Lords accepted that Mr McKew's act of jumping in an emergency was within the chain of causation. That is, liability of the employers continued from the accident to the situation where because of the condition of his leg leg he might have to take the action he did in order to avoid a fall. Where, however, he put himself in a position so that an emergency could arise this was an intervening act. In this situation Mr McKew could have sought assistance from the other members of his family or he could have descended the stairs on his own taking greater care.

In the 'rescue' cases considered earlier the defences have sought to avoid liability by pleading that the rescuer's actions were new acts which intervened so as to break the chain of causation. These attempts have been unsuccessful since the courts protect the rescuer's position by holding that such a person was acting on moral grounds and the policy was to support such actions.

Contributory negligence

Before the passing by Parliament of the Law Reform (Contributory Negligence) Act 1945 the position at common law was that if it could be shown that a person making a claim for negligence had in any way contributed to the accident then that fact defeated his claim. The injustice of this rule was obvious but it took time before Parliament corrected the matter. The Act now provides that if a plaintiff in some way contributed to the injury suffered then that fact is not to defeat the claim. Instead the amount of damages that would otherwise be awarded is to be reduced by the percentage of blame the court attaches to the plaintiff. The percentage is determined by the judge having heard the evidence of the accident. There is no upper limit and reductions of 70 per cent and above have been made. If the plaintiff was wholly to blame then it is not a matter of contributory negligence.

Under the Act contributory negligence refers not just to negligence but also to breach of statutory duty or other act or omission which gives rise to liability in tort. Contributory negligence applies to loss of life, personal injury and damage to property. The provisions do not apply to a breach of contract action. Some judges have applied the provisions in such actions but the Court of Appeal has now ruled that Parliament never intended the Act to apply to contract disputes.

Although the fixing of the reduction is the responsibility of the judge the Court of Appeal has indicated appropriate percentages in motor accident cases where seat belts were not worn. If the injuries would have been totally avoided if a seat belt had been worn then the reduction is 25 per cent; if however the injuries would have still occurred but have been less severe the reduction is 15 per cent. In the case of *Capps v Miller* 1989 the Court of Appeal dealt with a claim by a motor cyclist who had been injured by a motorist's negligence. He had been wearing a crash helmet but the chin strap was not fastened. This resulted in his injuries being more severe than would have been the case if the strap had been fastened. A reduction of 10 per cent was considered appropriate.

In assessing the plaintiff's negligence the courts apply, in general, the same standard of care as in cases of negligence. So consideration and, where appropriate, concession is made when a claim is made by children, the elderly and those with some disability. In a number of cases the courts have refused to apply contributory negligence to children. The ground for this has been an acceptance that the children could not appreciate dangers.

Two cases concerning the construction industry show how contributory negligence applies. In the case of *Jones v Livox Quarries Ltd* 1952 Jones was riding on the towbar of a taxcavator when another vehicle bumped the back of the towed vehicle. He fell off and the towed vehicle ran over him. His award of damages was reduced because of his contributory negligence. In the case of *Kensington and Chelsea and Westminster Area Health Authority v Adams, Holden and Partners and Others* 1984 some defective building work was done to a hospital building. The remedial works cost £250,000 and the Health Authority sued the architects and others for this sum. The judge, having heard the evidence, was of the opinion that the Health Authority's clerk of works had been negligent in failing to detect the defective work whilst it was being done. As he was an employee of the authority they were vicariously liable for his failure to discharge his duties properly. His contributory negligence, which was that of his employers, was fixed at 20 per cent. So the award of the court was not the £250,000 claimed but £200,000 only.

BREACH OF STATUTORY DUTY

Since the middle of the last century Parliament has produced, and continues to produce, a huge quantity of legislation with the aim of protecting individuals. Although these provisions cover a range of individuals, many apply to persons in employment. A prime example of this is the Health and Safety at Work etc Act 1974. In addition to provisions in Acts of Parliament there are many regulations of great complexity which affect employees. For example, the Control of Substances Hazardous to Health Regulations 1988 and the Construction (Working Places) Regulations 1966.

The aim of this legislation is, in the main, to protect employees and others. There is little evidence that in producing this legislation Parliament has the intention to provide a means for injured persons to be compensated. The courts have, however, interpreted various Acts of Parliament as not only creating criminal offences for breaches of their provisions but also giving injured persons a right to sue for damages. Where the court's interpretation is that a particular act does not give an injured person that right, such as has happened with road traffic legislation, then the injured person has to sue for the tort of negligence.

Where some statutory provision does create a statutory duty the great advantage to an injured person is that once it can be shown that that person is protected then it is much easier to succeed in the claim than it would if the claim were made for negligence. This may be seen from the case considered earlier, that of *Ferguson v John Dawson and Partners (Contractors) Ltd* 1976, where Ferguson fell from a roof 15 feet above the ground. Once Ferguson was able to prove that he was an employee and not self-employed his claim succeeded. As an employee he was protected by the Construction (Working Places) Regulations 1966. These require that a person shall be protected if he is working above two metres high, which Ferguson was, so there was a breach of statutory duty.

Before considering the courts' approach to the interpretation of statutory provisions to determine if there exists a right to sue for breach of statutory duty we can note some provisions which are beyond doubt. Section 38 of the Building Act 1984, which is not yet in force, has provisions which make a breach of building regulations a civil matter. So a person who has suffered injury could sue for breach of statutory duty. Section 209 of the Water Industry Act 1991 places a strict liability on a water undertaker for damage caused by the escape of water, provided the escape was not the fault of the person who suffered the loss. There are a small number of other Acts of Parliament where there is a definite right for injured persons to sue for breach of statutory duty.

Where there is no explicit right to sue set out in a statutory provision, the courts have to interpret the provision to ascertain if there is such a right despite Parliament's failure to specify it. In doing this the court will examine the whole of the statutory provision in order to determine its general aim. In addition the law that existed previously will be considered. If, as is often the case, a statute states that a breach of a provision shall be punishable by fine and that appears to be aimed at punishing the offender and to deter other possible offenders, then that punishment might be the sole purpose of the statute.

When considering Acts of Parliament which place duties on public bodies the courts have been unwilling to treat those Acts as also imposing civil liabilities on them. If, however, a statute does not impose a penalty for a breach of a provision then there is a strong case for holding that there was an intention that a claim for breach of statutory duty may be made.

If a statute is so framed as to be protective to a particular class of person, usually employees, then it is likely to be interpreted as being a statute which permits a civil claim to be made. For a person to bring a claim in this circumstance it is necessary to show that he comes within this particular class. This rule may be seen in the decision of the Court of Appeal in *Keating v Elvan Reinforced Concrete Co Ltd and Another* 1968. Here Keating fell into a trench which Elvan had dug acting as contractors for the local council. Protective barriers had been erected but these had been removed by a stranger. Keating sued the council claiming that they were in breach of a duty under the Public Utilities Street Works Act 1950. His claim was dismissed. The court interpreted the Act as creating obligations between the council as the highway authority and contractors employed by them. It was not intended to protect individuals.

Where there have been difficulties in a person seeking to make a civil claim, and justice demanded that he should be able to sue, Parliament has given that right. This however has occurred only rarely. An example is the Highways Act 1980 which gives an injured person the right to sue the highway authority where there has been a failure to maintain the highway properly.

From what has been considered so far it will be apparent that the courts have difficulty in determining whether or not a statutory provision gives a person the right to sue for damages. It might reasonably be asked why Parliament when creating the statutory provision does not indicate clearly whether or not there should be a right to sue for damages. At the moment there is no indication that they have any such intention.

In order to make a successful claim a plaintiff must prove that the statutory provision is one which was intended to protect him from that injury. This can lead to an unusual result in some circumstances. The House of Lords in *Nicholls v F. Austin (Leyton) Ltd* 1946 decided that when a drill on a drilling machine broke and came through the guard injuring the worker there was no liability. The reason for this was that Section 14 of the Factory Act 1937, which required every dangerous part of machinery to be securely fenced, was intended to keep the worker out and not keep the machine or product in.

Each statutory provision must be applied strictly as the Court of Appeal indicated in *Larner v British Steel PLC* 1993. Here Larner was an experienced mechanical fitter who was carrying out work on a heavy piece of equipment. This piece of equipment was known by his employers to be cracked. It fell and severely crushed his leg. Section 29 of the Factories Act 1961 places the duty on an employer to keep a place of work safe for any person working there. The defence sought to show that the plaintiff had to prove that the danger was reasonably foreseeable by British Steel. The court, however, refused to accept this, which was based on negligence. The duty under Section 29 was a strict duty; there was no question of introducing reasonable foreseeability. To do so would defeat the objective of the Section which was to provide a safe working place.

To succeed in a claim for breach of statutory duty it is necessary to prove that the person under the duty is in breach. If that is not possible then the claim must fail. In *Ginty V Belmont Building Supplies Ltd* 1959 Ginty was an experienced roofer employed by the defendants who were roofing contractors. The regulations in force at that time, the Building (Safety, Health and Welfare) Regulations 1948, required employers to provide and use crawling boards for roof work. This the defendants had done. Ginty however did not use the boards and fell through a roof on which he was working. He sued for his injury. The court dismissed his claim. His injury was his own fault. The employers had provided all the equipment required by the regulations and so were not liable. This decision may be compared to the House of Lords decision in *Boyle v Kodak Ltd* 1969 where Boyle, an experienced painter, fell from a ladder whilst painting an oil storage tank. The ladder slipped because it was not lashed at the top. The Building (Safety, Health and Welfare) Regulations 1948 required that it should be lashed. This obligation applied to both employer and employees. The employers were held to be liable since they were held not to have done all they ought to have done to make the requirements of the regulations known to Boyle. Boyle, however, was held to have been contributorily negligent since he ought to have been more aware of the regulations. The award to him was reduced by 50 per cent for his contributory negligence.

A person sued for breach of statutory duty may use the defence of contributory negligence as provided by the Law Reform (Contributory Negligence) Act 1945. In addition, as we have just considered, if the plaintiff is entirely to blame no award will be made. The defence of *volenti non fit injuria* is not available except where an employee is suing the employer for the tort of another employee, that is for vicarious liability. At one time it was believed that if a statutory duty had been delegated to another that was a defence. This is not now accepted as good law.

As will be appreciated, an injured employee suing for damages for an industrial accident he has suffered would not wish to fail in the claim on some legal technicality. For this reason it is the practice with cases of this nature to sue for negligence and/or breach of statutory duty. By doing this the plaintiff has a greater chance of being successful with the claim.

5 OCCUPIERS' LIABILITY ACTS 1957 AND 1984

INTRODUCTION

We saw in our examination of the common law tort of negligence that in certain circumstances a duty of care can be owed by one person to another and a breach of that duty can lead to an award of damages. We also noted that there could be a duty of care under an Act of Parliament. A breach of any such statutory duty can lead to an award of damages. Two Acts of Parliament which create duties of care which are of particular importance to the construction industry are the Occupiers' Liability Act 1957 and the Occupiers' Liability Act 1984.

Before Parliament passed the Act of 1957 there was a duty of care owed by occupiers to those who came on their lands. This duty of care existed at common law and varied according to circumstances. At that time those who went on to the land of another were placed in one of three categories. The categories were: invitees, licensees and trespassers. Invitees were those who went on to land at the direct invitation of the occupier and the occupier was under a duty to guard the invitee against harm from any unusual danger he knew of or ought to have known of. Licensees were those who went on another person's land with the occupier's express or implied permission. To such a licensee the duty of care was to warn him of any concealed danger or trap of which the occupier was aware. A trespasser was a person who went on another person's land without the occupier's permission or invitation. To a trespasser the only duty owed was not to create a danger. Added to these three categories there was the separate one of the contractual relationship. If an occupier, such as a hotel owner, made a contract with a guest the duty of care was to use reasonable skill and care to make the premises safe.

It was inevitable that with these different categories difficulties would arise. In some cases judges held a person, often a child, to be a licensee to whom a duty was owed rather than a trespasser. In other cases judges took the view that a person on another person's land was a trespasser and so could not claim damages for an injury suffered whilst on the land.

The only way in which the position could be corrected was by Parliament legislating. The courts had too many conflicting decisions to be capable of defining a clear approach. It is for this reason Parliament passed the Occupiers' Liability Act 1957 and why the Act's provisions are as they are. It later became necessary for Parliament to pass the Occupiers' Liability Act 1984 in order to clarify the law with regard to trespassers.

APPLICATION OF THE 1957 ACT

Section 1 of the Act states that the rules of the Act shall replace the rules of common law with regard to the duty an occupier of premises owes to visitors in respect of dangers due to the state of the premises or to things done or omitted to be done on them. What the rules do not change are the common law rules as to whom a duty is owed and on whom the duty is placed. As will be seen, the rules under the Act regulate the nature of the duty owed by an occupier of premises and of any invitation or permission the occupier gives or is to be treated as giving to another and the consequences.

The Section provides that the occupier is to treat as his visitors those persons who at common law would be treated as the occupier's invitees or licenses. So the occupier's lawful visitors are those who would formerly have been placed in these two categories. An exception to this is that a person who enters land under provisions in the National Parks and Access to the Countryside Act 1949 is not a visitor to whom a duty is owed. The 1984 Act, however, has imposed a lesser duty on an occupier to a visitor under the Act.

Lawful Visitors
As the duty of care under the Act is owed only to lawful visitors some consideration of this classification is necessary. It covers any person who goes on premises at the express or implied invitation of the occupier or it can be implied that the person, although not expressly or impliedly invited, is present by the occupier's permission. In this last circumstance a person is on the premises as a licensee. That is, the person is on the premises without being expressly invited by the occupier but the occupier knows of the presence of that person and takes no steps to exclude that person.

So a residential developer who expressly or impliedly invites prospective purchasers to visit the site so as to view the houses owes them a duty of care under the Act. The only way in which such a developer could avoid a duty of care would be to expressly exclude visitors by fencing or notices which would make entry a trespass. As a trespasser is not a lawful visitor to whom a duty of care is owed under the 1957 Act, any person who goes on a site as a trespasser has no claim. The fact that a person has gone on premises as a trespasser over a period of time does not change his classification under the

Act into a licensee so that he becomes a lawful visitor. It should also be recalled from our previous consideration of trespass to land that a person can become a trespasser if after entry as a lawful visitor he stays on the premises after the permission to be there is withdrawn or if that person has acted in a manner which is inconsistent with the reason for being there.

An occupier owes the duty of care to those who come on premises as a right conferred by law. Those who are included here include a building control officer, an inspector under the Health and Safety at Work etc Act 1974 and entry under other Acts of Parliament. Clause 11 of the JCT 1980 Form of Contract gives an express power to the architect to have access to the site of the contract works. So far as domestic premises are concerned visitors such as the postman, the meter reader and someone delivering goods would be lawful visitors. If an occupier wishes to exclude those who would otherwise be lawful visitors he may do this by a notice specifically excluding them. An example would be a notice which stated 'No hawkers or Circulars'. This would make those who then entered to try and sell something or to leave leaflets not lawful visitors.

Premises to which the 1957 Act applies

Section 1 of the 1957 Act deals with the premises for which an occupier is to be under a duty of care. These are not just buildings but also any fixed or moveable structure, including any vessel, vehicle or aircraft. This is a wide definition and has great significance to a construction site. In most cases a main contractor takes possession of the site and so becomes the occupier for the purposes of the Act. He is also the occupier of, for example, canteen huts he erects which may be used by his own employees and others. He is the occupier of the scaffold he erects and which is used not only by his employees but all others, including, for example, the clerk of works. The extent to which the definition applies may be seen from the decision of the High Court in *Bunker v Brand (Charles) and Son Ltd* 1969 where Bunker was not an employee of the main contractor who was using a tunnelling machine in the construction of the Victoria Line Underground. He was an employee of a company that installed the machine. A modification was required and Bunker, together with other workers, was required to pass over moving rollers of the machine to get to the face of the machine where the modification was required. He lost his balance and fell from the machine suffering injury. He sued the main contractor under the Occupiers' Liability Act 1957. The court agreed to his claim that the main contractor was the occupier of the machine and that Bunker was a lawful visitor. Bunker succeeded in his claim subject to a 50 per cent reduction for his own contributory negligence.

In the case of *Page v Read* 1984 Page was a self-employed painter who was working on a newly constructed terrace house which had a stepped gable. He was not using a roof ladder but was leaning over to paint a fascia board and the connecting soffit. He slipped down the roof and fell off suffering injury. He sued Read who had the contract for the paintwork on the site under a number of grounds. One of which was that Read owed him a duty of care in tort. Page lost his claim. The Court ruled that Read was not the occupier of the roof under the Occupiers' Liability Act 1957.

A further example of the application of the definition in the Act as to the premises to which the Act applies is found in the High Court case of *A.M.F. International Ltd v Magnet Bowling Ltd and Another* 1968. Here a bowling alley was to be laid within a newly constructed building. The main contractors were, as part of their contract, required to exclude the entry of water within the building. This was of particular importance to A.M.F. who had purchased expensive timber for the floors of the bowling alley. The efforts made to exclude water were inadequate with the result that water damaged the timber stored in the building. The main contractors were held to be occupiers of the building under the Occupiers' Liability Act 1957 and so liable under the Act.

Who is the occupier
Section 1 of the 1957 Act states that the rules under the Act which impose a duty are to apply in consequence of a person's occupation or control of premises. So the matter is not solely that of actual occupation of the premises but also of control of the premises. In most circumstances the person in physical occupation of the premises will be the occupier under the Act. There are, however, circumstances where some person not in actual physical occupation of the premises will also be an occupier under the Act simply because that person has some degree of control over the premises.

The leading case on this topic is the House of Lords decision in *Wheat v Lacon and Co Ltd* 1966. Here Lacon and Co, a brewery company, owned a public house the ground floor of which was run as the public house by Mr Richardson as manager. The first floor was used by Mr and Mrs Richardson as their living accommodation. Mrs Richardson had permission from the brewery company to take in paying guests. Mr and Mrs Wheat were staying as guests of Mrs Richardson. At about 10 p.m. one evening Mr Wheat fell down the private staircase which led to the Richardsons' accommodation. He was killed. The High Court decided that his death was the result of someone having taken the bulb from the lamp at the top of the staircase and the fact that the handrail finished three steps short of the bottom of the staircase. The question arose as to whether the brewery company owed any duty of care to Mr Wheat. Was the brewery company an occupier of the accommodation on the first floor so that a duty was owed to Mr Wheat if he was a lawful visitor? The House of Lords decided that Mr and Mrs Richardson were occupiers of the first floor and that the brewery company was too. The reason for reaching this decision was that the brewery company had a degree of control over the first floor from the fact that the Richardsons had not been given a lease of their accommodation. They occupied by a licence from the brewery company. The brewery company had a right to carry out repairs to the first floor which meant that they had retained a degree of control. In the circumstances, however, the duty of care had not been breached since the brewery company did not know and could not reasonably have known of the absence of the bulb to the lamp.

The common duty of care

Section 2 of the 1957 Act contains the provisions setting the standard of care an occupier owes to his lawful visitors. Unlike the previous common law position there is just one standard of care, referred to as the common duty of care.

Sub-section (1) states:

> An occupier of premises owes the same duty, the 'common duty of care', to all his visitors, except in so far as he is free to and does extend, restrict, modify or exclude his duty to any visitor or visitors by agreement or otherwise.

From this it can be seen that the Act allows the common duty of care to be changed. Before the passing of the Unfair Contract Terms Act 1977 it was usual practice to exclude liability when visitors were allowed to enter premises where there was a possible danger. For example, a construction company would permit visitors to go on a site where there were dangerous activities only if they all signed an agreement excluding liability. Now, by reason of Section 2 of the Unfair Contract Terms Act 1977, any notice which seeks to exclude or restrict liability for death or personal injury resulting from negligence is ineffective. In the case of other loss or damage an exclusion for liability for negligence will only be effective if that term or notice satisfies the test of reasonableness under the Act. These provisions, however, only apply to a business or from the occupation of premises used for business purposes. This means that a private individual can exclude or restrict liability to lawful visitors to his private premises.

An example of the way in which liability was excluded is seen in the case of *Ashdown v Samuel Williams and Sons* 1957. Here Mrs Ashdown used a path on Williams' land as a licensee. This path crossed a railway line on the land. Notices were placed at different places on the land warning people that they were on the land at their own risk and that they had no claim against Williams if they suffered an injury. Mrs Ashdown was knocked down and injured by some railway trucks which had been negligently shunted. Those notices were held to be sufficient to exclude liability on the part of Williams. Now, because of Section 2 of the Unfair Contract Terms Act 1977, that notice would be ineffective and a plaintiff would probably be successful in a claim.

The common duty of care is defined in sub-section (2) as:

> The common duty of care is a duty to take such care as in all the circumstances of the case is reasonable to see that the visitor will be reasonably safe in using the premises for the purposes for which he is invited or permitted by the occupier to be there.

From this it should be noted that all the circumstances of the occurrence have to be taken into account. Two other important points are that the duty is reasonable to see that the visitor will be reasonably safe. So the duty is not one of strict liability. If, therefore, the occupier does what in the circumstances is reasonable to see the visitor will be reasonably safe then the duty of care has been discharged. This could mean that a lawful visitor who suffers a serious injury would not be successful in a claim.

The last point to note is that the lawful visitor has to be using the premises for the purposes for which he was invited or permitted by the occupier to be there. In one case a judge said that if you invite a person to your house you do not expect him then to slide down the banisters of the stairs. An indication of the approach of the courts on this point is the decision of the House of Lords in the case of *Ferguson v Welsh and Others* 1987. In this case a local authority required the demolition of a building on land which they intended to develop as a sheltered housing project. A contractor was awarded the contract which was subject to a number of restrictions as to the manner of the demolition, insurance and approval if there was to be a sub-contracting. All these provisions were disregarded and when Ferguson, a sub-contractor, was injured by a collapse of the building he sued the local authority. The House of Lords decided that the local authority were occupiers of the site. This did not, however, mean that they were liable to Ferguson. There was no liability to an employee of a contractor working on the occupier's premises where there was an unsafe system of work. The Law Lords did suggest that if the occupier of the premises had reason to suspect that work was being done in an unsafe manner it might be that there would be a duty to see a safe system of work was instituted.

A further point with the duty of care is found in sub-section (3):

> The circumstances relevant for the present purpose include the degree of care, and of want of care, which would ordinarily be looked for in such a visitor, so that (for example) in proper cases:
>
>   (a) an occupier must be prepared for children to be less careful than adults; and

(b) an occupier may expect that a person, in the exercise of his calling, will appreciate and guard against any special risks ordinarily incident to it, so far as the occupier leaves him free to do so.

This guidance is most important to construction operations. In the first case, because children are attracted to all the things on a construction site and the activities carried out there. In the second case, the carrying out of work by a person with some skill or training is a circumstance where reliance can be placed on that person to guard against certain risks.

In considering paragraph (a) in more detail it is necessary to note the judgment in *Phipps v Rochester Corporation* 1955 which, although decided before the Occupiers' Liability Act 1957, is accepted as a correct interpretation of the common law with regard to children and still correct law. In the case Phipps was a five year old boy who was out with his seven year old sister. Some land near to their home belonged to the council and was being developed as a housing estate. The local authority had dug a trench about nine feet deep for a sewer. The trench was about two feet six inches wide and about a hundred yards long. The local authority knew that people walked across the field and apparently took no objection to it. The children's parents were aware of the development. When the children went on the land and came to the trench, rather than walk round the excavation they tried to jump across it. The girl did this successfully but the boy fell into the trench and broke his leg. He sued but his claim was dismissed. He was held to be a trespasser to whom no duty of care was owed.

In the course of his analysis of the law on the duty owed to children the judge indicated that there might in law be a distinction between children who had some appreciation of danger and knew what they were doing and those who were too young to have this reason or understanding. These children could be described as being 'children of tender years'. These children were in a special class and ought not to be allowed out unaccompanied by an adult. In these particular circumstances the parents must have known that the building operations were going on nearby and ought to have realised that holes and trenches were likely to be dug. The parents ought not to have allowed the children to go where there were obvious dangers. The corporation was entitled to assume that parents would behave in a naturally prudent way and that they would not be obliged, in effect, to take on parental duties.

The decision in *Phipps v Rochester Corporation* suggests that children can be put into three categories. These are: those children who are sufficiently mature to appreciate usual dangers, say, the 15 or 16 year olds; those children of 'tender years' who are too young to appreciate dangers and ought to be accompanied by an adult; and those children who are of an age or maturity that knowledge and appreciation of dangers has to be judged on an individual basis.

A point of importance with construction operations is the rule with regard to allurements. An allurement in law is something which is attractive and dangerous to children. An occupier of land who has on the land something which is an allurement has to be aware that that could attract children and that they could be unaware of its danger. The average construction site contains many articles which are allurements. Included are concrete mixers, hoists, scaffolding and stored material.

An example of the operation of the rule with regard to allurements, decided before the introduction of the 1957 Act but still of importance, is the House of Lords decision in *Glasgow Corporation v Taylor* 1922. Here a seven year old child was in a public park under the control of the corporation. A shrub had been planted which produced berries which looked like cherries. These, however, were poisonous. The child was tempted to the shrub and ate some of the berries. The child died as a result of this. The decision was that the shrub was an allurement. It had not been fenced off nor had a warning notice been erected. The corporation was liable.

There are a number of cases where the courts have declined to hold that certain things were allurements. An example is the case of *Latham v R. Johnson and Nephew Ltd* 1913 where a pile of stones had been left by the side of a road. Latham, a child, was playing on the stones and fell, cutting his hand. His claim was dismissed, the pile of stones was not an allurement.

Paragraph (b) of sub-section (3) allows an occupier, in the application of the common duty of care, to treat someone who comes on his premises to carry out work to be aware of and guard against the risks usually found in his work. So an occupier who calls in an electrician to attend to a fault in an electrical system is under no duty to warn the electrician of the danger of electrocution if he works on the system without first switching off the main supply. That danger is one inherent in the work of an electrician and he ought to be aware of it and guard against it. If, however, the occupier knew of some possible danger in his premises, say, some weakened woodworm-infested floorboards, then the occupier would not be complying with his duty of care if he failed to warn of that danger.

Subject to this kind of circumstance, the occupier is entitled to rely on the specialist he has called in to appreciate and guard against dangers associated with his work. The Court of Appeal in the case of *Roles v Nathan* 1963 dealt with this particular point in the Occupiers' Liability Act 1957. The facts in the case were that some premises, owned and occupied by Nathan, had a coke-burning boiler which was smoking badly. Two chimney sweeps were brought in to sweep the chimney but there was no improvement. An expert was brought in to assist. He immediately realised that there was danger in the boiler room from fumes. He ordered the chimney sweeps to leave the boiler room. He gave instructions as to the sealing-off of parts of the flues before the boiler was re-lighted. The sweeps agreed to do this but they did not and they were later found dead in the boiler room with the fire burning in the boiler. The court dismissed a claim for damages made by the widow of one of the sweeps. The court decided that danger from fumes coming from the boiler was something the sweeps ought to have known and guarded against. In addition to this, the sweeps had been warned of the danger but had chosen to ignore the warning.

Warning

As we have already seen, the posting of a warning notice may avoid liability of an occupier at common law. The Occupiers' Liability Act 1957 also provides for the use of warning notices.

Sub-section (4) (a) of Section 2 states:

> In determining whether the occupier of premises has discharged the common duty of care to a visitor, regard is to be had to all the circumstances, so that (for example):
> (a) where damage is caused to a visitor by a danger of which he had been warned by the occupier, the warning is not to be treated without more as absolving the occupier from liability, unless in all the circumstances it was enough to enable the visitor to be reasonably safe.

The provision recognises the use by an occupier of premises of a warning which, in considering the discharge of the common duty of care, may be sufficient to free the occupier of liability. Two points need to be noted with the provision. The first is that all the circumstances have to be taken into account, so no single factor is decisive. The second is that the warning will not be effective unless it enables the visitor to be reasonably safe. The warning does not, therefore, have to guarantee safety to be effective.

As we have just seen with *Roles v Nathan*, the warning given about the dangerous fumes was one reason for the claim being dismissed. For a warning to be adequate it should warn the visitor of the particular danger, be given well in advance of the danger and be prominent and permanent. A warning which simply states 'Danger Ahead' will probably not be enough since it does not warn of the particular danger. A warning which states 'Danger Steep Stairs' does warn the visitor of the danger. The notice should be well in advance of the danger so that the visitor can take appropriate action to avoid the danger. A warning on a notice board exposed to the elements should be properly protected so that it does not become unreadable.

The effect of a failure to warn of a danger is to be seen in the decision of the High Court in *Rae v Mars (UK) Ltd* 1990. The facts of the case were that Mr Rae was an experienced surveyor who went to make a survey of an unused factory. He had not received any warning from the owner of the factory as to any dangers he might encounter. Unknown to him the factory ground floor had a submerged area which was situated very close to the entry door. When he opened the door and stepped inside he fell into the submerged area and injured his leg. When he sued for damages the judge upheld his claim but held him to be 30 per cent contributorily negligent. In the judgment the judge said that Mr Rae should have received warning of the danger. He also was of the opinion that there should have been a warning on the entry door for all visitors, and a further notice or barrier immediately inside the factory.

Finally it should be recalled that any notice which seeks to avoid liability for death or personal injury from negligence is of no effect because of the provisions in Section 2 of the Unfair Contract Terms Act 1977.

Independent contractor

The 1957 Act does not change the general rule that a person who engages the service of an independent contractor is not liable for wrongful actions by the independent contractor. There are, however, provisions in the Act dealing with the use of an independent contractor.

Sub-section (4) (b) of Section 2 states:

> where damage is caused to a visitor by a danger due to the faulty execution of any work of construction, maintenance or repair by an independent contractor employed by the occupier, the occupier is not to be treated without more as answerable for the danger if in all the circumstances he had acted reasonably in entrusting the work to an independent contractor and had taken such steps (if any) as he reasonably ought in order to satisfy himself that the contractor was competent and that the work had been properly done.

This provision follows the general rule at common law and subject to two requirements absolves the occupier of liability when he uses the service of an independent contractor. The first requirement is that the occupier should appoint a competent independent contractor. That is, an electrician for electrical work and not a handyman who would undertake work of that nature together with a wide range of other activities. The second requirement is that where it is reasonable for the occupier to do so, he should satisfy himself that the work of the independent contractor has been properly done. As we saw earlier with the case of *Haseldine v Daw and Sons Ltd* 1941 an occupier is not expected to have the electrical or mechanical knowledge to check that the work by an apparently competent company of lift engineers has been done properly. With the case of *Woodward v Mayor of Hastings* 1945 we saw the clearing of snow from the steps of a building could be checked by the occupier to see that the task had been done properly.

Other provisions of Section 2

Section 2 preserves the defence of *volenti non fit injuria*. It is provided so that the common duty of care does not impose on an occupier any obligation to a visitor in respect of risks willingly accepted as his by the visitor. The question as to whether a visitor has accepted a risk is to be decided by the application of the principles used in these cases. These principles were examined earlier when the defence of *volenti non fit injuria* was considered.

The section concludes by stating that any person who enters premises in the exercise of a right conferred by law is to be treated as if permitted by the occupier to be there. This provision means that even if the occupier has not and would not give permission to such a person, that person nevertheless is to be treated as a lawful visitor.

Effect of contract on occupier's liability to third party

Section 3 of the 1957 Act deals with the position of a person making a contract with the occupier of premises and that contract entitling persons who were not parties to the contract to enter those premises. Where this occurs the Section states that the occupier owes to those persons the same duty of care as he owes to visitors and this cannot be restricted or excluded by that contract.

The section also applies to a tenancy so as to bind either the landlord or tenant who have, under the tenancy, to permit persons to enter the premises to treat them as visitors and so protected under the Act.

LIABILITY TO TRESPASSERS UNDER THE OCCUPIERS' LIABILITY ACT 1984

We saw earlier that the passing of the Occupiers' Liability Act 1957 did not affect the position of a trespasser. The common law rule was that a trespasser took the premises as he found them. The only duty on the occupier of premises was not to do some act with a deliberate intention of harming the trespasser or with reckless disregard for his presence.

This position was changed by the House of Lords decision in *British Railways Board v Herrington* 1972 where the Law Lords decided that an occupier did owe to trespassers what was described as the 'common duty of care'. This was not to the standard of the common duty of care under the Occupiers' Liability Act 1957 but better than the duty previously owed to trespassers. The new duty of care, unfortunately, had principles which were so broad they created practical difficulties in application. For this reason Parliament sought to put the matter beyond doubt by passing the Occupiers' Liability Act 1984.

The scope of the Act is such that it applies not only to trespassers but also to those who are not the occupier's visitors but enter under some other right. So the Act applies to persons exercising private rights of way and those who enter under the powers in the National Parks and Access to the Countryside Act 1949.

The 1984 Act states that under the Act the same persons shall be treated as occupiers of premises and visitors as they are under the 1957 Act.

Sub-section (3) of Section 1 states that an occupier of premises owes a duty to another who is not his visitor in respect of death or personal injury if:

(a) he is aware of the danger or has reasonable grounds to believe that it exists;
(b) he knows or has reasonable grounds to believe that the other is in the vicinity of the danger concerned or that he may come into the vicinity of the danger (in either case, whether the other has lawful authority for being in that vicinity or not); and
(c) the risk is one against which, in all the circumstances of the case, he may reasonably be expected to offer the other some protection.

The duty owed by an occupier to the other is the duty to take such care as is reasonable in all the circumstances of the case to see that he does not suffer injury on the premises by reason of the danger concerned. Injury means anything resulting in death or personal injury, including any disease and any impairment of physical or mental condition.

Although it is a number of years since the Act was passed there is no case law which gives guidance as to how these provisions are interpreted. In general terms there has to be a danger which the occupier is aware of or has reasonable grounds to believe exists. So if there is a danger which he could not know of then there is no liability. The occupier has to know or have reasonable grounds to believe that the other person is in the vicinity of the danger or may come into the vicinity of the danger. If, therefore, in the circumstances the occupier could not know that this was so there is no liability. The last point that the risk is one against which, in the circumstances, the occupier might reasonably be expected to offer the other some protection is a point of some difficulty. Clearly this is where some guidance from judicial decisions is essential. A standard of some kind will have to be obtained if an occupier is to know what he has to do to comply with the provisions in the Act.

Section 1 of the Act allows the duty of an occupier to be discharged from liability by taking reasonable steps to give warning of the danger concerned or to discourage persons from incurring the risk. This provision allows the occupier to avoid liability by giving warnings which are appropriate in the circumstances or, for example, by erecting barriers to exclude people from the danger.

The Act also allows the defence of *volenti non fit injuria* to be applied. So any person who under the principles applicable willingly accepts to run the risk has no claim against the occupier.

COMMON LAW TORT OF NEGLIGENCE AND THE OCCUPIERS' LIABILITY ACT 1957

The tort of negligence and the duty of care under the Act are two separate civil wrongs. Although there is no great distinction between the duty at common law and the common duty of care under the Act it might well be an advantage to an injured person to claim under both torts. It is still possible to sue a person who is on another person's land for the common law tort of negligence on its own, whether or not the person sued would be an occupier under the Occupiers' Liability Act 1957.

A case which was decided before the 1957 Act became operative and was based on the common law tort of negligence was the House of Lords decision in *A.C. Billings and Sons Ltd v Riden* 1958. Here Billings were contractors carrying out work to the entrance to a building. This and the storage of material made the garden path and steps difficult to use. The builders advised the caretaker of the building to use next door's path and steps to gain access to the building. A visitor to the caretaker's accommodation used the recommended route but when leaving after darkness had fallen, stumbled from the path and fell into a depression in the garden suffering injury. She sued the builders and was successful. The builders were held liable because their work had forced visitors to use an adjoining path and they had failed to warn and protect users of the danger with the adjoining path. Mrs Riden's award was reduced substantially for her contributory negligence in refusing the offer of assistance to see her to the highway.

In the Court of Appeal decision in *Pannett v P. McGuinness and Co Ltd* 1972 a child fell into a fire of burning rubbish on a demolition site when the demolition contractor's employees had, contrary to instructions, left it unattended. A claim was based on negligence. It was claimed that the presence of children was expected, and in fact had occurred, and the measures to exclude them from a hazard such as a fire had been inadequate. The claim was successful. In his judgment Lord Denning said that there was also a duty on the builders as occupiers but this did not affect the liability under negligence.

Finally, we saw with the House of Lords decision in *Ferguson v Welsh and Others* 1987 that the Law Lords suggested that the local authority might have had a liability under the 1957 Act when a claim for negligence was brought by an injured worker.

6 PROPERTY LAW

INTRODUCTION

In English law property occupies an unusual position in that it recognises rights to physical objects such as buildings and rights in non-physical things such as the right of light which gives the holder the right to restrict his neighbour from building so as to affect his right of light. As we shall see later, this right in non-physical things covers the right of an architect to protect the copyright of his plans.

At times property law seems unnecessarily complex and it gives rise to legal disputes which seem to the ordinary individual to be beyond comprehension. Added to this is the fact that the average landowner will contest most strongly any infringement of his rights in his land.

The reason for the complexity of English property law is that the law has developed over almost one thousand years. Over this period of time there have been advances and retreats in the development of the law. Originally most of this law was based on common law and equity but in the last hundred years or so Parliament has legislated increasingly on these different topics which form property law.

Parliament has made determined efforts to bring property law up to date. The cost of transferring the ownership of land, apart from the difficulty, caused Parliament in 1925 to pass five major Acts of Parliament. The Acts had the aim of modernising the law and making it easier and cheaper to convey the ownership of land. Since then further Acts of Parliament have sought to continue the process of modernization.

At common law the owner of land owns not only the surface of the land but also the air space above to a reasonable height above and the ground below to the centre of the earth. It was this, and the attitude to rights in property, that brought about the belief that 'An Englishman's home is his castle'. In the middle ages there was certainly a strong element of truth in this. Today, however, this is not so. The position now is that the rights of individual landowners have to give way to the interests of the public. The prime example of this is the demolition of private houses against the wishes of their owners in order to construct a motorway. The public benefit to be gained from its construction is held to override private rights.

The rights of individual landowners were first reduced by our monarchs making claims on things in the ground. So any gold or silver in its raw state in the ground is claimed by the Crown. Treasure trove, which is gold or silver in manufactured form which has been hidden and the owner of which is unknown, is also claimed by the Crown. The greatest restrictions on a landowner's right to use and enjoy his land are contained in Acts of Parliament. Oil is claimed for the Crown and has been since the first Act passed by Parliament, the Petroleum (Production) Act 1934. That Act was passed when it was first suspected that oil could be found on land. Since then, with the finds of large deposits both on land and under the sea, other Acts have been passed to control the finding of oil deposits and their exploitation. Coal, too, has been subject to control for many years. In this case the ownership of coal beneath the land of a landowner belongs to British Coal. It was first taken out of private control by the Coal Act 1938 which placed ownership in the control of a body specially formed for that purpose known as the Coal Commission. Water was first subject to statutory control by the Water Resources Act 1963.

The effect of these common law rules and statutory provisions is to deprive a landowner of any advantage if some valuable find, such as an oil deposit, is made on his land. Indeed other than for ordinary compensation, he will suffer loss from the use of his land to remove or extract some find. So, unlike those in a number of other countries, an English landowner gains nothing from the discovery of a valuable product in his land.

The most extensive form of control over a landowner's use and enjoyment of his land is the control provided by the Town and Country Planning Act 1990. As we shall see later, these particular provisions are so extensive as to stop a person building on his land and to control the way in which he may use his land and buildings. The importance of these provisions is such that Parliament made a number of them criminal offences with power for the courts to impose severe penalties.

There are a number of other Acts of Parliament, such as the Highways Act 1980, which can restrict a person's use and enjoyment of his land. Under the Highways Act 1980 a landowner can be prevented from developing his land if it will be needed for some highway improvement. Land may also be acquired compulsorily for highway construction or improvement.

ESTATES IN LAND

English land law started with the Norman Conquest in 1066. The King took the whole of the land into his personal ownership. He then rewarded those who had helped in his conquest by giving them the use of land in return for them performing certain services. Those who were initially rewarded by the King in this way then repeated the process so that a system arose of people working on small plots of land and performing services in return for this benefit. In this way land was farmed and benefits paid to the lord of the manor.

Although it is of little practical importance today, this system still applies. In theory all land in the country is owned by the Crown. The Crown will take back any land which a person owns on his death if that person has not made a will or left relatives who could claim the land.

As a result of this historical development English land law has 'estates', which indicate the duration of the holders' interests in the land, and 'tenures' which indicate the services which had to be performed for the use of the land. Tenures now are of no practical importance and those that remain are solely of ceremonial importance. With estates, however, the position is different. Here a number of different types existed and this led to great difficulty in the conveyance of ownership of land. It was for this reason the Law of Property Act 1925 reduced the number of legal estates which could exist in English land law.

Section 1 of the Law of Property Act 1925 states that the only legal estates which may exist in land are:

(a) An estate fee simple absolute in possession;
(b) A term of years absolute.

The estate fee simple absolute in possession is known as the 'freehold estate'. It is the highest form of estate which exists in English law. The word 'fee' means that the estate is capable of inheritance. That is, the holder of the estate may by his will leave his estate to anyone he wishes. The word 'simple' means that the estate is not limited, for example, to the male side of the family only. The word 'absolute' means that the estate is perpetual. That is, it does not come to an end on the occurrence of some event. The word 'possession' means not only physical possession but the right to possession. The estate of fee simple absolute in possession is often referred to as the fee simple or just freehold.

The estate term of years absolute means an estate which is leasehold. It can be of any period of time, which is fixed at the time the lease is made. This estate is usually referred to as leasehold or a lease or a tenancy. As compared with the estate of fee simple absolute in possesion it is an inferior estate in land. Unlike freehold it is limited in duration and is subject to a number of restraints which seek to protect the landlord. The landlord also has the right to require the tenant to leave the land in certain circumstances and, if necessary, can obtain a court possession order. In addition, the tenant will have to pay the landlord a rent in return for the right to occupy the land.

Landlord and tenant

The relationship with the parties to a lease is that with a long lease they are referred to as lessor and lessee. With short leases the relationship is usually referred to as landlord and tenant. As the use of land and buildings by leases is very common some consideration of the position between the landlord and tenant is necessary.

A lease may be created by the person who has the fee simple absolute in possession, the freeholder, carving out of his estate the lease. So the freeholder may grant to another person a lease, say, of 21 years. That gives the other person a legal right to occupy the land for that period of time. When that period of time has expired the tenant's right to occupy the land ends and the freeholder then assumes the right of occupancy. It is also possible for a lease to be carved out of a lease. So a person who has a 21 year lease may give another person a seven year lease out of his 21 year lease. For the period of the seven years the original holder of the lease gives up possession. When that period has expired the property reverts to the holder of the 21 year lease.

A lease, to be validly created, must have a fixed period of time and give exclusive possession. The period of time of the lease will be that agreed by the landlord and tenant. A lease may be for a day or it may be for 999 years. Leases for periods of a week or a month are usual with residential properties. Leases for a year or a number of years, say, up to 21 years are usual with commercial buildings. Leases of land for the purpose of erecting buildings, known as building leases, are usually for 999 years.

The requirement that a lease shall have a fixed duration means that at the time the lease was created there must be a known beginning and ending. The importance of this is to be seen from the case of *Lace v Chantler* 1944. The case arose from an arrangement where a dwelling was let 'for the duration of the war'. The Court decided that this was insufficient to create a lease. There was a known beginning but an uncertain end. No one knew when the arrangement was made just when the 1939–45 war would end. To this extent there was a lack of certainty. Because this form of words had been used on a wide scale, with the intention to return the dwellings when the war ended, Parliament had to intervene. This it did by passing the Validation of War-Time Leases Act 1944. The Act applied retroactively and put a date for the lettings to end so as to give them the status of leases.

In the case of a lease for a week or a month, known as a periodic tenancy, it is not uncommon for the tenancy to run for many years. Here the view is that the lease runs on by enlarging itself by new periods of time until either party serves on the other a valid notice to quit.

A lease, to be valid, must give the tenant exclusive possession of the land. If exclusive possession is absent, such as a shared occupation, a lease does not exist. The importance of the right to exclusive possession is seen from the fact that with that right the tenant can exclude everybody including his landlord. It is for this reason a lease usually gives the landlord the right, either by himself or by his surveyor, to enter the property at certain intervals for the purpose of inspecting the state of the property and if necessary carrying out repairs.

When there is an absence of exclusive possession the person occupying the premises will have a lesser right in law known as a licence. Landlords of dwellings have for many years sought to prevent a person occupying the dwellings as a tenant under a lease. The reason for this was the degree of protection given to tenants by the provisions in the Rent Act 1977. Since the introduction of the Housing Act 1980 it has been possible for the landlord of a dwelling to let it on a shorthold tenancy, which avoids the provisions in the Rent Act 1977.

The House of Lords in *Street v Mountford* 1985 dealt with a case where the parties to an agreement for the occupation of a flat had agreed that it was to be a licence. If effective as a licence it would allow the owner of the flat to require the occupier to leave on minimum notice. It would also prevent the occupier asking the Rent Officer to fix a 'fair rent', which could be substantially less than the agreed payment. The fact that in this case the occupier had exclusive possession of the flat was conclusive in the opinion of the Law Lords that, despite the written and signed agreement, a lease of the flat had been created. This decision demonstrates the fact that it is the substance of the agreement that counts and not the form of agreement.

Form and content of a lease

Section 52 of the Law of Property Act 1925 requires, subject to an exception, that a lease shall be created by deed. A deed is now governed by the provisions in the Law of Property (Miscellaneous Provisions) Act 1989. These require that the deed shall be in writing and state that it is a deed, and be signed by the parties. The signatures are to be witnessed. The exception to Section 52 is in Section 54. This allows a lease to be made in writing or by word of mouth provided it is for a period not exceeding three years, at the best rent obtainable and without taking a premium. As will be understood, this allows ordinary dwellings to be leased in a simple form and avoids the expense of the execution of a deed.

The contents of a lease vary according to the kind of premises being leased. The lease of a large commercial building over a long period will require many provisions, whereas the lease of a dwelling for a short period will contain far fewer provisions. All leases will state the rent payable and how and when it is to be paid. Both the landlord and tenant, particularly the landlord, will seek to protect their interests in the lease and premises by means of covenants in the lease. An example of a tenant's covenant is to repair the premises. On the part of the landlord an example is the convenant to insure the premises against fire damage and to use the insurance money to repair the damaged premises. If the tenant should be in breach of a covenant in the lease the landlord may take action to require the tenant to remedy the breach. If the tenant fails to remedy the breach or is in breach of the covenant to pay the rent the landlord may forfeit the lease and obtain a court order to remove the tenant.

There are provisions in the Rent Act 1977 and Protection from Eviction Act 1977 which give extensive protection to the tenants of residential properties. To a lesser extent, there is protection for tenants of business premises under the Landlord and Tenant Act 1954.

Fixtures

A matter of possible dispute between a landlord and tenant, and to a lesser extent between the seller and purchaser of property, is the ownership of fixtures. The law of fixtures is based on the rule that 'whatever is attached to the soil becomes part of it'. This means that if an object, which could be a building, is attached to land that object becomes part of the land. This results in the owner of the land becoming also the owner of the object.

The extreme example of this is the owner of land who leases to his tenant so that his tenant can build on it. When the lease comes to an end the land, and the building on it, reverts back to the owner. The harshness of this rule, particularly with small dwelling-houses, led Parliament to pass the Leasehold Reform Act 1967 which allows tenants to either buy the freehold of their houses or have a new lease granted to them.

The question as to whether or not an object has been so attached to land as to become a fixture is often difficult to answer. There are two tests used to answer this question. The two are:

1) the degree of annexation; and
2) the purpose of annexation.

With the first test it is a matter of how firmly an object is attached to the land. The firmer the attachment the more likely it is that it is a fixture. So a building which is of normal construction with concrete foundations will be a fixture. If, however, it is a lightweight building which rests on its own weight with, perhaps some securing bolts into the ground it will not be a fixture.

The second test brings into consideration why the object is there and what purpose it serves. Does it improve the land or building in a permanent way or is it there simply as an object of enjoyment? If it was intended to be a permanent improvement it is a fixture. If it was to be temporary or enjoyed only then it is not a fixture. Objects which are not fixtures include statues in gardens as part of an ornamental layout. Internally they include firegrates, bookshelves and blinds.

A leading case on this topic is the House of Lords decision in *Leigh v Taylor* 1902 where two inch strips of wood were nailed to the papered walls of a mansion house. Canvas was then stretched across the strips of wood and nailed to them. From this a tapestry was fastened and secured with edgings of wood. When the house was sold the question of ownership arose. If the tapestry was a fixture it was part of the house. If it was fixed to display it as an object of beauty it was not a fixture. The House of Lords decided that the tapestry was not a fixture but an object so fixed as to allow its beauty to be observed. The way it was fixed allowed its removal without causing injury. The case of *H. E. Dibble Ltd v Moore* 1970 may be compared with this decision. Here a greenhouse was attached to the land solely by securing bolts which were let into the concrete foundations. This was held not to be a fixture.

There is a limited right for tenants to remove fixtures when a lease ends. Tenants' fixtures, which include objects such as those needed for a trade such as boilers and machinery, can be removed during the tenancy. Domestic objects which can be removed without causing injury to the building, such as window blinds, may be removed during the tenancy. In the case of agricultural fixtures the Agricultural Holdings Act 1986 allows the tenant to remove them either during the tenancy or up to two months after the tenancy ends.

INTERESTS IN LAND

English land law recognises that one plot of land may exercise a right over another plot of land. Such rights are not personal to the owner of the land but are attached to the land. Thus when land which has a right over another plot of land is sold the new owner has the benefit of that right. Interests in land are created by the original owners of the lands concerned. There are also some rights which are personal (and so ownership of land is not necessary) which can be exercised over another person's land.

Easements

An easement is the right to use or restrict the use of another person's land. Easements cover a wide range of matters but the main ones, and the one of greatest importance to the construction industry, are rights of support, rights of way and rights of light. Other rights have been accepted by the courts as coming within the classification of easements. Included are such things as the right to hang washing on another plot of land. It has been said that the class of easements is never closed. So it is open to the court at any time to recognise something as an easement.

There are a number of rights which resemble easements but which do not come within the classification. A right to go on land and take part of the land or of the produce of the land is known as a profit à prendre. This right includes the right to go on land to dig peat, to collect firewood and to catch fish. Profits à prendre can exist as a personal right and this distinction means that it cannot be an easement. A licence is permission for a person to go on land without which the entry on land would be a trespass. A licence is a personal right and that together with its informal manner of creation means that it cannot be an easement. Restrictive covenants are agreements made to benefit land. They are similar to an easement but the manner of creation in some respects is different. Public rights may resemble easements but in an important respect differ. The difference may be seen in connection with public highways. The right to use a public highway is a public right and so not dependent on the existence of a plot of land to benefit from the public highway. In addition, a public highway is available to all members of the public and not restricted to a limited number of persons as is a right of way.

Essential features of an easement

In the case of *Re Ellenborough Park* 1956 Mr Justice Danckwerts defined the essential features of an easement and his definition has been accepted since as the authoritative analysis. He said for an easement to exist there must be:

1) a dominant and a servient tenement;
2) an easement must accommodate the dominant tenement, that is, be connected with its enjoyment and for its benefit;
3) the dominant and servient owners must be different persons; and
4) the right claimed must be capable of forming the subject matter of a grant.

1) The requirement that there must be a dominant and a servient tenement indicates clearly the relationship of the right to land law. An easement is a right affecting two plots of land. One plot, the dominant, makes use of the other plot, the servient. An example here is of one plot of land having a right of way over another plot of land. The dominant has the benefit of the right of

way and the servient the burden of the right of way. Where there is one plot of land only and the owner of that land allows someone to walk over the land that permission is not an easement. It is a licence only and can be brought to an end by notice. It is a personal right only.

2) For a right to exist as an easement it must be shown that it benefits the dominant tenement in some way. The fact that it might be to the personal advantage of the owner of that plot is not sufficient. It has to benefit the plot itself. To use the example of a right of way, the existence of that right makes the dominant tenement a better plot of land. Without that right of way the plot of land might have great access difficulties.

The fact that a right benefits a person is not sufficient in itself to create an easement. In the case of *Hill v Tupper* 1863 a person who owned a canal leased land on the canal bank to Hill and purported to grant him a 'sole and exclusive' right to put pleasure boats on the canal. Hill claimed that he had an easement in respect of the canal which allowed him to bring an action against Tupper, the landlord of a nearby inn, who had puts boats on the canal in competition with his. The court decided that Hill did not have an easement. He had a licence which gave him rights against the person who had granted the licence and no one else. In addition, what Hill was doing was a commercial venture which did not fit within the concept of easements.

3) The requirement that the dominant and servient tenements are to have different owners is based on the definition of an easement as being a right in another person's land. It is not possible in law to have an easement in your own land. If, therefore, a person owns and occupies both plots of land there cannot be an easement. A person cannot have rights against himself. If, however, the same person owns both plots of land but occupies one only and has a tenant on the other an easement could come into existence.

4) The requirement that an easement must be capable of forming the subject matter of a grant brings in a number of matters. The first is that there must be a capable grantor and grantee. That is, each must have the necessary capacity in law to grant and receive an easement. The right claimed must be sufficiently definite. This means that something which cannot be defined will not be accepted as an easement. It is not possible to have an easement to a view or to privacy. The right claimed must be one which either comes within the accepted class of easements or is something the courts will be willing to accept as an easement. As we have seen, the class of easements is never closed. The courts, however, are unwilling to allow a right to be accepted as an easement when it possibly goes beyond using another person's land. In the case of *Copeland v Greenhalf* 1952 Greenhalf had a

business repairing vehicles. For 50 years he had parked on a strip of land, owned by Copeland, vehicles which were awaiting repair or being repaired. The court refused to accept that this was an easement. The reason for this was that what Greenhalf was doing amounted to joint use of the land with Copeland. It was almost a claim to possession. In *Ward v Kirkland* 1967 Ward claimed to have a right to go into Kirkland's farmyard in order to carry out maintenance work to the wall of his cottage which abutted the farmyard. In this case the number of visits was very infrequent but was sufficient to create an easement.

Creation of easements

Easements may be created in a number of ways. In some cases by direct action and in other cases by indirect action.

Acts of Parliament may contain provisions which allow easements to be created. For example, bodies which provide services such as gas, water and electricity which have their powers in Acts of Parliament may create easements.

Express Grant   Express grant is a method of creation in frequent use. It may arise when land is sold and in the conveyance an easement is granted to the purchaser over land which has been retained by the seller. Another example is where a property which is not connected to a public sewer can be connected if the adjoining landowner would allow a drain to be laid down across his land. If the owner of that land is willing to allow the drain to be laid the easement will be created by a deed of express grant between the two owners. As this is a private matter between the two owners it is entirely for them to agree. They will have to agree the price to be paid for the right to lay the drain, where it will be laid and the arrangement for maintenance works.

Implied grant   Implied grants of easements come into existence where the courts are willing to accept that a purchaser of land ought to be granted an easement. The absence of an express grant in a conveyance of land is, in effect, made good by the courts' intervention. The courts are sometimes asked to imply a grant when land has been sold which does not have access to it. The land is 'landlocked'. This is dealt with by the courts granting an easement of necessity, that is, giving the purchaser a means of access over the land retained by the seller of the land. A form of this grant which is based on the common intention of the parties was dealt with by the Court of Appeal in *Wong v Beaumont Property Trust Ltd* 1965. The case is also an example of how owners and occupiers of land are bound by what their predecessors arranged earlier. In the case Beaumont's predecessor in title had leased premises to Wong's predecessor in title. An express provision in the lease was that the tenant would use the premises for a restaurant. When Wong took over the lease he intended to use the premises as a Chinese restaurant. He promised to comply with public health regulations and to eliminate all offensive smells and odours. What was not known to Wong and Beaumont at the time the lease was transferred was that these obligations could only be complied with by the provision of a new ventilation system. This system would have to pass through the upstairs part of the building which had been retained by the landlord. The Court of Appeal decided that Wong was entitled to claim an easement of necessity with regard to the construction of the ventilation system. This was necessary in order to allow him to comply with obligations under the lease and to satisfy the public health regulations.

Included in the category of implied grant is the rule in *Wheeldon v Burrows* 1879. This rule, which may by express provision be excluded from an agreement, provides that if a person sells a piece of land but retains part of the original whole, then he must allow the purchaser those rights that are continuous and apparent. An example will demonstrate the application of the rule. Suppose X owns and occupies two plots of land on one of which there is a house. Access to the house is only by passage over both plots of land. If X sells the plot of land on which the house stands then, under the rule, it is implied that the new owner Y has a right of way over the other plot of land. In effect the original owner X is not allowed to sell land so that the new owner Y is not able to use the land.

Another point to note with implied grant is that Section 62 of the Law of Property Act 1925 provides that on the conveyance of a legal estate in land a number of rights, including easements, are deemed to pass with the land. These provisions may however be expressly excluded. If, therefore, there is no exclusion a property which has a right of way over an adjoining plot of land will take with it when sold that right of way.

Express and implied reservation   Express reservation arises when a person sells a plot of land and reserves with the sale some right for the benefit of land he has. In the case of implied reservation the court implies that the seller of a plot intended to reserve for land he has some right which would benefit his land. For example, he might have sold land over which there is a path the use of which is essential to land he has. If he failed to reserve the right to use the path in the sale the court will imply a reservation.

Prescription   Another method of acquiring an easement is by prescription or passage of time. The basis of this method is that English law will recognise that use over a long period of time suggests a legitimate right. In the appropriate circumstances the courts will give a legal standing to a use so that a plot of land thereby acquires a right which benefits that land.

In order to establish a right in this way a number of requirements must be satisfied. The first is that there must have been continuous use as of right. The matter of continuous use has been interpreted widely by the courts. Use of rights of way have been accepted even though there have been substantial intervals between the uses. The second requirement is that the use must be by or on behalf of the fee simple owner against a fee simple owner. The justice of this may be seen from the fact that a fee simple owner may rent his property to a tenant and be unaware of the use being made of his land. The other requirements are that the use must be without force, without secrecy and without permission. The use without force is an obvious requirement since the courts can hardly give legal authority to some use which is exercised solely by force or the threat of force. The requirement that the use must not be secret is seen in the case of *Union Lighterage Co v London Graving Dock Co* 1902. Here the Dock Co in the construction of a dock drove underground rods into the land of Union Lighterage. This was not discovered until more than 20 years afterwards. The claim to have established a right from long use was dismissed because of the secret way in which the work had been done. The requirement as to a use to be without permission is based on the fact that if, in general, a landowner gives his permission to another to use his land that ought not to be taken to be the acquisition of a legal right.

The ways in which a right under prescription may be claimed are: 'from time immemorial', by Lost Modern Grant and under the Prescription Act 1832.

Time immemorial is from 1189 which was the beginning of the reign of Richard I. It was fixed as a starting point and operates on the principle that a period of 20 years use which could be shown to have started before 1189 established a legal right. If, however, as is more often the case, the use is in connection with a building erected after that date that means this type of claim cannot be made.

Lost Modern Grant is a legal fiction. That is, it is a means created by the courts to provide an authority to accept a use as a legal right. It was introduced to deal with claims which could not be brought under time immemorial. It is based on 20 years use which arose from a deed of grant which has since been 'lost' and so cannot be produced as evidence to the court as justification for the use.

The Prescription Act 1832 sets out certain periods of time which, in the appropriate circumstances, establish the existence of easements. The first point to note is that easements of light are dealt with differently to other forms of easement. With easements of light the actual enjoyment of access of light for a period of 20 years without interruption makes the right absolute. This, however, is not so if the light is enjoyed by written consent or agreement. For easements, other than light, a period of use as of right for 20 years without interruption establishes the easement. If the use started because of oral consent then a period of 40 years use is necessary for the easement to be established. If the use started from written consent or agreement then the period of 40 years use does not establish an easement.

Extinguishment of easements

Easements may be extinguished in a number of ways. Since easements are rights in another person's land it follows that when the two plots of land are in the ownership and possession of the same person then what was an easement ceases to be so. It is not possible to have an easement in one's own land.

Most easements that are extinguished are by means of release. That is, the landowner with the right either expressly releases the right or the circumstances are such that there is implied release. Express release is where there is a formal expression, a deed, that the right is extinguished. So if a landowner has a right of way over adjoining land and he is willing to give up the right, probably in return for a sum of money, that extinguishment would be by a formal deed.

In the case of implied release it is necessary to distinguish mere non-use from a definite intention to release the right. With implied release there has to be abandonment and something further to show the intention to give up the right. An example of this could be a right of way used by means of a gate in a wall. If the use of the way is abandoned and the gate walled up this would be taken to be implied release.

Right of support

In considering rights of support it is important to note that there are two forms of rights of support. The first is the natural right of support and the other the acquired right. A natural right of support is not an easement but a right possessed by a landowner. It is an inherent right in land. Unlike an easement it is not acquired over a period of time. As we have already noted, an easement can only come into existence in one of a number of recognised ways.

A case dealing with the natural right of support is the House of Lords decision of *Redland Bricks Ltd v Morris* 1969. Here Redland operated a quarry for the extraction of clay next to land owned by Morris. A decision was made to stop extraction at a point about 80 feet from the boundary with Morris's land. It was believed that this left a safe margin so that no damage would be caused to Morris's land. In fact this was not sufficient and a landslip withdrew support to Morris's land and an area of that slipped too. This area was used for growing soft fruits so there was a loss of profit as well as the disturbance to the land.

Morris made a claim for damages and for injunctions. A mandatory injunction was granted by the county court requiring the reinstatement of the land. A prohibitory injunction was also granted. The House of Lords decided that the natural right of support had been infringed but that the mandatory injunction, which required about £35,000 of expenditure when the whole property was worth some £13,000 only, was in the circumstances unreasonable. This, therefore, was struck out of the award. The other parts, the prohibitory injunction and the award of damages were upheld. Morris's claim was successful even though there was no evidence of negligence on Redland's part. The right of support had been infringed and that entitled Morris to protection.

A case which dealt with an easement of support was *Bradburn v Lindsay* 1983. Here two semi-detached houses were built with a dividing wall between them. Under the Law of Property Act 1925 this wall was deemed to be divided between the two owners and each had cross-rights of support. The house owned by Lindsay was left unoccupied and became neglected to an extent that the local authority eventually made a demolition order and then themselves demolished the house. This left the dividing wall both unsupported and unprotected. Bradburn brought an action claiming, amongst other things, a breach of a right of support. The High Court agreed that Bradburn's house had a right of support from Lindsay's house and that this right had been infringed. It was decided that Bradburn was entitled to have three buttresses built to provide the support the wall had previously enjoyed.

The Court of Appeal in the case of *Phipps v Pears* 1965 made a ruling on a matter which whilst not a claim for a right of support was closely linked to such a claim. The case arose from a terrace house being demolished and rebuilt. On rebuilding the flank wall was not bonded to the existing wall of the other house. This wall was constructed of single brick and was not waterproofed in any way. When the older house was later demolished the new flank wall was exposed to the elements and damage resulted. Phipps, the owner of the house with the exposed flank wall, claimed to be entitled to an easement of protection. The Court of Appeal rejected the claim on the ground that the law did not recognise any such right. Lord Denning, the Master of the Rolls, said that to recognise such a right would mean that an owner could be prevented from pulling his house down, and this would put a brake on desirable improvements.

Right of light

A right of light is an easement which allows the dominant owner to
prevent a building being erected on the servient land if that would
obstruct his right. The right can only exist with regard to light
coming through a defined aperture. So this form of easement can
only exist with buildings. In the case of *Allen v Greenwood* 1980 the
Court of Appeal decided that a right of light could be acquired by an
ordinary domestic greenhouse.

The difficulty with rights of light is at what stage is there an
actionable obstruction which will allow a court to grant a remedy.
Over the years the courts have been asked to accept various forms
of scientific measurement. In the case of *Colls v Home and Colonial
Stores Ltd* 1904 the House of Lords refused to accept that
obstruction to light could be determined by projecting a line from a
window sill at an angle of 45 degrees. If an area of 45 degrees was
unobstructed it was claimed there was no nuisance. In the case of
Carr-Saunders v Dick McNeil Associates Ltd 1986 the High Court
refused to accept a 50–50 rule; that is, light is taken away which
leaves more than 50 per cent with a low standard of lighting. The
approach of the courts is that of not how much light has been taken
away but how much remains. In the case of *Carr-Saunders v Dick
McNeil Associates Ltd* 1986 Mr Justice Millet said that the dominant
owner is entitled to that access of light 'as will leave his premises
adequately lit for all ordinary purposes for which they may
reasonably be expected to be used'.

As will be appreciated, to allow a building to acquire a right of
light can have a most damaging effect on what becomes the servient
land. The development of the servient land could be severely
restricted because of that right of light. Such restriction would be a
financial loss to the owner of the servient land.

One way of preventing a right of light arising is to erect on the
land which would otherwise be the servient land a physical screen,
which cuts off the light that would otherwise go to the windows of
the building. The difficulty with this action is the erection of a screen
to windows above ground level; added to this is the problem of
maintenance. A more usual way is to use the provision in the Rights
of Light Act 1959. This allows a notice to be registered with the local
authority. The notice has the same effect as the erecting of a
physical screen and so prevents the acquisition of a right of light.
The notice is entered in the Local Land Charges Register kept by
the local authority and so available to anyone who makes a search of
the register.

Restrictive covenants
When land is leased the landlord can, and invariably does, protect
his interests in the land by the insertion of clauses in the lease. In this

way the landlord protects the land when it is out of his possession and ensures that when it is returned it will be in the state desired. A clause often inserted restricts the way in which the tenant uses the land. A breach of such a clause allows the landlord to take action against the tenant and might lead to the lease being forfeited.

In the case of freehold land the person who sells a plot of land may wish to restrict the way in which that land will be used. In order to do this, since there is no lease, the person selling the land imposes in the conveyance a restrictive covenant. As the term implies it is a promise by the purchaser that in the future use of the land its use will be restricted in the way agreed.

Restricted covenants may take various forms but probably the commonest is to use the land for residential purposes only. Another not uncommon use is where a house owner with a large garden sells off part of the garden for development. In this circumstance it is likely that in order to preserve his privacy the seller will restrict the development to a single dwelling and limit its height. Other circumstances are where land is sold and is not to be built on and where land has trees which are to be preserved.

Before we had a system of planning law to control development restrictive covenants were used extensively to form a body of private law binding all landowners within a certain area. Residential developers still make use of restrictive covenants and quote them as a sales promotion feature.

In some respects a restrictive covenant is similar to an easement in that two plots of land have to exist, one of which is under a burden which benefits the other plot. A restrictive covenant cannot, however, be acquired by long use as easements can. It comes into existence by an agreement being made between the owners of the two plots of land.

A restrictive covenant comes, usually, into existence when X sells land to Y and in the conveyance inserts a covenant. In this case Y is the covenantor since he has given the covenant to use the land in a particular way. X is the covenantee since he has received the benefit of the covenant. In this type of arrangement, if Y should take steps which showed his intention to break his covenant X has the right to go to court and get an injunction to restrain the threatened breach. In certain circumstances X may also be able to claim damages.

Difficulties arise with restrictive covenants when either of the original parties to the covenant disposes of the land to another. The rules on these matters are found in the common law and in equity. They had developed over time and are somewhat complex. It is for this reason a restrictive covenant made after 1925 has to be registered. In the case of unregistered land registration has to be in the Land Charges Register kept under the Land Charges Act 1972, and for registered land under the property register kept under the Land Registration Act 1925. Failure to enter the restrictive covenant in the appropriate register means that the convenantee loses the benefit of it against a person who buys the land subject to the burden, provided he was unaware of its existence.

When a covenantee assigns the land which has the benefit of the covenant it may be expressly mentioned in the conveyance of the land. This transfers the benefit of the restrictive covenant to the new owner.

A further method of transferring the benefit of the restrictive covenant is by the provisions in Section 78 of the Law of Property Act 1925. These provide that a covenant relating to land is deemed to have been made for the benefit of the covenantee and his successors in title. This covers the situation where there has been a failure to expressly transfer the benefit of the covenant. The application of the provisions is to be seen in the Court of Appeal decision in *Federated Homes Ltd v Mill Lodge Properties Ltd* 1980. Here a property company sold three plots of land for residential development. One plot was sold to Mill Lodge subject to a covenant which restricted the development to not more than 300 dwellings. The other two plots of land were sold to Federated Homes without however expressly transferring the benefit of the covenant. When Mill Lodge indicated that they intended to build more than the 300 dwellings Federated Homes sought to restrain them claiming the benefit of the covenant. The defence of Mill Lodge was that as the benefit of the covenant had not been expressly transferred it could not be enforced by Federated Homes. The decision of the court was that the provisions in Section 78 operated to pass the benefit of the covenant with land.

In the case of an estate development it is possible to create restrictive covenants which bind all the plots on the estate. This type of creation is known as a building scheme and is based on the decision in *Elliston v Reacher* 1908. The case laid down a number of rules the application of which has been eased over recent years. The requirements are:

1) both the plaintiff and the defendant must have derived title from one common vendor;
2) that the common vendor laid out the estate in defined plots in advance of the sales of the plot to the plaintiff and defendant;
3) the restrictions imposed by the common vendor were intended to be for the benefit of all the plots within the scheme;
4) that the plaintiff and defendant, or their predecessors in title, purchased their plots on the footing that the restrictions imposed were mutually enforceable by the owners of all the plots in the scheme;
5) the scheme must apply to a defined area.

In practice a building scheme applies in a simple way. The

prospective purchaser is shown a plan of the whole residential development and on that plan it is marked that all the plots are to be sold subject to the same restrictive covenants. If not marked on the plan the prospective purchaser must be told in some other way, such as the sales particulars, of the restrictive covenants.

A restrictive covenant may also be enforced under the rule in *Tulk v Moxhay* 1848. This is an equitable rule which operates on the basis that if a purchaser has notice of the existence of a restrictive covenant then he is bound by that covenant even though he has not been bound at common law in the purchase. The case arose from the sale in 1808 by Tulk to Elms of a vacant piece of Leicester Square. Elms covenanted for himself, his heirs and assigns with Tulk, his heirs and assigns that he, Elms, would keep the vacant piece of land in an open state and uncovered with buildings. Elms sold the land and eventually, after it had been sold several times, it was bought by Moxhay. In the conveyance of the land to Moxhay, unlike the earlier transactions, there was no stipulation concerning the covenant. Moxhay admitted that he had knowledge of the covenant. When he threatened to build on the land Tulk sought an injunction to restrain him and to make him comply with the covenant. The House of Lords decided that Tulk was entitled to the injunction to restrain the threatened breach of covenant by Moxhay. Tulk retained some land in Leicester Square which benefited from the covenant and it would be inequitable to allow Moxhay who had notice of its existence to avoid its operation. It was a negative covenant, that is one which does not require the expenditure of money, and so required nothing of Moxhay other than to refrain from building on the land.

Discharge and modification of restrictive covenants

With the passage of time it is inevitable that the purpose and usefulness of some restrictive covenants diminishes. There may, for example, be a change in the nature and character of a district so that a restrictive covenant that a plot of land be used for residential purposes only serves no good purpose. It may, in fact, reduce the proper use of land. For these reasons there needs to be a means of either discharging or modifying restrictive covenants in appropriate circumstances.

Under Section 84 of the Law of Property Act 1925 it is possible to apply to court for a declaration stating whether land is or is not still subject to any restriction. The declaration by the court will state what the position is with regard to the nature, extent and enforceability of a covenant. By making this application a person may discover whether or not a restrictive covenant, possibly made many years ago, is to be treated as still in force and to what extent.

The more usual way of challenging a restrictive covenant is by an application to the Lands Tribunal under the provisions in Section 84 of the Law of Property Act 1925. The Lands Tribunal have the power to discharge or modify a restrictive covenant with or without the payment of compensation. The Lands Tribunal may act if they consider the covenant to be obsolete or if the continuance of the covenant would impede some reasonable use of the land for public or private purposes or it is of little practical benefit or contrary to the public interest. In these cases the loss has to be such that compensation by money will be adequate.

Two other grounds where the Lands Tribunal may discharge or modify are where all those entitled to the benefit of the restrictions have agreed, expressly or impliedly, to them being discharged or modified, and where modification or discharge would not cause injury to those entitled to the benefit of the covenant.

When using their powers the Lands Tribunal must take into consideration the development plan and any pattern of planning policy for the area and any other material circumstance. This requirement means, for example, that if in an area the local planning authority has been granting planning applications for commercial development that fact has to be taken into account in considering a covenant which restricts use to residential only. In addition, in deciding to modify or discharge a covenant the Tribunal can require the person making the application to compensate the persons who would suffer a loss from the removal or reduction of the benefit of the covenant. The Tribunal may also require the applicant to accept new reduced restrictions.

The matter of money compensation and the acceptance of new reduced restrictions arises more often with fairly recent restrictive covenants. It is not unusual for a person to buy land subject to a restrictive covenant that a limited number of houses are to be erected on the land. A few years later that person, having not built on the land, may obtain planning permission to build a block of flats. Without the restrictive covenant being discharged or modified that development cannot take place. An application may, therefore, be made to the Lands Tribunal for discharge or modification. If compensation is ordered it will take into account the fact that the land had been sold at a low price because of the restrictive covenant and that the loss of the benefit of the covenant will affect the covenantee's enjoyment of his land.

Mortgage

A mortgage is an arrangement whereby a loan is made to a person who in return offers property, which is usually land, as security for the loan. If, therefore, the borrower defaults in repayment of the loan the lender has rights which might be exercised against the property. The lender, known as the mortgagee, may be a building society, bank, insurance company or private person and the borrower, known as the mortgagor, may be a person, company or trustees.

The law concerning mortgages is partly common law, equity and statute. So far as the ordinary person is concerned, who invariably needs a mortgage to buy his home, certain protection is given by the Building Societies Act 1986. The Act requires building societies, which are the usual lenders to individuals, to take steps to protect borrowers. For others this protection is not considered necessary since this kind of transaction is part of commercial life.

A mortgage may be created for freehold land by giving the mortgagee a long lease in the property, with a provision to bring it to an end on repayment of the loan, or by means of a legal charge on the property. In this way the mortgagee has a legal estate, a term of years, in the property which gives certain rights. In the case of leasehold land the mortgagor who has a lease, say, of 99 years creates out that lease another shorter lease. This again means that the mortgagee has a legal estate in the property. As with freehold land, it is possible to mortgage leasehold land by means of a legal charge on the property.

The creation of mortgages by leases as security is the traditional way of providing the security the mortgagee needs. The more recent provision of a legal charge, which gives the same protection, powers and remedies to the mortgagee, is a simpler, short and less expensive form of mortgage.

The mortgagee requires protection of his security. In the case of unregistered land he will take possession of the title deeds of the property, which will prevent the mortgagor creating a further mortgage without the second mortgagee being aware of the existence of the first mortgage. It is also possible to register the mortgage under the Land Charges Act 1972. In the case of registered land the Land Certificate is deposited with the Land Registry until the mortgage is brought to an end.

On occasions property is offered as security for a short term loan. This is not a legal mortgage since the circumstances do not justify the creation of a formal mortgage deed or legal charge. Instead it is possible to obtain a loan from, for example, a bank by the security of depositing the title deeds with them. This is a form of equitable mortgage.

The mortgagee has a number of remedies available if the mortgagor should default. He may sue for the money due on the basis that the mortgagor promised in the mortgage to repay the loan. The more usual remedy used is to sell the property. This power of sale carries the right to take possession of the property. The proceeds of the sale are used to pay off the mortgage debt, the mortgagee's expenses, with any surplus being paid to the mortgagor. Under the Building Societies Act 1986 building societies are under a duty to obtain the best price that can reasonably be obtained. In the case of other mortgagees there is not the same duty. A mortgagee may also take foreclosure proceedings in the court. This remedy, if it is granted, ends any claim the mortgagor may have. The property is taken from him. As it is a harsh remedy the court has power to refuse the application and instead order a sale of the property.

The mortgagor has the right to redeem the mortgage by paying off the loan. He also has the right of possession of the property. This fact is accepted as indication of his ownership of the property.

CONVEYANCING

The word conveyancing is the legal description of the transaction which transfers the ownership of land from one person to another. Traditionally it was a lengthy and expensive process but more recently because of the legal changes we have already noted it has become less expensive and easier to do. This has been mainly because of the system of land registration being applied throughout the whole country.

The process of conveyancing falls into two parts. The first part is pre-contract. The second part proceeds on the basis that the first part is satisfactory and consists of all the work from the contract being made to the formal completion.

Pre-contract

The position of a prospective purchaser before the exchange of contracts is now governed by the provisions in the Law of Property (Miscellaneous Provisions) Act 1989. Before this Act came into force it was essential to conduct all negotiations 'subject to contract'. The reason for this was that at that time a binding contract to buy land could be made by an exchange of letters or the signing of some note or memorandum. Now the 1989 Act states that a contract for the sale of land must be in writing. That is a formal contract document. Until there is such a contract there is no legal relationship to buy the land. This means that either the seller or prospective purchaser can withdraw without there being any possibility of a breach of contract.

During the period before the contract is signed the prospective purchaser will make arrangements for a mortgage, if that is necessary, and to have the property surveyed.

The solicitor for the prospective purchaser will make a search with the local authority of the local land charges register kept under the Local Land Charges Act 1975. Other questions may also be asked of the local authority at the same time. Information will be sought as to planning matters, liability for road maintenance, matters concerning drainage of the property and whether any charges are owed to the local authority in connection with the property.

Questions are also asked of the seller's solicitor, which are known as 'preliminary enquiries'. Specific questions are asked as to matters such as boundaries, disputes concerning boundaries, drains which run through the land, any guarantee which exists, such as dry rot treatment, and whether any alterations have been made to the property and if so whether the necessary permissions and consents were obtained.

At the conclusion of these measures the solicitor for the prospective purchaser will be able to advise that it will be safe to sign and exchange contracts. When this is done a deposit of 10 per cent of the purchase price is paid. This deposit will be forfeited if, for any reason, the prospective purchaser decides not to proceed with the purchase. At this time also the date for completion is agreed. This time is usually four weeks but can be varied as the parties decide.

Contract to completion

Once contracts have been exchanged, and it is usual to use standard forms of contract for this purpose, the property has been legally sold. The fact that the buyer has not yet taken possession does not alter this fact. If, however, the purchaser seeks to withdraw from the contract the seller may retain the deposit as damages for the breach or sue asking the court for a decree of specific performance. The next stage is the formal completion of the transaction. The exact procedure of this varies according to whether the title to the land is unregistered or is registered under the Land Registration Act 1925.

In the case of unregistered land it is necessary to ensure that the seller has in fact the right to sell the property. This is done by requiring the seller to produce a good root of title. That is one which is recognised as proving the ownership of the legal and equitable interest sold, and provides identifiable description of the property and does not show anything which casts doubt on the title of the seller. Under Section 23 of the Law of Property Act 1969 the title must begin with a good root at least 15 years old. A good root is a conveyance for sale or a legal mortgage. So if X is selling his property to Y and X bought the property 20 years earlier the root of title is the conveyance to him of the title 20 years earlier. The process can mean the examination of several documents in order to ensure that the title to the property has properly been obtained. For example, if the property has been left in a will has the will been properly made and have the personal representatives acted properly? When satisfied that the title is as indicated, these documents are handed over and together with the new conveyance form the title deeds. In the case of a sale where part only of a plot of land is being sold the owner will retain the title deeds. In this case the sale of the part of the land is endorsed on the last conveyance.

An important feature with unregistered land is the need to make a search of the Land Charges Register kept under the Land Charges Act 1972. This register contains information, divided into classes, about the owner of the property. Included are restrictive covenants, legal mortgages not protected by the deposit of title deeds, estate contracts, pending legal actions and bankruptcy. Failure to register charges means, in general, that a purchaser is not bound by that matter. An official certificate of search provides protection in that any entry in the 15 days following the search will not bind the purchaser if the completion is within that time.

Registered land does not present the same difficulties as those just considered. Here there is a certificate of registration under the Land Registration Act 1925. The property certificate has a title number and the name of the registered owner. The certificate is divided into three parts. The first, the property register, describes the property and indicates whether it is freehold or leasehold. The second, the proprietorship register, gives the name of the registered proprietor and the type of title. The third, the charges register, gives details of certain matters concerning the property. Because of the existence of this last part there is no search of the Land Charges Register since all the information is on the certificate.

The buyer is given an official copy of the entries on the register. On being satisfied with regard to these the transfer of title takes place. The former title owner's name is crossed off the register and the new owner's name inserted. A search of the register is made before completion and this gives protection to the purchaser for a period of 21 days. Anything registered within this time will not bind the purchaser provided the transaction is completed within this time.

NEGOTIABLE INSTRUMENTS

The payment of cash for debts due to some one is not a satisfactory way of conducting business except on a small scale. It is for this reason other methods exist for payment without actual cash being handed over. A right to be paid a debt is, because it is not a tangible thing such as land or buildings, known as a chose in action. It is a right recognised by law and may be enforced by an action in the courts. It is possible to transfer the right if the provisions in Section 136 of the Law of Property Act 1925 are observed. These are: that the assignment is absolute and not by way of a charge; is in writing; and express notice in writing is given to the debtor. If these formalities are satisfied the assignee can sue the debtor in his own name. The assignee, however, cannot have any greater rights than the assignor had. It is also possible to have an equitable assignment, that is one which does not comply with the requirements of Section 136. It comes about by the assignor handing over the document and indicating in writing or orally that he intends to assign it. Equity law looking at the intent rather than the form treats that transaction as an assignment. The background to negotiable instruments is the transactions between merchants which took place in earlier times. They recognised the benefits to be obtained by having documents which allowed debts to be paid in this way and to be able to transfer debts. The law which had been part of the common law eventually was put into statute law. The most important types of negotiable instruments are bills of exchange including cheques and banknotes.

A bill of exchange is defined in Section 3 of the Bills of Exchange Act 1882 as:

> A bill of exchange is an unconditional order in writing, addressed by one person to another, signed by the person giving it, requiring the person to whom it is addressed to pay on demand or at a fixed or determinable future time a sum certain in money to or to the order of a specified person, or to bearer.

From this it can be seen that it has to be an order not subject to any condition; it has to be in writing; it has to be signed by one person, the drawer, requiring another person, the drawee, to pay a sum of money to a specified person or bearer, the payee. The sum of money is to be paid on demand or at a fixed time or a determinable time.

To put this into a practical example Adam, the drawer, instructs his bank Utopia Ltd, the drawee, to pay Eve, the payee, a certain sum of money on a fixed date. When the bank, Utopia Ltd, accepts the bill of exchange the bank then becomes liable to pay the sum specified. Until a bill is accepted, which is done by writing on the bill, the drawer remains personally liable. Once accepted, the drawer will be liable only if the drawee, the bank, defaults on payment.

As we have seen, a bill may be made payable to a specified person to his order or to bearer. If a bill is made payable to a specified person only then it cannot be transferred. When the bill matures that person has to recover payment. If, however, it is made payable to a specified person or order then it can be transferred. So if a bill names Jones as the payee or order Jones can transfer the bill the Smith by signing the bill, so endorsing it. In endorsing it the name of the person to whom it is endorsed must be given. The effect of this is that Jones becomes liable on the bill if the drawee, the acceptor, defaults in payment. On the transfer the person who has given value for the bill and is unaware of any defect or irregularity in the bill can sue on the bill in his own name. He is known as a 'holder in due course'.

With a bill which is made payable to bearer, whoever is the bearer at the time the bill matures is entitled to payment. A bill may also become a bearer bill. This happens when a bill has been made out to a specified person or order and that person just puts his signature on the bill. This is known as 'endorsement in blank' since the bill has been endorsed without naming a person to whom it has been transferred.

A cheque is a bill of exchange. It is drawn on a banker and payable on demand. Unlike a bill of exchange a cheque is never 'accepted'. Furthermore the payee has no right against the banker. The debt which the debtor seeks to pay by a cheque is not paid until the bank has honoured the cheque. If a cheque is post-dated the bank is not entitled to debit the drawer's account until that date has arrived.

It is the practice of banks not to pay cheques which have not been presented for payment within six months of their dates. This is good practice and the banks ask for assurances that the cheques are still valid before they will be honoured.

A cheque may be crossed by drawing two parallel lines across its face. The effect of this is to mean that it can only be paid to a bank. It cannot, unlike an 'open cheque', be used to obtain cash over the counter of a bank. When a cheque has the two parallel lines drawn across its face or when the words 'and company' or 'not negotiable' are written within the lines, the cheque is said to be crossed generally. By the use of crossed cheques the possibility of dishonest handling is reduced since payment has to be through a bank account. A further protection is to cross the cheque specially by writing within the lines the name of a banker to whom it is to be paid.

It is also the practice to mark cheques 'not negotiable'. Where this is done it does not prevent the cheque being transferred. The transferee, however, cannot have a better title to it than the transferor had and is subject to any defects which exist in his title. This means that if a cheque has been transferred and for some reason the bank will not pay on it the transferee has to look to the transferor and not the drawer of the cheque for a remedy.

Another practice is to mark within the crossed lines the words 'account payee' or 'account payee only'. These words did not have any legal significance until the passing of the Cheques Act 1992, other than to secure that the money was paid into the payee's account. Now, however, Section 1 of the Cheques Act 1992 states that a crossed cheque with the words 'account payee' or 'a/c payee' either with or without the word 'only' is not transferable. The cheque is valid between the parties only. This is a further measure to reduce the possibility of dishonest use of cheques.

In addition to these measures it is the practice of banks now to issue cheque books to personal customers without the words 'or order'. These cheques are payable to a payee only. Again this is a measure to reduce fraud and dishonesty. Cheques can be altered but if they are the alterations must be initialled by the drawer. Failure to do this means that the bank, the drawer or any endorser are not liable on the cheque.

The Cheques Act 1957, Section 1, provides protection to a banker paying cheques which have not been endorsed or have been endorsed irregularly. The banker has to be acting in good faith and in the ordinary course of business. The application of this provision may be seen in the situation where John draws a cheque on his account with the X bank in favour of James. The cheque however is stolen by Jasper. Jasper then opens an account in the name of John at the Y bank and pays in the cheque. The Y bank then passes the cheque to the X bank. If the X bank then in good faith and in the ordinary course of business pays on the cheque to Y bank so that Jasper obtains the money the X bank is not liable. In order to guard against these difficulties it is the practice of banks to require cheques paid into a payee's account to be endorsed.

When a person discovers that a cheque has been stolen or lost or some other reason precludes payment, the drawer should stop the cheque by telling the bank not to pay it. In the case of a cheque issued on the basis of a cheque guarantee card the drawer has agreed with the bank that he will not be able to stop such a cheque. In stopping a cheque the usual bank practice is to require any oral instruction to be confirmed in writing. A bank will automatically stop a cheque once it receives notice that the drawer has died, become bankrupt or become mentally incapable. Other circumstances include a company winding up or a court order.

Banks will refuse to pay cheques when the amount drawn is greater than the credit balance or any authorised overdraft. In this case the cheque will be returned, usually marked 'refer to drawer'. If a bank wrongly refuses to honour a cheque, or returns a cheque with words indicating that there are insufficient funds when this is not so, then there is a breach of contract between the bank and customer. In addition the customer may be able to sue for defamation of character.

BANKRUPTCY

The law relating to bankruptcy is mainly contained in the Insolvency Act 1986, added to which are various rules and case law. The 1986 Act changed the law of bankruptcy in a substantial way. It has made it easier for a person to avoid bankruptcy and also to be discharged from bankruptcy earlier than was previously the case. The limitations on business activities placed on a bankrupt still remain and, of course, the stigma of public exposure as a person who is insolvent.

Interim action

It is not always in the best interests of the creditors to make a person bankrupt. Arrangements can be made whereby a person remains in business but his financial affairs are managed by his creditors. In this way the creditors have a better chance of being paid their debts in addition to which the person avoids bankruptcy.

The Act allows an application to be made to the court for an interim order in respect of an individual debtor. The interim order prevents, during the period it is in force, a bankruptcy petition being either presented or proceeded with, and any other legal proceedings being commenced or continued against the debtor or his property except with leave of the court. The application may be made by the debtor and if he is an undischarged bankrupt by the trustee in bankruptcy or the official receiver. The application may only be made if the debtor intends to make a proposal to his creditors for composition in satisfaction of his debts or a scheme of arrangement of his affairs.

An application cannot be made if a bankruptcy petition has been presented by the debtor and an insolvency practitioner has been appointed to inquire into the debtor's affairs. The purpose of this restraint is to prevent a conflict between two provisions in the Act. Once an application is made the court may stay any legal action against the debtor.

In order to prevent the interim order being used as a delaying tactic by a person who is insolvent the Act states that an interim order ceases to have effect 14 days after it is granted and no fresh application can be made within 12 months of a previous application.

The making of an interim order depends on a person, referred to as a 'nominee', being appointed to submit a report on the debtor's affairs. The debtor has to submit a statement of his affairs to the nominee. If the nominee needs extra time to do his work the interim order may be extended. The nominee reports to the court and on the report the court may discharge the interim order or call a meeting of the creditors.

If a meeting of creditors is called they may approve the voluntary arrangement or they may approve it subject to modifications. If there are modifications the debtor must approve. The Act forbids modifications to the proposal which would alter the proposal so that it no longer was a proposal under the Act, or to make any secured or preferred creditors lose their priority in the order of claims.

The nominee may administer the arrangement or he may be replaced by another person provided he is a qualified insolvency practitioner. Whoever is appointed is referred to as the supervisor.

There is power given to the court to remove the supervisor. The supervisor is given power to apply to the court for directions on any particular matter arising under the voluntary arrangement.

Bankruptcy petition

Where the situation is such that formal proceedings of bankruptcy are necessary a petition may be presented to the court which is either the High Court or County Court. A bankruptcy petition may be presented by the debtor himself, by a creditor or creditors jointly, by the supervisor of a voluntary arrangement or by a criminal bankruptcy order made against the person. The petition must relate to a person present in the country or who has carried on business in the country within the last three years either as an individual or as a member of a partnership.

The petition must be in respect of one or more debts owed by the debtor to a creditor if it is a creditor's petition. The debt must not be less than the 'bankruptcy level', which is at present £750, but which may be changed. The debt has to be for a liquidated sum. Before a creditor can present a petition he must have served on the debtor a demand, 'the statutory demand', requiring payment of that debt, and three weeks must have elapsed since that demand was served and the demand has not been complied with or set aside.

The court is not to make a bankruptcy order on a creditor's petition unless satisfied that the debt has not been paid or secured or compounded or that the debtor has no reasonable prospects of being able to pay the debt. The court may dismiss the petition if satsfied that the debtor's offer to secure or compound the debt has been unreasonably refused.

In the event of the debtor making a petition for his own bankruptcy it is required that in addition to the petition the debtor has to present a statement of his affairs. If in considering the debtor's petition because of the small amount involved the court believes that, on the report of an insolvency practitioner appointed by the court, summary administration is appropriate then the court shall so order. A bankruptcy order is made which is subject to a certificate for summary administration of the bankrupt's estate. Summary administration is a simpler and less costly method of dealing with bankruptcy.

A supervisor of a voluntary arrangement may present a petition to the court if the debtor has failed to comply with his obligations under the voluntary arrangement, or has given false or misleading information or has failed to do things reasonably required of him under the voluntary arrangement.

When the court makes a bankruptcy order any disposition of property or payment made by the debtor after the day of presenting the petition is void. As this could operate unfairly against a person who was unaware of the debtor's financial state and consequent bankruptcy there are exceptions to the provision. A person who received the property or payment before the day when the bankruptcy order was made, had acted in good faith, given value and without notice of the bankruptcy petition having been presented is protected.

As there may be circumstances where it is necessary to protect a debtor's property, the court has power after the presentation of the petition but before the making of a bankruptcy order to appoint an interim receiver. There is also a provision for the appointment of the official receiver after the making of a bankruptcy order and before the appointment of a trustee.

Trustee in bankruptcy

As the making of a bankruptcy order removes the control of his financial affairs from the debtor it is necessary for a person, of appropriate qualification, to be appointed to deal with the debtor's estate. In simple terms the trustee's responsibility is to get in money owed to the bankrupt and from the assets pay the creditors in accordance with an order of priority.

A person appointed as a trustee must be qualified as an insolvency practitioner in relation to bankruptcy. The court or in certain circumstances a creditors' meeting may appoint the trustee. If no trustee is appointed the official receiver is under a duty to act as interim receiver until a trustee is appointed. The debtor has to deliver to the official receiver possession of his estate and all books, papers and other records which relate to his estate.

The official receiver is under a duty to decide within 12 weeks whether to summon a meeting of the bankrupt's creditors. If he does not do so or decides against summoning a meeting of the creditors for the purpose of appointing a trustee, then he must do so if not less than one quarter in value of the creditors request the meeting.

The reluctance of the official receiver to call a meeting or of the creditors to request a meeting is bound up with the amount in the debtor's estate. If the amount is so small that there will possibly be nothing left, after expenses, to pay to the creditors there is no point in the creditors having a meeting. Time and expense spent in this way would be a total loss. The position would be different if the estate was of some value. Then the creditors would wish to appoint their own trustee and be involved in the matter.

On occasion, such as the failure to account properly for the spending of a large sum of money, a public examination of the bankrupt would be desirable. Such an examination allows questions to be put to the bankrupt under oath. A public examination may be requested by either the official receiver or by one half of the creditors in value.

Once a trustee is appointed the bankrupt's estate immediately vests in him. Any property acquired by the bankrupt after the commencement of the bankruptcy is also claimed by the trustee. The court may, on the application of the trustee, make an 'income payment order' so that part of a bankrupt's income may be claimed for the benefit of the creditor. Sufficient income, however, must be left to meet the reasonable domestic needs of the bankrupt and his family.

A trustee is not allowed to claim such tools, books, vehicles and other items of equipment as are necessary to the bankrupt for use personally by him in his employment, business or vocation. Nor can claim be made for such clothing, bedding, furniture, household equipment and provisions as are necessary for satisfying the basic domestic needs of the bankrupt and his family.

An important power of the trustee is the power to disclaim, by giving the prescribed notice, any onerous property. The description includes any unprofitable contract or unsaleable property. As this power affects others to a substantial extent the trustee can be required to give his decision within 28 days. If the period of 28 days has expired without the trustee making a decision it is deemed that he has not disclaimed the onerous property.

The trustee, in the performance of his duties, is accountable to the committee of creditors which was appointed by the creditors. He is also answerable to the court and in fact may be removed from his position by the court. The trustee, when he has made the distribution, has to call a final meeting of the creditors.

Distribution of the bankrupt's estate

When the trustee has got in all the assets of the bankrupt he is required by law to pay out a dividend to those creditors who have proved their claims. In deciding on the dividend the trustee must allow for the expense of the bankruptcy and allow for any debts which are still in doubt. If the creditors' committee agrees the trustee may divide amongst the creditors property which because of its special nature or other circumstance cannot easily be sold. If a creditor proves his debt after the dividend has been paid his claim cannot affect previously paid dividends.

The claims have to be paid in an order of priority. Preferential debts must be paid before ordinary debts. Preferential debts include 12 months income tax and tax due in connection with sub-contractors in the construction industry; debts due to the Customs and Excise; 12 months social security contributions; money due for state and occupational pensions; remuneration, including holiday pay, due to employees for a period of four months.

Ordinary debts, which are paid only after the preferential claims have been satisfied, include trade debts. As will be appreciated, in practice, ordinary debts are often not paid since what money the trustee has recovered will be absorbed by the trustee's expenses and the preferential claims.

Discharge from bankruptcy

Under the previous law a person declared bankrupt found it difficult to be discharged from being a bankrupt until a considerable number of years had past. Now discharge is automatic after two years from the bankruptcy order in the case of summary administration. In the case where there was no summary administration the period is three years. It is possible, however, for the court to suspend the running of the time if the official receiver proves that the bankrupt has failed to comply with his obligations. The court may also exercise this power if a condition imposed by the court has not been fulfilled.

DEBT COLLECTION

The county courts were established in the middle of the nineteenth century in order to provide a simple, inexpensive system for a trader to recover debts owed to him. For a number of years it was known as the 'small traders' court'. Its procedure was, and still is, designed to allow ordinary individuals to sue and be sued without the use of lawyers. The jurisdiction of the county courts was extended by the Courts and Legal Services Act 1990 so that now claims in contract or tort for amounts up to £25,000 will be dealt with by the county courts.

An action in the county court has to be commenced in the court for the district where the defendant lives or carries on business or where the contract was made. If the action is commenced in the wrong court district there is a procedure to transfer the action to the correct court.

The action starts with completion of a form for a default summons. This is sent to the court with the appropriate fee, which varies according to the amount claimed, and two copies of the particulars of claim. The particulars of claim is a statement setting out the grounds for the making of the claim. The court then issues a plaint note with the number of the action and this is the action's reference thereafter. The summons, which is usually served by post, has to be correctly addressed. Individuals have to be properly named, partnerships are sued as firms and if an individual trades under another name that fact has to be stated. In the case of limited companies the summons has to be served at their registered offices.

Once the summons is served the defendant has 14 days within which to enter a defence. If the defendant fails to do this the plaintiff may ask for judgment in default. If the defendant admits the debt but offers to pay it by instalments then it is up to the creditor to decide whether to accept the offer. If a defence is submitted but the plaintiff believes that the defence shows no reasonable ground to resist the claim he may ask the court for judgment. If the defence appears reasonable and the claim is for less than £1,000 the claim may be dealt with by a system of arbitration within the court system. Above this amount it will go for trial before either a district judge or circuit judge.

Enforcement of judgment

It is one thing to obtain a court judgment, it is another thing to recover the amount awarded by the judgment. Even with the assistance of the court some creditors never get paid. It is for this reason solicitors will sometimes advise clients not to proceed with justifiable claims since either the amount claimed is too small or the person to be sued is not worth suing.

A frequently used form of enforcement is to execute on the defendant's goods. This is done by the county court bailiff who seizes goods to the value of the amount. If the defendant is in employment there is the possibility of obtaining an attachment of earnings order. This court order requires the employer to deduct from the defendant's earnings a stated sum. The amount deducted must not reduce the defendant's earnings below a fixed sum so as to provide sufficient for him and his family to live.

A less used means of recovery is by a garnishee order. This is where the creditor is aware that the debtor has money owing to him. The person owing the money, the garnishee, is ordered to pay the money into court for the benefit of the creditor. An example of this would be where a creditor discovered that a debtor, against whom he had a court judgment, had a bank account. Here the creditor could by the garnishee order require the bank to pay the amount into court for his benefit.

Where a debtor has property such as a building or shares in a company it is possible to obtain a charging order against the property. This is notice to everybody that the property is charged with the payment of the debt. It also gives protection in that it makes the creditor a secured creditor in the case of bankruptcy.

A commonly used means of obtaining payment is to inform the debtor that bankruptcy is being considered. For this to be made the debt must not be less than £750. The possibility of bankruptcy, with its associated effects, is often sufficient to secure payment. A number of professions will not allow a bankrupt to practise the profession.

Where the debtor conducts a business which is viable and cash producing it is possible to obtain the appointment of a receiver. The receiver has power to take profits from the business for the benefit of the creditor.

Rather than go through all these procedures in order to obtain payment of debts some traders make use of commercial arrangements. These arrangements are conducted by companies whose line of business is debt recovery. The arrangements take two forms. The first is where a company actually buys the debt from the trader. Here the trader gets paid at an agreed percentage of the sum on the invoice. This arrangement will only work if the trader has been dealing with good customers who are likely to pay their debts. The other arrangement is for a company to seek to recover a trader's debts and if successful to take a percentage of the amount recovered. Because of all the work involved in recovering the debt the percentage retained is usually substantial.

PATENTS AND COPYRIGHT

Both patents and copyright are forms of property recognised and protected by law. They can be of considerable value and both are of some importance to the construction industry.

Patents are governed by the provisions in the Patents Act 1977. A patent is defined in Section 1 as an invention which is new, involves an inventive step, is capable of industrial application and the grant of a patent is not excluded by other provisions in the Act.

Any person may make an application for a patent to protect an invention. The application may be made alone or jointly. The application is made in the prescribed manner with the prescribed fee to the Patent Office. The fact that the application has been made is published and the examination of the application then proceeds. If the grant of the patent is made the invention has a protected status. The period of time this continues is 20 years. The grant of a patent is to be entered in a register kept at the Patent Office.

Many inventions are discovered by employees in the course of the duties of their employment. The Act states that in this circumstance the invention belongs to the employer. If, however, the employee makes the discovery in other circumstances then the invention belongs to the employee. When an employee's invention is properly claimed by the employer, the employee is entitled to compensation. The patent has to be of outstanding benefit to the employer and it has to be just that the employee be awarded compensation. The amount awarded has to give the employee a fair share of the benefit the employer derives from the patent.

The holder of a patent may authorise others to make use of the patent by means of a licence. In return for this licence the person authorised makes a payment for the granting of that right.

An infringement of a patent may be dealt with by the holder in a number of ways. If the infringement has not yet occurred an injunction may be obtained. If the infringement has occurred damages may be claimed or a sum for each action which has profited the infringer.

The law with regard to copyright is contained in the Copyright, Designs and Patents Act 1988. It is of particular importance to the construction industry with regard to plans of buildings. Section 1 of the Act states that copyright is a property right which subsists, amongst others, in original literary, dramatic, musical or artistic works. The expression 'artistic work' is defined in Section 4 as including 'a work of architecture being a building or a model for a building'. The expression 'building' includes 'any fixed structure, and a part of a building or fixed structure'.

So the plans prepared by an architect or a building surveyor of a building, a part of a building or structure, if original, will be copyright under the Act. It is usual for building plans to be marked as being the copyright of a named person.

The duration of copyright is fixed at the period of 50 years from the end of the calendar year in which the author dies. During this period the holder of the copyright may protect his rights by action in the courts. A proposed infringement may be restrained by an injunction. An actual infringement allows the holder of the copyright to sue for damages.

The holder of a copyright may authorise others, by means of a licence, to make use of the copyright. An example of this is a book of house designs produced by various architects. Each design is protected by copyright and the individual architects will license someone to make use of the copyright design.

In the case of an architect the copyright exists not only in the plans but in the building itself. So a person who has not seen the plans but inspects the building and then goes off and builds in a similar manner has infringed the architect's copyright. If the architect is an employee then the copyright in his design belongs to his employer.

The question as to copyright if a building has to be rebuilt was considered in the case of *Meikle v Maufe* 1941. Here a building, which had a number of distinctive architectural features, was destroyed by fire. The architect was of the opinion that his permission was required before the building could be rebuilt to his original design. The court decided that to rebuild on the same site would not be an infringement of copyright and that it would be implied that the architect had given the copyright for this purpose to the building owner.

This situation is now dealt with by the provisions in Section 65 of the Act. These stated that anything done for the purposes of reconstructing a building does not infringe any copyright in the building or in the plans in accordance with which the building was, by or with the licence of the copyright owner, constructed.

The question as to whether the architect retains copyright in his plans depends on the contract. In general he will retain the copyright. He may, however, agree to assign the copyright to the person who commissioned his work. This would be the case with a developer of residential estates who commissioned an architect to design houses of different types and wished to use the plans on other developments in the future.

The need to be certain as to the right to use copyright plans is to be seen from two Court of Appeal decisions. In the first case *Blair v Osborne and Tompkins* 1971 two owners of a plot of land wished to erect two houses on it. They engaged Blair as architect for this purpose. He was to prepare detailed plans for the purpose of obtaining planning permission. His contract of engagement was by the use of the Royal Institute of British Architects (RIBA) Conditions of Engagement and Scheme of Provisional Charges 1962. These allowed either party to end the contract by giving reasonable notice. Blair obtained full planning permission. He sent a copy of the plan, the certificate of planning consent and his account for £70 to the owners. The owners paid the account. They then sold the land together with the plans. The architect when he learnt of this claimed that his copyright had been infringed. The court refused to accept his claim. Their ruling was that in return for his fee he had impliedly promised that the owners were licensed to use the plans for the buildings and that this licence extended to a builder or purchaser of the site.

In the case of *Stovin-Bradford v Volpoint Properties Ltd* 1971 Stovin-Bradford, an architect, agreed by an oral contract for 100 guineas to prepare drawings in order to obtain planning permission for an extension to a factory. The architect obtained the planning permission mainly as a result of a distinctive feature of his design. He sent his account marked with the words: 'Agreed nominal fee 100 guineas'. He also added words indicating that he had retained the copyright in the drawings and that his permission was necessary for their reproduction. If the contract had been under the RIBA scale of fees he would have been entitled to £900 for what he had done. Not long afterwards he withdrew from the project. The factory was extended using part of his design. He discovered this fact some months later. He sued claiming infringement of copyright. The court awarded him £500 damages. The court was satisfied that he had retained the copyright since not only had he indicated this in writing but he had charged a nominal fee. The amount, 100 guineas, was substantially less than the amount he would have been entitled to under the RIBA scale of fees. It could not, therefore, be implied that his drawings could be used by the owners.

As these cases showed a somewhat uncertain and unsatisfactory position regarding the architect's copyright, the RIBA in their conditions of engagement 'Architect's Appointment' set out to correct the matter. Now the architect expressly claims copyright and the client's entitlement depends on the work undertaken and the fees of the architect having been paid or tendered. In a specified circumstance the architect may withhold his consent to the use of his copyright. This, however, must not be unreasonably withheld and the question as to whether the architect has been reasonable or not is to be determined by arbitration.

7 PLANNING LAW

INTRODUCTION

It is not possible these days to consider property law without examining some aspects of town and country planning law. This body of law regulates in some detail the construction and use of buildings. Modern planning law started with the Town and Country Planning Act 1947 and since then had been added to and continues to be amended. At the present time the principal Act is the Town and Country Planning Act 1990, which has been amended by the Planning and Compensation Act 1991. In addition there is a substantial body of law in the form of rules and regulations.

LOCAL PLANNING AUTHORITIES

Ever since the introduction of the Town and Country Planning Act 1947 it has been considered appropriate that the central government should be involved in the policy and control of planning matters. This still applies and the Secretary of State for the Environment has duties and powers under the 1990 Act.

The main burden of administration of planning law is placed on local authorities. Since the passing of the Local Government Act 1985 the Greater London Council and the six metropolitan county councils have been abolished. The remaining county councils, referred to as the 'shire' counties, are county planning authorities. Within these county planning areas the district councils are the local planning authorities for their own areas. There are, therefore, two local planning authorities for these country areas, each with its own responsibilities. In the former metropolitan county areas the district councils now have sole responsibility for planning matters. In the Greater London area the boroughs have sole responsibility.

There are circumstances where planning decisions for two or more local authorities would be better made by a single body. The Secretary of State therefore has power to constitute a joint planning board. This he has done and formed the Lake District Special Planning Board and the Peak Park Joint Planning Board.

In practice a local planning authority does much of its work by means of a committee. Under the Local Government Act 1972 such a committee may be authorized to discharge the planning functions.

Under the same Act the local planning authority can delegate planning functions to an officer of the authority. This is frequently done with regard to routine matters. The decision of the officer binds the authority.

DEVELOPMENT PLANS

Development plans are intended to indicate the local planning authority's policy with regard to planning development. By consultation of such plans the ordinary individual can see what development is likely to be permitted within an area. By adhering to the proposals in the plans there will be consistency on planning matters in an area over a period of time.

Development plans have taken various forms since they were introduced with the 1947 Act. More recently, changes have had to be made to take account of the abolition of the Greater London Council and the metropolitan county councils.

The non-metropolitan county planning authorities have the responsibility of preparing and keeping under review structure plans. In making surveys for this preparation the counties are required to take into account specific matters, including economic characteristics, population, transport and traffic systems. A structure plan is a written statement of general policies in respect of the development and use of land. In the preparation of the plan a number of requirements regarding consultation, publicity and examination in public have to be satisfied.

District council planning authorities in non-metropolitan county areas are responsible for the preparation of local plans. A local plan is an extension in detail of the policy provisions set out in the structure plan. Because of its detailed provisions the local plan is the plan the ordinary individual will consult for information as to the future of his property. The local plan is prepared in accordance with instructions from the Secretary of State. The local plan can designate any area where comprehensive treatment is required within a prescribed time as an action area. An area thus selected is marked down for comprehensive treatment within an early date. In the preparation of a local plan there has to be public participation, the right to object and a public inquiry.

In the metropolitan district councils, because they are responsible for all the planning functions in their areas, the arrangement for development plans is different. The councils have to produce a unitary development plan. This is a combination of the important elements of the structure plan and the local plan. After making the required survey of the area and taking into account certain directions from the Secretary of State the unitary plan has to be prepared. The plan has two parts. The first is a written statement of the council's general policies, and the second a written statement in detail of the proposals and a map and other information justifying the proposals. The plan is subject to public participation, objection and a public local inquiry.

Two recent innovations where authorities, other than the recognised local planning authorities, have certain planning powers are urban development areas and enterprise zones. Both of these are set up under powers in the Local Government, Planning and Land Act 1980. The purpose of these authorities is to have special powers in order to deal with run-down areas where energetic and swift action is necessary. The powers of the authorities are confined to the areas to be dealt with.

DEVELOPMENT

The general rule, to which there are a number of exceptions, is that any proposal which comes within the definition of development as set out in Section 55 of the Town and Country Planning Act 1990 is subject to planning control.

Development is defined as:

1) the carrying out of building operations, engineering operations, mining operations or other operations in, on, over or under land, or
2) the making of any material change in the use of any buildings or other land.

Certain other matters are specially mentioned as being development or not development. Of particular interest to builders is the provision that the use of a single dwelling-house as two or more separate dwellings is to constitute development. Matters which are not to constitute development of interest to builders are improvements, alterations or maintenance works which do not materially affect the external appearance of the building; maintenance or improvements carried out to a road by a local highway authority; and the breaking open of streets for the inspection, repair or renewal of sewers, mains etc by a local authority or by a statutory undertaker.

In order to assist in the application of the law the term 'building operations' is defined in some detail. It covers all the usual operations ordinarily understood as builders' work, including demolition.

There is a substantial body of case law on the application of the term 'development' to different circumstances. In order to avoid the necessity of persons making applications for developments which are such that they will inevitably be given permission, certain matters are classed as 'permitted development'. For these planning permission is not required provided certain conditions are satisfied. All these are set out in the Town and Country Planning General Development Order 1988.

APPLICATION FOR PLANNING PERMISSION

An application for planning permission must comply with the Town and Country Planning (Applications) Regulations 1988. The application has to be made on a form from the local planning authority. The form has to provide certain information and to be accompanied by a plan or drawings as necessary. The application is made when it is actually received by the authority. Fees have to be paid with applications on a fixed scale.

An application may be made for full permission or outline permission. An application for full permission contains all the necessary details sufficient to allow consideration to be given to it. In the case of outline permission the application consists simply of a plan of the land concerned and a request to be allowed to use that land for a particular development. This allows an application to be made without the expense of preparing plans and drawings. If this application is granted it will then be subject to a later approval by the authority of 'reserved matters'. These relate to siting, design, external appearance, means of access and landscaping of the site.

In certain circumstances an application must be advertised in a prescribed manner. It is the practice of most local planning authorities to notify members of the public if an application might affect in some way their interests.

PLANNING PERMISSION

When an application for planning permission is made the local planning authority must acknowledge its receipt. The authority then has to give notice of its decision within eight weeks from the date of receipt. This period, however, may be extended by agreement in writing between the parties. If the decision is to refuse the application or to grant it subject to conditions the decision notice must given full reasons for the decision. There is a right of appeal to the Secretary of State within six months or such longer period as may be allowed. Failure to make the decision within the period may be treated as refusal and the right of appeal arises.

In order to assist a person who is considering development of land or the use of buildings the 1990 Act allows that person to request the local planning authority to issue a certificate of lawfulness for his proposal. If such a certificate is granted the applicant can then proceed on the basis that planning permission will be granted when eventually it is sought. If the application is refused there is a right of appeal to the Secretary of State.

Mention was made earlier of the power of the Secretary of State in planning matters. A point of importance with planning permission is the power of the Secretary of State to deal with applications himself. This is known as 'calling-in' the application. This is done when the application concerns a matter of national importance or it is something which gives rise to strong local feeling. When the Secretary of State has 'called-in' an application he deals with it in the usual way subject, however, to there being no right of appeal. The applicant and authority may both have a private hearing before a person appointed by the Secretary of State before he makes his decision.

In dealing with a planning application the local planning authority may:

1) grant permission for the development;
2) grant permission subject to conditions;
3) refuse permission.

The granting of permission subject to conditions has given rise to much case law. In general it may be said that the authority must act reasonably in imposing conditions and those conditions must relate to some planning feature and be shown to be necessary in those circumstances. There is the same right of appeal against permission granted subject to conditions as there is for refusal.

A local planning authority has to keep a register of planning permissions which have been granted. This register is to be available for public inspection free of charge. By the use of the register any person may discover whether planning permission has been granted in connection with a building or land which he is interested in buying. It is also helpful in disclosing the pattern of permissions granted by a local planning authority.

Planning permission when granted is of a limited duration. If full planning permission is granted development must be begun within five years unless the local planning authority direct that some other period, longer or shorter, shall apply. In the case of outline planning permission application must be made for reserved matter's approval within three years of the grant of the original approval. The development must be begun within five years of the original grant or two years of the final approval of any reserved matter, whichever period is the longer.

In Section 56 of the Act various activities are specified as being 'material operations' which are ones which begin a development. Included is digging a trench for a foundation of a building.

If a development has been begun but has not been completed then the local planning authority has the power to serve a 'completion notice'. This notice terminates the planning permission unless the development is completed within a stated time, which must not be earlier than 12 months.

PLANNING APPEAL

As we have noted, there is a right of appeal against a refusal to grant permission or granting it subject to conditions. The right must be exercised within six months of the receipt of the authority's decision notice or the time for making the decision has expired. The appeal is to the Secretary of State for the Environment.

Although the appeal is to the Secretary of State the hearing of the appeal is by a person appointed for that purpose, usually an inspector of the Department of the Environment. In dealing with the appeal the Secretary of State has all the power to deal with the matter as had the local planning authority. He may, therefore, impose conditions which the authority did not impose or refuse permission which the authority had granted subject to conditions.

The decision may also, in specified circumstances, be made by one of his inspectors and this is of the same effect as if made by the Secretary of State himself. The majority of appeals are now dealt with in this way.

The hearing of the appeal may be by a public local inquiry, a private hearing or by written representation. The importance of the appeal and the expense involved determines which form of hearing is used.

The Secretary of State's decision is final. There is, however, a limited right of appeal to the High Court, on a point of law only, within six weeks of the decision.

ENFORCEMENT OF PLANNING CONTROL

Breaches of planning control are not uncommon and the 1990 Act provides a number of means whereby any breach of planning control may be dealt with. The means of enforcement is by notices. The local planning authority may serve, as appropriate, a planning contravention notice, a breach of condition notice, an enforcement notice and a stop notice.

A planning contravention notice may be served with the intention of discovering the ownership of land, what activities or operations are being carried out on the land, when any such activity or operation began, to discover whether planning permission was granted and when, and to give the owner of the land an opportunity to apply for planning permission. Failure to comply with a planning contravention notice is a criminal offence.

A breach of condition notice may be served by a local planning authority when they become aware that a planning permission granted subject to a condition is not being complied with. The notice is served on the person responsible who may be either the developer or the person having control of the land. The notice may specify the steps necessary to comply with the condition and state the time for compliance which must be not less than 28 days. Failure to comply with a notice is a criminal offence.

The more formal way of dealing with a breach of planning control is by the service of an enforcement notice. Before considering the use of this procedure it is important to note that there are time limits on the making of enforcement notices. These are:

1) If the breach of planning control is development involving the carrying out of operations without planning permission, no enforcement action can be taken after four years from the date the operations were substantially completed;
2) If the breach of planning control is development involving the change of use of any building into use as a single dwelling-house, no enforcement action may be taken after four years following the date of the breach;
3) In the case of any other breach of planning control no enforcement action can be taken after ten years following the date of the breach.

If an enforcement notice is served it must be not later than 28 days after its issue and is to take effect not earlier than 28 days after it was served. The notice has to be served on the owner and occupier of the land to which it relates and on any other person who has an interest in the land.

An enforcement notice must specify the matters said to constitute a breach of planning control, the steps needed to remedy the breach, and the period within which the steps specified in the notice are to be taken. The notice must also give the local planning authority's reasons for issuing it and draw attention to the right of appeal to the Secretary of State.

An example of the use of the enforcement notice procedure would be where the local planning authority discovered that some building work had been carried out for which planning permission had not been obtained. Provided not more than four years have elapsed since the building work was carried out the authority may serve the notice. The notice could require the removal or alteration of the building work.

Since the circumstances which cause a local planning authority to serve a notice may change or the authority reconsider the matter, there is power for the authority to withdraw the notice.

If an appeal is made to the Secretary of State the enforcement notice is of no effect until the appeal is either finally decided or withdrawn. The notice of appeal must be in writing and specify the grounds of appeal and give such other information as may be prescribed.

Both appellant and authority have the right to be heard by an inspector appointed by the Secretary of State. If the Secretary of State so decides there may be a public local inquiry. In determining the appeal the power of the Secretary of State is extensive, including the granting of planning permission as he considers appropriate.

If an enforcement notice is not complied with the local planning authority may take the steps specified in the notice and recover their expenses so incurred. In addition the owner and other persons having control or an interest in the land may be prosecuted in the criminal courts.

A stop notice is a provision which is a supplement to an enforcement notice. A stop notice is a measure designed to prevent a person 'playing the system' as is possible under the enforcement notice procedure. A stop notice may be served at the same time or after the service of an enforcement notice, but not after the enforcement notice has taken effect. The stop notice cannot prohibit the use of a building as a dwelling-house and cannot prohibit certain activities if they have been carried on for more than four years.

A stop notice can be served on any person appearing to have an interest in the land or who is engaged in any activity prohibited by the notice. The notice cannot take effect until the date specified in the notice. This date is not, unless there are special circumstances which must be stated, to be earlier than three nor later than 28 days from the date of service on any person. The stop notice may be withdrawn at any time.

As the effect of a stop notice can be damaging to a developer, builder or owner of land the Town and Country Planning Act 1990 contains provisions for the payment of compensation for loss or damage directly due to a stop notice. Compensation is payable in limited circumstances, including the withdrawal of the stop notice, the quashing of the enforcement notice, and the variation of the enforcement notice so that there is no longer a breach of planning control.

A register has to be kept by local planning authorities containing information about enforcement and stop notices in their areas.

LISTED BUILDINGS

Ever since the introduction of the Town and Country Planning Act 1947 planning legislation has recognized that certain buildings should be subject to special planning control because of their historic or architectural interest. The present planning control is contained in the Planning (Listed Buildings and Conservation

Areas) Act 1990 and the Planning (Listed Buildings and Conservation Areas) Regulations 1990.

Section 1 of the Act requires the Secretary of State for the
Environment to compile lists of buildings of special architectural or
historic interest or to approve, with or without modification, lists
prepared by the Historic Buildings and Monuments Commission
for England (English Heritage) or by other persons or bodies of
persons. Any list compiled or approved may be amended.

As can be seen from the above, the Secretary of State can
consider lists prepared by other persons or bodies than English
Heritage. This allows civic or other societies in our ancient towns to
prepare lists and submit them for approval. In the normal course of
events it will be English Heritage which will prepare the lists of
buildings considered suitable for listing by the Secretary of State.

In considering whether to include a building in a list the Secretary
of State may take into account not only the building but also its
exterior which contributes to the architectural or historic interest of
any group of buildings of which it forms part and the desirability of
preserving on the ground of architectural or historic interest any
feature of the building which is a man-made object or structure fixed
to the building or forming part of the land within the curtilage of the
building.

The purpose of this provision is to allow the listing of a building
not just for itself but also for the part it plays with other buildings.
The fixing of objects or structures is also included. This means that,
for example, ornamental gates and railings may be listed.

It would be incorrect to believe that the buildings listed have to be
centuries old or designed by eminent architects. Buildings which
have been in existence for 20 or 30 years only may be listed. A
building may have a special feature, architecturally or historically,
which justifies its listing even if it is only 30 years old.

In the listing of buildings there are two classifications. Grade I are
those buildings of exceptional interest. Grade II are those of special
interest. Those buildings which are considered to be particularly
important in Grade II are marked as Grade II*.

As soon as a building is included in a list the Secretary of State has
to send a copy of that list to the local planning authority for the area
where the building is situated. Any copy of the list deposited is to be
a local land charge under the Local Land Charges Act 1975. By this
provision a prospective purchaser of the building becomes aware
that it is listed.

The importance of knowing that a building is listed and the
difficulty which arises when it is may be seen in the Court of Appeal
decision in *Amalgamated Investment and Property Co Ltd v John
Walker and Sons Ltd* 1976. Here a warehouse was sold with the
purchasers intending to redevelop the building. The day after
contracts of purchase were exchanged the vendors were informed

by the Secretary of State that the warehouse was to be listed. The following day the formal listing took place by the Secretary of State signing the list. The effect of the listing was to reduce the value of the building substantially. The purchaser's attempt to get out of the contract was unsuccessful.

When the Secretary of State has informed the district council or the London borough council of the listing of a building, the council have to serve a notice on the owner and occupier of the building informing them that the building has been listed. The exclusion of a building from a list by the Secretary of State has also to be notified in the same way. Copies of the lists are to be available for inspection free of charge at reasonable hours at council offices.

There is no appeal by the owner or occupier as to the listing of a building. Until recently the inspector who was making the survey of a building prior to its possible inclusion in a list did not even inform the owner or occupier. Now the practice is to make the inspector's presence known. Although there is no formal right of appeal it is possible for a person to request a review of the decision. This is done by a different inspector viewing the building.

As will be seen, the listing of a building can have an expensive and restrictive effect. Planning control is strict and permission for change of use of the building or its alteration will be difficult to obtain. Repairs will have to be done in such a way that they are consistent with the character of the building. For example, lead-work to a building which requires replacement will have to be replaced with the same material.

Experience has shown that a building which is not listed, but which might justify inclusion, will need protection until its future inclusion in a list is determined. Not infrequently, a local planning authority hears of a proposal to demolish or alter a building which is not listed but which possibly ought to be listed. Unless rapid action is taken the building may be destroyed or damaged.

In order to deal with this situation the Act allows a local planning authority, other than a county planning authority, to serve a building preservation notice on the owner and occupier of a building which is not listed. The building must appear to be of special architectural or historic interest and to be in danger of demolition or alteration so as to affect its character as a building of such interest. The building preservation notice comes into force as soon as it is served on the owner and occupier and remains in force for six months from the date it is served or until the Secretary of State gives notice of his decision to either include or not include the building in a list. In a case of urgency the notice, instead of being served on the owner and occupier, may be affixed to the building. The effect of the notice is to treat the building as if it were listed. If the Secretary of State decides not to list the building the owner and occupier must be immediately informed of that decision.

Section 6 of the Act contains provisions which may be used to remove uncertainty about the possible listing of a building. The provisions allow a prospective developer or any other person to make an application to the Secretary of State for a certificate that he does not intend to list the building. Such application may be made when an application has been made for planning permission to alter, extend or demolish the building, or where any such planning permission has been granted. If the Secretary of State grants an application his certificate prevents him for a period of five years from listing the building, and it precludes the local planning authority from serving a building preservation notice.

Listed building consent

The Act forbids the carrying out of works of demolition, extension or alteration to a listed building without the appropriate consent. An application for listed building consent must be made to the local planning authority. There is, however, power given to the Secretary of State to deal with the application himself and for this reason he must be notified of the intention to grant an application and a period of 28 days allowed for him to decide whether to intervene and use his power.

The application has to be made on a prescribed form and give required information. If an application is refused or if it is granted subject to conditions the applicant may appeal to the Secretary of State. The local planning authority may, provided the consent has not been acted upon, revoke or modify the consent.

As circumstances may arise whereby urgent works are necessary to a listed building, there are a number of defences available to a person charged with the offence of doing work without consent. Included are works urgently necessary in the interests of health and safety or for the preservation of the building.

Listed building consent may be granted with or without conditions. If conditions have been imposed the local planning authority may reserve specified details for later approval. The local planning authority may vary or discharge the conditions on the application of a person having an interest in the listed buildings.

In considering whether to grant listed building consent the local planning authority or the Secretary of State must have special regard to the desirability of preserving the building or its setting or any features of special architectural or historic interest which it possesses.

Once listed building consent is granted it remains of benefit to the building. So the purchaser of a building which has the benefit of such consent does not have to make a fresh application in his own name. The consent is subject to a condition that the work must be begun within five years from the date of the consent or such other period, longer or shorter, as the authority considers appropriate.

Where application is made for listed building consent for alteration or extension and the works do not constitute development, or planning permission would not be necessary because what is proposed would come within 'permitted development', then if consent is refused compensation may be claimed. The compensation is based on the value of the building being less than it would have been had listed building consent been granted. Compensation may also be claimed where listed building consent has been revoked or modified and a person interested in the building has thereby suffered loss or damage. A similar right exists for a person who suffers loss or damage because of the making of a building preservation notice which does not result in the building being listed.

Listed building purchase notice

A person who owns a listed building can suffer substantially if he is refused consent or consent is restricted. He may be unable to use the building as he wishes and the building may therefore become a burden rather than an asset. To make an individual suffer in this way is unfair and so power is given to him to require the building to be purchased from him.

The power to require the authority to purchase the building arises when consent is refused, or granted subject to conditions, or is revoked or modified. The owner has to serve a notice on the authority requiring them to purchase the building. The owner has to show that the building has become incapable of reasonably beneficial use in its existing state or in the case of conditions that the building cannot be rendered capable of such use by the carrying out of the works in accordance with the conditions.

The authority on whom the purchase notice has been served has three months within which to decide whether to accept the purchase notice or not. If it is to be rejected a counter-notice is served stating the grounds for the rejection. The matter then goes to the Secretary of State for his consideration as to whether or not to confirm the purchase notice.

Listed building enforcement notice

Local planning authorities are sometimes faced with the situation that a person has carried out work to a listed building, whether deliberately or not, in such circumstances that an offence has arisen. There is, therefore, need for power to control and deal with any such situation.

A local planning authority, where it appears to them that any works have been or are being executed to a listed building and the works constitute an offence, may, if they consider it expedient to do so having regard to the character of the listed building, issue a 'listed building enforcement notice'. The notice must specify the contravention and require steps to be taken: to restore it to its former state; or to execute specified works needed to alleviate the works done to the building; or bring the building to the state it would have been in if any listed building consent which had been granted had been complied with. The notice must be served within 28 days of it being issued and not earlier than 28 days of its service it is to come into effect. Within this period an appeal may be made to the Secretary of State on a number of specified grounds.

The making of an appeal suspends the notice until the Secretary of State has determined the appeal. The Secretary of State may confirm, quash or vary the terms of a notice.

Failure to comply with a listed building enforcement notice is a criminal offence punishable on summary conviction to a fine of £20,000 and on conviction on indictment to an unlimited fine. In addition to this power to prosecute the authority may, when the works specified have not been carried out within the compliance period, enter the land and carry out those works. The expense incurred in executing those works may be recovered from the owner of the land.

Repair of listed buildings

In the past, owners of listed buildings have tried to obtain permission to demolish them and when their applications have been refused have left the buildings to deteriorate in the hope that their worsened condition will support a later application to demolish. In addition there would be a saving of maintenance costs. In order to discourage this practice the power of local planning authorities has been strengthened. Now immediate action can be taken to deal with urgent repairs and a building may be compulsorily purchased.

If it appears to a local authority that work is urgently necessary to a listed building for its preservation then, subject to giving the owner seven days notice in writing, they may carry out such works. These works, which must not be to part of a building which is occupied, can include works to provide support or shelter. The Secretary of State also possesses the same power. Once the works have been executed the expenses incurred can be recovered from the owner. The owner has the right to make representation, within 28 days of the demand, to the Secretary of State with regard to the demand.

If it appears to the Secretary of State that a listed building is deteriorating because of failure to take reasonable steps to preserve it, either he or a local planning authority may compulsorily acquire the building. Before exercising this power a repairs notice must be served on the owner giving him two months to carry out the works specified in the notice. If a building is compulsorily acquired and it is apparent that the building has been deliberately allowed to fall into disrepair for the purpose of justifying its demolition and the development or redevelopment then the Secretary of State may direct that there shall be minimum compensation for the building. What this means in effect is that the compensation is limited to the value of the building as it is disregarding any redevelopment value.

CONSERVATION AREAS

Unlike the other provisions of planning law we have considered, the concept of conservation areas was not introduced until 20 years after the main body of planning law became operative. The Civic Amenities Act 1967 was the statute which introduced conservation areas. It was a recognition that the protection of buildings of special architectural or historic interest was not sufficient in itself.

Section 69 of the 1990 Act requires every local planning authority to determine from time to time which parts of their areas are areas of special architectural or historic interest the character or appearance of which it is desirable to preserve or enhance. Any such area is to be designated a conservation area.

From this definition it can be seen that it is not a matter of considering individual buildings. It is simply a question of an area, which can be in an urban or rural area. The area itself can be large or small. A small group of buildings can be a conservation area just as can the whole of a small village.

When a local planning authority designates an area to be a conservation area that fact must be published in a local newspaper and the *London Gazette*. The Secretary of State must also be informed.

The importance of a conservation area is the degree of control exercised over planning matters. Any proposal to demolish a building in the area is subject to the need to have consent. Any tree in the area is protected in that consent is needed for certain works to be carried out to them. If a planning application relates to a development which would affect the character or appearance of the area there must be publication of the application. Certain forms of permitted development are also controlled.

Certain provisions allow financial assistance to be given to enhance the character or appearance of the conservation area. By these means an area can actually be improved and not just preserved.

TREE PRESERVATION ORDERS

The Town and Country Planning Act 1990 provides for the making of tree preservation orders. The order is made by the local planning authority when the authority is satisfied that it is expedient to do so in the interests of amenity. When granting planning permission for development the authority is under a duty to see that adequate provision is made for planting or preserving trees. Residential developers frequently find that their layouts have to take into account the existence of trees protected by an order.

When an order is in force it will prohibit the cutting down, lopping, uprooting, wilful damaging or wilful destruction of trees except with consent. The prohibition does not apply to trees which are dying or dead or have become dangerous or have become a nuisance. An order may provide for replanting.

The procedure for the making of a tree preservation order requires the authority to take into account any objections or representations made. When it is confirmed, the owners and occupiers of land on which the trees stand are to be informed of the order.

Experience has shown that some landowners when they become aware that trees on their lands might become subject to tree preservation orders will cut down the trees. Such action prevents any restriction on development of the land from the making of an order. To prevent such action an order may be made which comes into immediate effect and operates for six months or until the order is confirmed.

A contravention of a tree preservation order is a criminal offence. On summary conviction a fine of £20,000 may be imposed. In the case of conviction on indictment the fine is unlimited. In imposing the fine the court is to take account of any financial benefit accruing to the defendant.

8 HIGHWAY LAW

HIGHWAYS AND HIGHWAY AUTHORITIES

At common law a highway is a way over which the public have a right to pass and repass only. Any stoppage on the highway must be that that is incidental to the use of the highway. As can be seen from the definition it is not stated that the way must be over solid land. It has to be a way the public can use. This means that certain stretches of water, over which the public have rights of passage, are highways at common law.

It can also be noted that there is no mention of the use to which a highway may be lawfully put. It is, however, the case that certain highways can be used in limited ways only. A footpath is restricted to use by people on foot and cannot be used as a vehicular way. Some footpaths may be used not only by foot passengers but also by animals.

It is important not to confuse a public highway with a private right of way, which we considered earlier in connection with easements. A public highway is a way open to all members of the public and ownership of land is irrelevant to its use. With an easement, as we noted, ownership or occupation of land is essential.

Most of the law concerning highways is found in the Highways Act 1980. Section 328 of the Act defines 'highway' as, except where the context otherwise requires, the whole or a part of a highway other than a ferry or waterway. This definition means that for the purposes of the Act, except where it is otherwise required, a highway is a way over solid land.

The Highways Act 1980 also defines various classes of highways. A footpath is a way over which the public have a right of way on foot only, not being a footway. A footway is part of a carriageway over which the public have a right on foot only. A carriageway means a way constituting or comprised in a highway, being a way (other than a cycle track) over which the public have a right of way for the passage of vehicles.

There is no definition of what constitutes a road but the expression trunk road means a carriageway of national importance. A street is defined as including any highway and any road, lane, footpath, square, court, alley or passage whether a thoroughfare or not. In the case of *Attorney General v Laird* 1925 it was decided that for a way to come within the classification of a street there must be houses or other buildings on at least one side of the way.

Highways may also be defined in the 1980 Act as being highway maintainable at public expense. Any such highway has to be maintained, to an appropriate standard, by the highway authority which has responsibility for that highway. A highway which does not come within this classification is still a highway available for use by the public but the highway authority has no liability for its maintenance.

Originally all highways were created by common law. Some still are but most are created by the use of powers in different Acts of Parliament, principally the Highways Act 1980. To create a highway at common law there has to be dedication by the landowner and the acceptance by the public of that dedication. The dedication by the landowner can be express, in which case it will be in a formal document, or it may be implied. In the case of implied dedication the public start to cross land and the landowner, fully aware of what is happening, takes no action to exclude them. If this use continues for a period of time, now fixed at 20 years use, then under Section 31 of the Act it is presumed to have created a highway, unless the contrary is proved.

An example of the creation of a highway at common law would be where the local landowner dedicated a way over his land to allow people to get to church more easily. The acceptance of this dedication by the public using it freely and openly completes the requirements for it to be a highway.

Most highways are constructed by the use of powers in Section 24 of the Act. The section empowers the Minister of Transport to construct highways, including trunk roads and special roads. A trunk road is part of the national road system and a special road is a motorway. The same section authorises a local highway authority to construct highways. Other provisions in the Act allow for the necessary land to be acquired, either by negotiation or compulsorily. All the associated matters with the construction of a highway are authorised by the Act.

Section 1 of the Act defines those authorities who are to have powers under the Act. The allocation of this responsibility depends on the importance of the local authority.

The Secretary of State for Transport, referred to in the Act as the 'Minister', is the highway authority for trunk roads and any other road which is made by some other statutory provision to be his responsibility. The Minister may delegate to county councils his functions with regard to the maintenance and improvement of trunk roads. The county council may in turn, with consent, delegate the functions to district councils.

The section also makes county councils and metropolitan district councils, which are district councils in the former metropolitan county council areas, highway authorities for the highways in their areas other than those which are the responsibility of the Minister of

Transport. If the Minister of Transport delegates functions to these authorities then they may discharge those obligations too.

In the Greater London area the London borough councils are the highway authorities for all highways in their areas other than those which are the responsibiilty of the Minister of Transport.

Non-metropolitan district councils are not local highway authorities. They may, however, claim certain highway functions from the county councils.

MAINTENANCE OF HIGHWAYS

Section 36 of the Act defines those highways which are to be highways maintainable at public expense. These include all those highways which before the 1980 Act came into operation were highways maintainable at public expense under the previous Act, the Highways Act 1959. Others are highways constructed by highway authorities; a highway constructed under the Housing Act 1985; a trunk road or special road; and a highway which is a footpath or bridleway created by an order made under the Town and Country Planning Act.

Under Section 37 a person who proposes to dedicate a way as a highway may give notice, not less than three months before the date of the proposed dedication, to the council who would be the highway authority if that way were a highway. The council then decides whether or not the highway will be of sufficient use to the public to justify it being maintained at public expense. If the council refuses to certify that the way has been made up and maintained for a period of 12 months then the person may appeal to the magistrates court. If the way is, however, satisfactory then it becomes a highway maintainable at public expense.

In the case of those highways which are not maintained at public expense the Highways Act 1980 contains provisions whereby highway authorities may require those responsible for the main-tenance of the highway to take action to put it in good repair. This usually means that either an individual landowner or the owners of land which fronts on to the highway have to bear the cost of maintenance.

The obvious advantage of having a highway accepted as one maintained at public expense is that the cost of maintaining the highway comes from public funds. In addition to this, liability for any accident due to failure to maintain the highway falls on the highway authority.

Section 41 imposes a duty on highway authorities to maintain highways which are maintainable at public expense. Failure to do so means that there has been a breach of that duty and so the highway authority will be liable to a person for any injury received as a result of that failure to maintain. Section 58 of the Act provides a defence in any action for damages. If a highway authority had taken reasonable care to see that the highway was not dangerous for traffic that is a defence. In order to have the benefit of the defence the highway authority must have had regard to the character of the highway, the standard of maintenance appropriate, whether the authority knew or could reasonably have been expected to know of the condition which gave rise to the danger, and whether the authority could reasonably have been expected to repair the highway or warn of the danger.

A matter concerning the maintenance of highways which is of particular importance to the construction industry is that of extraordinary traffic. In normal circumstances highways require maintenance consistent with usual use. Busy town roads will require more maintenance than country roads or roads in residential areas.

When, however, the expense of maintenance works can be shown to be beyond that that would normally arise and can be directly related to some unusual use the question arises, should the highway authority have to pay that expense. Most people would think that it would be unreasonable to require this.

In order to deal with this situation Section 59 contains provisions to allow the recovery of expense due to extraordinary traffic. The highway authority for a highway maintainable at public expense may recover the extraordinary expenses which have been or will be incurred in maintaining the highway because of damage caused by excessive weight passing on the highway or other extraordinary traffic on it. The extraordinary expense may be recovered from any person by or as a result of whose order the traffic has been conducted.

The section also allows arrangements to be made, where it is accepted that traffic will cause damage, for the expense which will arise to be paid. This provision allows a person who is about to carry out work where he accepts that the traffic he will generate will cause damage to make arrangement with the highway authority for payment to cover the damage. By this prior arrangement time and expense is saved. If either party so requires the sum may be determined by arbitration.

The section requires that any proceedings by a highway authority to recover any sums payable to them are to begin within 12 months of the damage having been done or in the case of a building contract or work extending over a long period not later than six months from the date of completion of the contract or work.

The application of the provisions in Section 59 to building work can be seen to apply when a heavy piece of plant or a piece of equipment for installation in the building is conveyed to a site. If the transporting of this heavy load causes damage to a highway, which would not otherwise have arisen, then the section applies. Where, however, the damage is caused by a flow of traffic, greater than normal, which causes damage then this would be extraordinary traffic. In many cases with building projects damage will be caused by lorries delivering materials over the period of the contract.

It is usual in building contracts to make the contractor liable for any extraordinary expense which might arise from damage caused to a highway by his use and the manner of use of a highway.

A somewhat similar provision to that just considered is found in Section 60. This is applicable where traffic has been prohibited or restricted under powers in the Road Traffic Regulation Act 1984 or some other Act. If, therefore, the traffic has to make use of an alternative route which is of a lower classification and that requires the highway authority to either strengthen the highway or make good any damage caused, then the expense involved can be recovered. Any dispute as to liability to pay the expenses, the amount or whether it was reasonably incurred may be settled by arbitration.

ADOPTION OF HIGHWAYS AND STREETS

As we have already noted, Section 37 of the Highways Act 1980 allows a person to dedicate a way as a highway maintainable at public expense. Unless the highway authority is of the opinion that the way will not be of sufficient utility to the public then the way will become a highway maintainable at public expense. The authority can specify what works are to be done and require the person making the dedication to maintain it for 12 months from the date of the authority certifying that it has been dedicated.

The adoption of a highway is a matter of importance to residential developers and builders. When a residential estate is constructed the estate roads are highways in that they are used by the public at large. They are not, however, highways maintainable at public expense. For them to become such there must be dedication to and acceptance by the highway authority. It is, therefore, in the interests of the buyers of the houses that the estate roads should become highways maintainable at public expense. Otherwise they would be responsible for the maintenance of the roads and liable for any accident which resulted from inadequate maintenance.

It was the practice at one time for builders and developers to build dwellings and not construct estate roads. These were to be constructed later at the expense of the owners of the dwellings. This practice created many difficulties; owners might not agree to the later construction or some may not be able to meet their share of the expense and when the dwellings were sold the question of responsibility for the expense created problems.

In order to prevent these difficulties arising with future developments highway law has for some time required that a person proposing to build has to satisfy the highway authority that any necessary highways will be constructed. The Highways Act 1980 provides two means whereby this can be accomplished. The first is by an agreement under Section 38 of the Act, and the second by the Advanced Payments Code under the Act.

A Section 38 agreement allows, amongst other things, a person who is constructing a way to dedicate that way when constructed as a highway and the highway authority will then accept it as a highway maintainable at public expense. The agreement is made so that on a specified date the highway becomes maintainable at public expense.

The great advantage for a developer with a Section 38 agreement is that there is no requirement to put down a deposit or give security as is the case with the advanced payments code. This means that the developer does not lose the use of part of his capital for a substantial period of time.

In making the agreement the highway authority can, and will, require provisions to be satisfied as to the bearing of expense of construction, the maintenance for a period of time and any other relevant matters. Although it is not required by Section 38 it is the practice of highway authorities to require the developer to support the agreement by a bond. The bond would be issued by a bank or insurance company and provide cover for the expense of completing the highway if the developer should fail to fulfil his obligation. The common example would be a developer who went bankrupt without having completed the construction of the highways on the development. Here the highway authority would be able to claim on the bond for the cost of completing the highways.

Some highway authorities require that the amount in the bond be index-linked so that if construction costs increase after the agreement is made, which might have been some years earlier, the amount payable will be increased also. Authorities also make charges for the agreement so as to cover their administrative costs.

Section 219 deals with the requirements of the advance payments code. It requires that when plans for the erection of a building are deposited with the local authority for building regulations approval, and the building will have frontage on a private street in which the street works authority have power under the private street works code to require works to be executed or to execute works, then no work is to be done unless the owner has paid to the street works authority or otherwise secured payment to the authority of, the sum required for the cost of street works in that street. It is a criminal offence punishable by fine to fail to observe these requirements.

There are a number of specified circumstances where the provisions in the section do not apply. Included are those where a Section 38 agreement has been made.

Unlike the Section 38 agreement the code requires payment to be deposited, so removing part of a developer's capital. The only way to avoid this is to secure to the satisfaction of the authority payment in some other way.

Section 220 provides that the local authority shall determine whether or not there is liability under the code, which must be done within six weeks of approval of the plans, and if there is liability the amount of payment to be made. An owner who believes that he has been required to make payment of an amount which is excessive may, within one month, appeal to the Minister.

The amount required to be deposited may, after a notice has been served requiring the deposit, appear to the local authority to be more than will be required or the whole sum may not be required. In this case the local authority may serve a notice to this effect. If payment has been made then the excess sum or the whole sum has to be repaid. In the case of security then the amount secured is to be reduced to the amount of the excess or, if no sum is due, the whole security released.

Section 221 deals with the situation where the street works have been carried out otherwise than at the expense of the street works authority. That is in most cases by the developer. Here the sum deposited or the security given may be refunded or released, in whole or in part, as in the opinion of the authority represents the liability of the owner. Where the person at whose expense the works were carried out is not the owner of the land there is to be no refund or release until the owner has been notified of the authority's intention to make the refund or release. The owner is also to be given an opportunity to make representations on the matter. The purpose of this provision is to make the owner of the land aware of what is going to happen and allow him to make claim to the whole or part of the sum to be repaid. It could well be that there is an arrangement in the purchase of the land between the developer and owner whereby some sum is due to the owner. If the owner were not informed and the sum paid to the developer the owner might have difficulty in obtaining his proportion.

Section 222 provides that where a sum has been paid or security given by the owner of land for street works to be carried out in a private street on which the land has frontage, the liability of the owner or subsequent owners is discharged to the amount paid or secured. If the sum paid or security given turns out to be insufficient when the works are completed then the authority will claim the shortfall. If the sum paid exceeds that that is needed then the balance is paid to the present owner of the land. This might mean that the sum deposited by the developer is more than is needed and when the time comes for the balance to be handed over the developer has sold the land. The present owner is entitled to that refund. In order to protect themselves against this happening developers may require in the contract of sale that any balance is to be paid to them.

The position of a development being abandoned or the approved plans being of no effect because more than three years have elapsed since approval is dealt with by the provisions in Section 223. In this case the sum deposited is to be repaid and security given is to be released to the owner for the time being of the land.

In conclusion two points need to be noted. The first is that most of the matters considered, such as service of notices and determinations, have to be registered as local land charges under the Local Land Charges Register 1975. This allows a prospective purchaser who makes a search of the register to be aware of the position regarding these matters. The second point is that interest has to be paid, at a rate fixed by the Treasury, on the sum deposited with the authority.

Private street works code

Section 204 of the Act states that the private street works code has effect for securing the execution of street works in private streets anywhere in England and Wales. It will be recalled that a street is a way which has a building or buildings on at least one side of the way.

Section 203 defines a 'private street' as a street that is not a highway maintainable at public expense, and it also includes land deemed to be a private street by the provisions in Section 232. These cover the circumstances where a development plan has defined land as the site for a proposed road or where land will be required for road widening. Section 203 also defines 'street works' as any works for the sewering, levelling, paving, metalling, flagging, channelling and making good of the street, and includes the provision of proper means for lighting a street. The expression 'street works authority' means in the Greater London area the London borough, and outside Greater London the county council of the area where the street is situated.

From the above we can see that a highway which is not maintainable at public expense and which comes within the definition of a street is subject to the private street works code. This code empowers the street works authority to require the execution of certain works defined as street works.

The essential part of the private street works code is found in Section 205. In general this states that where a private street is not sewered, levelled, paved, metalled, flagged, channelled, made good and lighted to the satisfaction of the street works authority, the authority may resolve to execute works to that private street. Those works are to be street works and the expenses incurred by the authority in executing them are to be recovered by the apportionment between the premises fronting the street.

The circumstances where an authority may encounter a private street which justifies action being taken are where the street was not originally constructed properly or where there are deficiencies which have developed since the street was originally laid out. For example, a private street might have had its carriageway constructed with material which has deteriorated and now presents a badly broken surface.

If the authority decides to execute works to only part of a street then the expenses incurred by the authority may only be apportioned between the premises fronting on that part of the street. By this provision those premises which will benefit from the execution of the works are the only premises which can have the expenses incurred apportioned against them.

The procedure required by Section 205 is that the authority passes a resolution that it is satisfied a private street is in need of the execution of street works. The surveyor then prepares a specification of the works together with plans and sections, an estimate of the probable expenses of the works, and the provisional assessment apportioning the estimated expenses between the premises liable to be charged with them under the code.

When this has been done the whole of the information is submitted to the authority. The authority then passes a further resolution, known as the 'resolution of approval', approving the particulars, with or without modification or addition as it thinks fit. The next step is for the particulars to be published in local newspapers, a notice to be posted in a prominent position in or near the street for at least three successive weeks, and within seven days of the publication in the local newspapers served on the owners of the premises shown in the provisional apportionment as liable to be charged. In addition, for one month after a date of the second resolution copies of the resolution and other approved documents are to be kept available for inspection free of charge at all reasonable hours at the offices of the street works authority.

When a notice is served on an owner of premises informing him of the resolution of approval the notice must be accompanied by a statement of the sum apportioned to those premises by the provisional apportionment.

The need for a street works authority to follow this procedure precisely is to be seen from the decision of the High Court in *Ware Urban District Council v Gaunt* 1960. Here the original resolution had not included street lighting. In the second resolution, however, there was reference to street lighting. The court decided that the approval of the surveyor's specification could not be taken to be approval of the state of the street lighting. The authority had not considered the existing state of the lighting and found it to be unsatisfactory as was required in the first resolution.

The matter of premises fronting on the street is one which has to be decided on individual facts. The word 'fronting' under the Act includes 'adjoining' and 'adjoining' includes 'abutting'. In practice what is looked for is actual contact between part of the premises and the private street. Where this is not the case apportioning the expenses presents difficulty. In the case of *Buckinghamshire County Council v Trigg* 1963 Trigg owned an upper maisonette. The ground floor maisonette was owned by another person who also owned the front garden which adjoined the street. Trigg had access to the street through the front garden. When the apportionment was made Trigg was not included on the grounds that his premises had no frontage to the street. The High Court accepted that Trigg was not liable on the matter of frontage. His premises did not adjoin the street, they were separated from it by the front garden.

The apportionment of the expenses of street works is clearly a matter of importance. Section 207 directs that the authority in making the apportionment of expenses between the premises to be charged shall, subject to provisions, make the apportionment according to the frontage of the premises. Although this is a simple rule, and one which is usually used by authorities, it does not take into account the benefit individual premises derive from the works carried out. For instance, a commercial property may have a short frontage but benefit much more from the works than a domestic building with a wider frontage.

In order to deal with this possible injustice the section allows the authority, if they think it just, in settling the apportionments to have regard to the benefit derived from the work, to any work done by the owner or occupier. They may also include in the apportionment premises which do not front the street but have access to it through a court, passage or otherwise. They can fix the amount based on the benefit gained by those premises.

Section 208 provides a right of objections, on a number of stated grounds, to an owner of premises shown in the provisional apportionment as liable to be charged. The objections are heard and determined by a magistrates court.

There is power given to the authority to amend the specification, plans, sections, estimate and provisional appointment. In this case the procedure considered previously has to be repeated.

On completion of the works when the expenses have been ascertained a final apportionment is made. This apportionment is to be made on the same basis as the provisional apportionment. The owner of any premises may object to this within one month on a number of stated grounds including that the amount demanded exceeds by 15 per cent the estimated cost. The objection is settled by the magistrates court.

The amount due from the owners of premises is recovered, in whole or in part, with interest. There is provision for the amount due to be repaid by instalments over a period of 30 years.

Sections 215 and 216 provide for exemption from liability for places of public religious worship and, in certain circumstances, some railways and canals. Section 236 allows a local authority to decide to bear the whole or part of the expenses of street works and so discharge or reduce an owner's liability for that payment.

Once the final apportionment has been made and the demand served, a charge arises which is registerable under the Local Land Charges Act 1975. Any prospective purchaser of premises searching the register may discover the existence of liability. So the registration binds the purchaser to the liability.

When a private street has had street works executed the adoption of the street as a highway maintainable at public expense may be made by the street works authority. This is done by display of a notice in a prominent position in the street. Unless objection is made not more than one month later the adoption occurs. The proposed adoption may be objected to by an owner or the majority of owners giving notice to the authority. The authority can within two months apply to the magistrates court for an order overruling the objection. An appeal can be made against an order overruling an objection. If no appeal is made the street becomes a highway maintainable at public expense.

IMPROVEMENT LINES AND BUILDING LINES

Experience has shown the need to have legal powers to control the erection of buildings on land which will be needed for road improvement and to prevent the erection of buildings too near to a road. The Highways Act 1980, like the Highways Act 1959, therefore contains provisions empowering a highway authority to prescribe improvement lines and building lines.

Section 73 states that where a highway authority is of the opinion that a street which is a highway maintainable at public expense is narrow or inconvenient, or is without a sufficiently regular boundary line, or it is necessary or desirable that the street should be widened the authority may prescribe on either one side or both sides or within a distance of 15 yards of a corner a line, an 'improvement line', to which the street is to be widened.

Once an improvement line has been prescribed no new building shall be erected and no permanent excavation made below the level of the street at a point nearer to the centre of the street than the improvement line. The term 'building' is defined as including any erection however, and with whatever material, it is constructed and any part of a building, and 'new building' includes any addition to an existing building.

There are two exceptions to the prohibition to erect a building within an improvement line. The first is that the authority may give consent to the erection of a building for such period and subject to such conditions as it thinks expedient. This provision would allow

consent to be given to the erection of a temporary building for a
limited period of time. The second exception is that there is no
prohibition on statutory undertakers excavating for the purpose of
laying, altering, maintaining or renewing pipes and other apparatus.

As the prescribing of an improvement line or the refusal of
consent or the period of consent or any conditions in the consent can
materially affect a person, a right of appeal to the Crown Court
exists for an aggrieved person. A contravention of an improvement
line or of any condition in a consent is a criminal offence punishable
by fine.

A highway authority which has prescribed an improvement line
may, if it is of the opinion that the line or part of it is no longer
necessary or desirable, revoke either the whole or part of the line.
Both the making and revocation of an improvement line has to be in
accordance with the provisions in Schedule 9 to the Act. These
provisions require proper notification and publication of the
intention to make or revoke the line, and require the authority to
consider any objections made within six weeks of notification of the
intention to prescribe or revoke a line.

The prescribing of an improvement line can seriously restrict an
owner's use of his land. For this reason there is a provision that
where a person's property is injuriously affected by the prescribing
of an improvement line compensation is to be paid for the injury
suffered.

This right to compensation was considered by the House of Lords
in the case of *Westminster Bank v Beverley Borough Council* 1971.
The facts of the case were that the bank submitted plans for
planning permission for an extension to their premises. The
application was refused on the ground that part of the land to be
built on would be needed for road widening. The bank took the
view that if they were not to be allowed to build they should be
compensated. If an improvement line had been made, which in fact
it had not, then the bank would have been entitled to compensation.
Under planning law, however, there was no provision for compensation on the refusal of permission. The question put to the House
of Lords was whether an authority had to use an Act of Parliament
concerned with highways and which required the payment of
compensation, or could the authority use an Act of Parliament not
directly concerned with highways where there was no right to
compensation. The decision was that there was no obligation on the
authority to use the Act which required payment of compensation.

The position now is that the Town and Country Planning Act
1990 allows an authority to exclude or to modify the operation of the
provisions in Section 73. In effect an authority can wait for an
application to be made for planning permission and then consider it
and reserve from it land which will be needed for future road
improvement.

A building line is somewhat similar to an improvement line in that both seek to control the construction of buildings within a certain distance of a highway. Where they differ is that an improvement line has as its purpose the keeping of land clear of buildings so that that land can be used for road widening. A building line prevents the construction of buildings nearer to the centre line of a highway than is prescribed. The purpose of the line is to keep all new buildings away from the highway so as to secure good layout and improve safety on the highway.

Section 74 empowers a highway authority to prescribe a building line on either or both sides of a highway maintainable at public expense. Once a building line has been prescribed no new building, other than a boundary wall or fence, is to be erected nor any permanent excavation made below the level of the highway, nearer to the centre line of the highway than the building line. The authority may, however, give consent for such period and subject to such conditions as it thinks fit for a new building or permanent excavation.

The prohibition of the building line does not affect the rights of statutory undertakers to lay, repair, alter, maintain or renew pipes and other apparatus. Contravention of the building line or of any consent given by the authority is a criminal offence punishable by fine.

Should the authority form the opinion that a building line or any part of it is no longer necessary or desirable then the authority may revoke the line or part of it. The revocation or prescribing of a building line is subject to the provisions in Schedule 9 to the Act. These provisions are the same as those considered earlier for an improvement line.

If a person can show that his property has been injuriously affected by the prescribing of a building line he is entitled to compensation. The claim for compensation must be made within six months of the date of the line being prescribed or within six months of the date of a notice under Schedule 9.

The prescribing of a building line or of any conditions in any consent given by the authority are registrable in the local land charges register under the Local Land Charges Act 1975.

CLOSURE AND RESTRICTION OF HIGHWAYS

Construction operations are of such a nature that it is inevitable that a highway has to be closed, and the closure may be permanent as well as temporary, or a restriction be placed on its use. The circumstances of each operation determine which course of action should be taken. As the use of a highway is a public right, an infringement of which could give rise to public nuisance, any interference with that use must be lawful. Parliament has, therefore, given powers in three Acts of Parliament to authorities to close or restrict the use of highways.

The Town and Country Planning Act 1990, in Section 247, gives power to the Secretary of State for the Environment to make an order stopping up or diverting any highway if he is satisfied that it is necessary to do so in order to enable development to be carried out. This development has to have been sanctioned by planning permission or by a government department. So provided there is a properly authorised development the Secretary of State can make an order so as to permit this development to take place. Whether the order should permanently stop up the highway or divert it will depend on the particular development. In the order the Secretary of State may make provision, as seems necessary or expedient, for the provision or improvement of any other highway. By this provision an order may stop up a highway so that the development can be carried out but require another highway to be constructed in order to accommodate the users of the highway which is to be stopped up. A highway so provided can be declared to be a highway maintainable at public expense. A person seeking the order may be required to pay or make contribution to the cost of any works required by the order.

The effect of an order may be seen from the decision of the High Court in the case of *Bothwell v County and District Properties (South West)* 1990. Here the owner of a shop whose direct access to a highway had been lost because of an order made under Section 247 by the Secretary of State sued the developers. The order had been made so as to permit the development of a shopping centre. An access road had been provided to the rear of the shop. The owner challenged the order on the ground that it was an unlawful obstruction of a highway. The court however rejected the challenge, holding that because the highway had been lawfully stopped up by the order there could not be an obstruction by the developers.

Section 252 sets out the procedure provisions which must be followed for an order to be made. In general these may be said to be publication in a local newspaper and in the *London Gazette* stating the general effect of the order; where it may be inspected free of charge; and stating that objection may be made to the Secretary of State. Notification must also be given to the local authority and statutory undertakers. A notice must also be placed in a prominent position at the ends of the highway to be stopped up. Objections to the order, which have to be made within 28 days of the order, have to be considered by the Secretary of State. After this consideration he may, if he so wishes, cause a local inquiry to be held. As a result of consideration of the objections or of the result of a local inquiry the Secretary of State may make an order with or without modification.

As the stopping up or diversion of a footpath or bridleway is likely to concern a development on a small scale a simpler system is provided for in Section 257. In this circumstance the order is made by the local planning authority. The same powers exist as considered previously and the procedure is similar. The difference is that if there are no objections then the local planning authority approves the order. If there are objectors then the confirmation of the Secretary of State is necessary.

The Highways Act 1980 contains provisions for the closure or diversion of highways. Unlike the provisions just considered these provisions are not concerned with planning development. It is simply a matter of whether a highway is still needed or not.

Section 116 empowers a magistrates court, after making a view if the court thinks fit, to make an order authorising the stopping up or diversion of a highway. No order can be made for a trunk road or special road. Before making the order the court must be satisfied that the highway is unnecessary or can be diverted so as to make it nearer or more commodious to the public. The application to the court is made by the highway authority. Notice of the making of an application has to be given to the local council, and to the owners and occupiers of land adjoining the highway not less than 28 days before making the application. Any person on whom a notice has been served has the right to be heard in the magistrates court. An order authorising the diversion of a highway is not to be made until the written consent of the owner of the land over which the highway is to be diverted has been produced and deposited in court. In general the existing highway shall not be stopped up until the new highway has been constructed. Special consideration is to be given to statutory undertakers who have apparatus in the highway.

As Section 116 requires applications to be made by the highway authority it is necessary if a landowner wishes to have a highway stopped up or diverted to provide for this. Section 117 therefore allows a highway authority, at the expense of that person, to make an application at his request.

The stopping up or diversion of footpaths or bridleways is often necessary, whether for development or not. As these highways are not of the same importances as those used for vehicular traffic a simpler procedure than that just considered is appropriate. For this reason Sections 118 and 119 allow a local council to make an order stopping up a footpath or bridleway on the ground it is not needed for public use, or an order of diversion when satisfied that it will lead to a more efficient use of land or provide a shorter or more commodious path or way. If the order is not opposed it does not require confirmation by the Secretary of State; otherwise his confirmation is needed.

Other provisions in the Act deal with the procedures for making these orders. The procedures follow very much the same pattern as those considered earlier for other orders.

The Road Traffic Regulation Act 1984, as amended by the Road Traffic (Temporary) Restrictions Act 1991, deals with the situation where it is necessary for a road to be closed or restricted temporarily. Construction operations either on the road or on land adjoining the road may require such action. Unlike the provisions considered earlier the provisions in this Act deal with a temporary need only. It may be for a single day in order to allow a piece of equipment to be lifted from the road into a new building or it may be for a number of months so as to permit the erection of a building.

Section 14 allows a traffic authority to restrict or prohibit temporarily traffic on a road. In order to use this power the authority must be satisfied that there is a need because of works which are being or are proposed to be executed on or near a road, or that there is a likelihood of danger to the public or there is a risk of serious damage to the highway. In making an order the authority must have regard to the existence of alternative routes. The order itself may cover a wide range of matters, such as prohibiting or restricting vehicles of any particular type or pedestrians. The order may also allow for exceptions to the prohibition or restriction.

The section also allows an authority to apply a prohibition or restriction by way of a notice. A notice is issued when the circumstances are such that a prohibition or restriction has to be applied without delay. The typical circumstance where this would be necessary would be the collapse or likely collapse of a building adjoining a road.

The difference between a notice and an order may be seen in their durations. A notice has a duration of 21 days if it is concerned with danger to the public or serious damage to the road; if it is for works being executed by a road the duration is of not more than five days. In the case of an order for works on or near a road then a period longer than 18 months may be allowed; in other circumstances it must not exceed 18 months. In the case of footpaths, bridleways, cycle tracks of byways the period is not to exceed six months. In limited cases the 18 month period may be renewed by another order. The Secretary of State may extend the six month period, and may also extend the 18 month period but not for more than six months. Contravention of an order or a notice is a criminal offence.

Section 16 and Schedule 3 require that certain publicity requirements have to be satisfied for both orders and notices.

CONSTRUCTION OPERATIONS AND USE OF HIGHWAYS

Construction operations may be carried out on highways or on land adjoining highways. Some of these operations may endanger users of the highway; others may inconvenience them. As the users' right to use the highway is a public right these operations have to be controlled so as to minimise danger and inconvenience and it must be specified how the operations may be lawful use of a highway.

Section 130 of the Highways Act 1980 makes it the duty of a highway authority to protect the rights of the public to use and enjoy any highway for which it is the highway authority.

Section 131 makes it an offence without lawful authority or excuse to, amongst other things, make an excavation in a highway which consists of or comprises the carriageway, or deposit anything whatsoever on a highway so as to damage the highway. Lawful authority exists in a number of Acts of Parliament for people to make connection to services in a highway.

Section 137 makes it a criminal offence, without lawful authority or excuse, in any way to wilfully obstruct the free passage along a highway. Guidance on the application of this offence may be gained from consideration of the Court of Appeal case, on a civil claim, *Harper v G. N. Haden and Sons Ltd* 1933. Harper, a shopkeeper, sued claiming nuisance from hoardings which had been erected in a street which, he claimed, was an unlawful obstruction. The court dismissed the claim. In the judgment the court said that reasonable use of a highway would not be unlawful. Reasonable use means that an obstruction should not be greater than it needs to be nor exist longer than it needs to. So a construction operation should not cause a greater obstruction than it needs to nor should it remain for longer than is necessary.

Builders' skips are a common sight in highways but their use has only been common in the last 25 years. Before the passage of the Highways Act 1971, now repealed by the Highways Act 1980, there was no statute law dealing with builders' skips. Action could be and was taken on the ground of their use constituting a public nuisance.

Section 139 of the Highways Act 1980 deals with the control of builders' skips. A skip is not to be deposited on a highway without the permission of the highway authority for that highway. The permission is given to a person to deposit it or cause it to be deposited on a particular highway. The permission may be granted unconditionally or subject to conditions which have to be specified in the permission. Conditions which may be specified with regard to the skip include: siting; dimensions of the skip; painting or other treatment to make the skip visible to the oncoming traffic; care and disposal of its contents; the manner of its lighting or guarding; and the removal of the skip at the end of the period of permission. When a skip has been deposited in accordance with permission of the highway authority the owner of the skip is to secure: that it is properly lighted during the hours of darkness; that it is clearly and indelibly marked with the owner's name and address or telephone number; its removal as soon as practicable after it has been filled;

and that any conditions in the permission are complied with. Failure to do these things or to deposit a skip without permission are criminal offences punishable by fine. Under the section the owner of a builders' skip does not include a person who has possession under a hiring agreement of less than one month.

The section also provides that where there is the commission of an offence by any person and that is due to the act or default of some other person, then that other person is guilty of an offence. The person whose act or default caused the offence may be prosecuted and convicted whether or not the other person is charged or not.

It is a defence for a person charged with an offence to prove that the offence was due to the act or default of another person and that he took all reasonable precautions and exercised due diligence to avoid the commission of that offence by himself or any person under his control. The use of this defence is seen in the case of *Lambeth London Borough Council v Saunders Transport* 1974 where Saunders hired a builders' skip to another person. The hire was subject to the condition that that person would be responsible for the proper lighting of the skip. This, however, was not done and Saunders was prosecuted as owner of the skip for failing to comply with a condition. The defence that the offence had been caused by the act or default of another person was accepted. Saunders had taken reasonable precautions in the circumstances.

Where the defence that the offence was due to the act or default of another person is to be used there is a requirement that a notice, at least seven clear days before the hearing, has to be served on the prosecution. The notice has to identify and give information and assistance regarding that other person.

Where a person is charged with an offence under some other Act of Parliament of leaving a skip without proper lighting during the hours of darkness, it is a defence to prove that the offence was the result of some act or default of another person and all reasonable precautions were taken and due diligence exercised to avoid the offence.

A person charged with obstructing or interrupting the use of a highway may use as a defence the permission to deposit the skip, and that the offence was due to the act or default of another person and that reasonable precautions had been taken and due diligence exercised to avoid the offence.

Finally the section states that nothing in the section is to be taken as authorising the creation of a nuisance or danger to users of the highway, or as imposing on the highway authority any liability for injury, damage or loss resulting from the skip being on the highway.

Section 140 deals with the situation where a skip properly placed on a highway under Section 139 ought to be removed or re-positioned. The highway authority or a police constable in uniform may require the owner of the skip to so act. Failure to do so is a criminal offence. In addition either may remove the skip. Then notification is to be given to the owner. If the owner does not then recover the skip it can be disposed of. Expenses incurred can be recovered; if there should be a surplus it is to be given to the owner.

Section 161 makes it an offence for a person, without lawful authority or excuse, to deposit anything whatsoever on a highway with the result that a user of the road is injured or endangered.

Section 168 makes it a criminal offence in carrying out any building operation in or near a street for an accident to occur which gives rise to risk of serious bodily injury to a person on the street or would have given rise to such risk but for action by the local authority under the Building Act 1984. It should be noted that for the offence to arise there does not have to be an injury caused; it is the risk of injury which gives rise to the offence. So if something was dropped from a building under construction into a street that could be an offence. There is a defence that all reasonable precautions were taken to avoid causing danger or that the offence was caused by the act or default of another person and that reasonable precautions were taken and due diligence exercised to avoid the offence. A defence that some other person was to blame requires seven days notice to the prosecution giving information regarding that other person.

Section 169 contains a number of provisions regarding the erection of scaffolding on a highway. These provisions are not concerned with safety but seek to minimise any obstruction from a scaffold to users of the highway. The scaffold has to be one which is to be erected for any building or demolition work or works of repair, alteration or maintenance to a building. A person who wishes to erect a scaffold must obtain a licence from the highway authority. The licence may be subject to conditions. The licence is to be granted unless the authority considers that the structure would cause unreasonable obstruction of a highway or the structure could be erected in some other way which would cause less obstruction than the structure proposed and be equally convenient for the works. A refusal to grant a licence can be the subject of an appeal to a magistrates court. A person who is granted a licence is under a duty to see that the structure is adequately lit at night, to erect traffic signs and to allow statutory undertakers access to their apparatus. Contravention of the provisions in the section is a criminal offence punishable by fine. No civil or criminal liability arises from a structure which has been granted a licence.

Section 170 makes it a criminal offence for a person to mix or deposit mortar or cement or any other substance which is likely to stick to the surface of the highway, or which if it enters drains or sewers connected with the highway is likely to solidify. There are certain specified exceptions to the application of the section. One exception is that any mixing or deposit in a receptacle or on a plate which prevents the substance from coming into contact with the highway and from entering any drains or sewers connected with the highway is permitted.

Section 171 deals with the deposit of building materials, rubbish or other things in a street that is a highway maintainable at public expense or making a temporary excavation. The doing of any of these things requires the consent of the highway authority and without that consent a criminal offence has been committed. In giving the consent the authority may impose conditions. Apart from the duty to comply with conditions, the obstruction or excavation must be properly fenced and lighted during the hours of darkness. The authority can direct in writing that the person given the consent shall erect and maintain traffic signs in connection with the deposit or excavation. The obstruction or excavation is not to remain in the street for longer than is necessary. A person refused consent or who objects to conditions in a consent may appeal to a magistrates court. Where an offence has been committed by failure to observe conditions or to follow directions to erect and maintain traffic signs or to fence and light the obstruction or excavation the authority may remove the obstruction or fill in any excavation. The expense incurred in these works may be recovered from the person convicted of the offence.

Where building works are to be carried out next to a street the risk of injury to users of the street is obvious and for this reason a builder would normally erect a hoarding simply to protect the public and to ensure that he will not have civil claims made against him. In addition to these matters builders have to have regard to the provisions in Sections 172 and 173 which create criminal obligations.

Section 172 requires every person proposing to erect or take down a building in a street or court, or to alter or repair the outside of a building in a street or court, before beginning the work to erect a close-boarded hoarding or fence to the satisfaction of the highway authority so as to separate the building from the street or court. The authority may dispense with this obligation. When a hoarding or fence has been erected it has to, if the authority so requires, have a convenient covered platform and handrail so as to form a footway for pedestrians. In addition the hoarding, fence or any platform and handrail has to be maintained to the satisfaction of the authority; if required by the authority the hoarding, fence or any platform and handrail have to be sufficiently lighted during the hours of darkness. Finally the hoarding, fence and any platform and handrail have to be removed if the authority so requires. A person who is aggrieved by the refusal of the authority to consent to dispensation of the requirement to provide a hoarding or fence or to the obligations imposed by the authority may appeal to a magistrates court. Contravention of the provisions in the section is a criminal offence punishable by fine.

Section 173 makes it a criminal offence, punishable by fine, to use any hoarding or similar structure which is not securely fixed to the satisfaction of the authority.

9 CONTRACTS FOR THE SALE OF GOODS

INTRODUCTION

The law concerning the sale of goods is found in three Acts of Parliament and in a substantial body of case law. The principal Act of Parliament is the Sale of Goods Act 1979. This Act replaced the Sale of Goods Act 1893 which had been the subject of considerable amendment. The 1893 Act was a piece of legislation which brought together various principles and judicial decisions into a single Act. The Misrepresentation Act 1967 and the Unfair Contract Terms Act 1977 both contain provisions which limit the right of parties to a contract of sale of goods to exclude terms in the contract which are intended to afford protection to the purchaser.

DEFINITION OF A CONTRACT FOR THE SALE OF GOODS

Section 2 of the Sale of Goods Act 1979 defines a contract of sale as 'a contract by which the seller transfers or agrees to transfer the property in goods to the buyer for a money consideration, called the price'.

The section also defines an agreement for sale as:

> Where under a contract of sale the transfer of the property in the goods is to take place at a future time or subject to some conditions later to be fulfilled the contract is called an agreement to sell. An agreement to sell becomes a sale when the time elapses or the conditions are fulfilled subject to which the property in the goods is to be transferred.

To examine these definitions in a little detail we can see that one person, the seller, transfers or agrees to transfer to another, the buyer, the property in goods. The thing that is being transferred or is agreed to be transferred is the property in goods. The word 'property' is defined in Section 61 as: 'means the general property in goods, and not merely a special property'.

This definition is not very helpful other than indicating it is general rather than special. What it means in simple terms, which is subject to some qualification, is that the seller has the right to transfer the title to the goods to the buyer. That is, the buyer acquires the right of ownership in the goods. As will be seen later, this is something which receives further consideration in the Act.

The word 'goods' is also defined in Section 61 as:

> 'goods' includes all personal chattels other than things in action and money, and in Scotland all corporeal moveables except money; and in particular 'goods' include emblements, industrial growing crops, and things attached to or forming part of the land which are agreed to be severed before sale or under the contract of sale.

This definition covers objects but excludes the right in law to bring an action, a 'chose in action', and money. It also includes crops which are agreed to be severed from the land before sale or under the contract.

It is also to be noted that for the transfer or agreed transfer of the goods there must be a money consideration, the price. This has the effect of excluding from the definition of a contract for sale, and the protection afforded by the Act, contracts where there is no payment of money. The best example of this is a contract of exchange, where something other than money is given for the goods.

The definition deals with an agreement for sale, where the property in the goods is to pass at some future date or some condition to be fulfilled later, by making it into a contract for sale when that date arrives or when the condition is fulfilled.

Difficulties have arisen in the past when claims have been brought in circumstances where there was doubt as to whether the contract was a contract for the sale of goods. As we have just noted, a contract of exchange is not a contract of sale. It has, however, been accepted that a part exchange with some money payment is a contract of sale. So buying a new car by trading in an old car and paying the balance in money is a contract of sale.

A contract of hire-purchase resembles a contract of sale of goods in that goods pass from one person to another. The important distinction is that unlike a contract of sale a hire-purchase contract does not pass the property in the goods; it simply gives possession. During the period of possession payments are made which count towards a purchase, if in fact a purchase is made. The contract does, however, give the possessor of the goods the right to buy the goods if that person so wishes. These contracts are now governed by the Consumer Credit Act 1974.

Where probably the greatest difficulty arose was with contracts which involved labour and materials. A contract whereby a person does work and supplies material is not a contract for the sale of goods. For instance, a builder might contract to build an extension by the use of his labour and the supply of the necessary materials. This is not a contract of sale of goods. In order to overcome the problems of contracts of this type Parliament passed the Supply of

Goods and Services Act 1982. This Act provides protection similar to that of the 1979 Act to those who have work done which involves labour and materials. Before the introduction of the 1982 Act action had to be taken on the basis of ordinary common law.

An example of work which created doubt as to whether it was a contract for labour and materials, and so outside the Sale of Goods Act 1893, or a contract for the sale of goods came before the House of Lords in the case of *Cammell Laird and Co Ltd v Manganese Bronze and Brass Co Ltd* 1934. In this case Manganese Bronze contracted to construct two propellers for two ships Cammell Laird were building. Cammell Laird had provided a specification for some of the work but some was left to be decided by Manganese Bronze. One of the propellers was found to be unsuitable because of a defect. The House of Lords decided that the supply of the propellers was a contract for the supply of goods. This then allowed the application of Section 14 of the Act which made Manganese Bronze liable.

TERMS IN A CONTRACT

The general position with contracts is that the parties to the contract put terms into the contract they wish to have included. Those are express terms. Terms may also be implied if, for example, the court believes these to be necessary in order to give the contract business efficacy. The Sale of Goods Act 1979, as did its predecessor the 1893 Act, implies that certain terms shall exist in a contract for the sale of goods. These terms may be excluded but only in the circumstances considered later.

The terms in a contract for the sale of goods are conditions and warranties. The difference between the two terms is important. A condition is something of substance in a contract. It is not given a particular definition under the 1979 Act so the common law understanding has to be used. It is often said to be something which 'goes to the root of the contract'. That is, a breach of it is a matter of major importance. An example of a condition would be where goods had to be delivered to a ship sailing on a stated date. A failure to deliver the goods in time for the ship's sailing would be a breach of condition. The remedy for a breach of a condition is that the injured party can repudiate the contract. He may, therefore, make other contract arrangements and then sue the party in breach for damages to compensate for the loss he has suffered. It should be noted that to describe a term in a contract as a condition does not mean that the court will accept it as such. The court looks at the contract and from that determines whether the term is truly a condition or whether it is not a matter of substance to the contract.

A warranty is defined in Section 61 of the 1979 Act as:

'warranty' (as regards England and Wales and Northern Ireland) means an agreement with reference to goods which are the subject of a contract of sale, but collateral to the main purpose of such contract, the breach of which gives rise to a claim for damages, but not to a right to reject the goods and treat the contract as repudiated.

As can be seen from the definition a warranty is a term of less importance to the contract than a condition. A breach of warranty does not allow the injured party to repudiate the contract. The contract has not been affected to a substantial extent so as to justify that course of action. A breach of warranty, therefore, permits the injured party to sue for damages for the harm suffered by the breach.

So far as the 1979 Act is concerned, as will be seen, certain matters which most people would recognise as being of fundamental importance are treated as conditions and other, less important matters, are treated as warranties. The parties can amend the terms which the Act implies but the effectiveness of these amendments depends on whether, in the circumstances, it is fair and reasonable to allow the amendments.

FORMALITIES OF A CONTRACT OF SALE

Before considering the matters of conditions and warranties some examination of preliminary topics is necessary. A contract of sale under the Act may be made in writing; in the form of a deed or otherwise; or by word of mouth; or partly in writing and partly by word of mouth; or may be implied from the conduct of the parties. In practice, most suppliers of goods do so by use of contract forms in writing which contain terms and conditions.

A contract of sale may relate to existing goods or goods to be manufactured or acquired after the making of the contract. There will be a contract of sale even if the acquisition of the goods depends on a contingency which may or may not happen. If a contract for the sale of specific goods is made and unknown to the seller of the goods at the time the contract was made the goods had perished, then the contract is void. This provision is dependent on the goods being specific; that is as defined in Section 61 'goods identified and agreed on at the time a contract of sale is made'. If, therefore, the goods cannot be identified then this provision does not apply. An example of this would be a contract to buy 5,000 bricks from a stock of 25,000. If the 5,000 are not separated and identified then they are not specific goods. Where there is an agreement to sell specific goods and later, without fault of the seller or buyer, they perish before the risk has passed to the buyer the agreement is voided.

Section 8 of the Act deals with the ascertainment of the price of the goods. The provisions apply not only when the price of the goods has been agreed but also in other circumstances.

(1) The price in a contract of sale may be fixed by the contract, or may be left to be fixed in a manner agreed by the contract, or may be determined by the course of dealing between the parties.

(2) Where the price is not determined as mentioned in sub-section (1) above the buyer must pay a reasonable price.

(3) What is a reasonable price is a question of fact dependent on the circumstances of each particular case.

With regard to sub-section (1) it can be seen that the price may be that that the parties have agreed and inserted in the contract. It may, however, be fixed in a manner agreed by the contract. This would cover the situation where a contract for the sale of goods had different prices according to the number bought. The greater the number the lower the price of the individual goods. The contract may also leave the price to be determined in the way in which the parties have dealt with each other over a period of time. An example of this would be where a seller has supplied goods to the buyer on the basis that the price would be a certain percentage below a price fixed by some other person or body. So if the price of some goods was fixed at £10 and the agreed percentage was 10 per cent then, even though no price had been agreed between them, the buyer would pay £9.

Sub-sections (2) and (3) state that where the price is not determined as just considered, then it is to be a reasonable price and that is dependent on the individual circumstances. This provision would apply by, for example, ascertaining the value of similar goods, for the same quantity, from other reputable suppliers.

CONDITIONS AND WARRANTIES

Section 10 deals with the stipulations as to time for payment and time in other aspects. The expression 'time shall be of the essence of the contract' means that the time of delivery, completion or payment of some other matter is of such importance that a failure to meet the obligation on the agreed date constitutes breach of condition. That breach allows the injured party to repudiate the contract.

The section states that unless a different intention appears from the terms of the contract, stipulations as to time of payment are not of the essence of a contract of sale. So if the seller wishes to make the date of payment a term of the contract which is of the essence of the contract then this must be done expressly. Without that stipulation payment is to be within a reasonable time.

The section also provides that whether any other stipulation as to time is of the essence of the contract or not depends on the terms of the contract. Applying this provision, if the buyer of the goods requires delivery by a certain date then that requirement should be made a term in the contract. To this, however, must be added the rule laid down in the case of *Hartley v Hymans* 1920 that in ordinary commercial contracts for the sale of goods the rule clearly is that time is prima facie of the essence with respect to delivery. The justification for this rule is to be seen in a contract to deliver goods to a ship sailing on a stated date. A commercial transaction of that nature requires proper delivery irrespective of whether the time of delivery was made a term in the contract.

Section 11 contains provisions dealing with a breach of a condition. In the case of a breach of a condition by the seller the buyer has the right to waive the condition or to treat the breach of condition as a breach of warranty and not as a ground for repudiating the contract. So the buyer could, if he so wishes, not exercise his right when a breach of condition occurs. This would be done when the buyer's interests would be best served by not exercising the right. For example, it might suit the buyer to waive a breach of condition with regard to the delivery of goods. Late delivery might be entirely acceptable to the buyer. The right to treat a breach of a condition as a breach of warranty again would be used when it suited the buyer's interests. Again late delivery when time is of the essence might be acceptable to the buyer but it would be right for him to sue for damages for the breach of warranty.

Section 11 also seeks to give guidance as to whether a stipulation is a condition or warranty. Unfortunately it is not guidance which leads to a clear-cut definition. What it states is that whether a stipulation is a condition, giving a right to repudiate the contract, or a warranty, giving a right to claim damages only, depends on the construction of the contract. And a stipulation may be a condition even though it is called a warranty in the contract.

From this it follows that the courts look at what the parties have put in the contract as being conditions and warranties. The courts, however, reserve the right to hold that a condition in the contract in fact is not because the court is of the opinion that it is not something which goes to the root of the contract. In addition, under the section, the court can treat a warranty in the contract as being a condition.

The section also deals with the situation where the buyer, in a contract which cannot be severed, has accepted the goods or part of them. In this case the breach of condition has to be treated as a breach of warranty. The right to repudiate the contract is lost. The effect of this provision is that the buyer who has accepted some goods by that action loses his right to repudiate the contract and has to treat a breach of condition as a breach of warranty and claim damages. Where, however, the contract is one which can be severed then this does not apply.

A final point in the section is that where a condition or warranty cannot be fulfilled because of frustration then its fulfilment is excused.

TERMS IMPLIED IN A CONTRACT FOR THE SALE OF GOODS

Sections 12 to 15 of the Sale of Goods Act 1979 contain provisions which are generally considered to be the most important in the Act. The sections imply certain conditions and warranties into contracts for the sale of goods. These conditions and warranties are to apply in the circumstances set out in the sections. This, however, is subject to the rights of the parties to the contract to avoid or modify them, so far as they are able. The provisions in Sections 12 to 15 are similar to the provisions in equivalent sections in the Sale of Goods Act 1893 so the cases decided on the 1893 Act are still applicable.

Implied terms as to title
Section 12 of the Act states:

(1) In a contract of sale . . . there is an implied condition on the part of the seller that in the case of a sale he has a right to sell the goods, and in the case of an agreement to sell he will have such a right at the time when the property is to pass.

(2) In a contract of sale, other than one to which sub-section (3) below applies, there is also an implied warranty that –

    (a) the goods are free, and will remain free until the time when the property is to pass, from any charge or encumbrance not disclosed or known to the buyer before the contract is made, and

    (b) the buyer will enjoy quiet possession of the goods except so far as it may be disturbed by the owner or other person entitled to the benefit of any charge or encumbrance so disclosed or known.

In sub-section (1) there is an implied condition that the seller has a right to sell the goods and, in the case of an agreement to sell, that the seller will have the right to sell the goods at the time when the property is to pass. A buyer may, therefore, repudiate the contract and, under Section 54, he may recover any money he has paid. He may also in addition to repudiation make a claim for damages.

A case which dealt with a breach of condition under sub-section (1) is *Rowland v Divall* 1923. Rowland bought a car from Divall for £334. Divall sold the car in the justified belief that he had a right to sell it and pass a good title to Rowland. Rowland had no reason to suspect that he was not acquiring a good title to the car. He sold the car to another person for £400. It was then discovered that Divall had not owned the car when he sold it to Rowland. He had bought the car in good faith from a person who did not have a good title to the car. The true owner then claimed the car. Rowland repaid the £400 to the person to whom he had sold it. He then sued Divall for the £334 he had paid for the car. The Court of Appeal decided that Rowland was entitled to recover the £334. The court rejected a submission that this amount ought to be reduced because of the four months use of the car enjoyed by the person sold the car by Rowland. The court's reason for this rejection was that Rowland had not received any part of what he had contracted for and what he was entitled to, namely the property in the car and the right to possession. This amounted to a total failure of consideration.

The application of the decision in *Rowland v Divall* 1923 and an indication of the way the sub-section is applied is seen in the case of *Karflex Ltd v Poole* 1933. Here Karflex Ltd bought a car from one person and then hired it by means of a hire-purchase agreement to Poole, Poole having the usual right to buy the car when all instalments have been paid. Poole however paid the first instalment only and so Karflex took proceedings against him. Evidence then came to light that the person from whom Karflex had acquired the car was not the true owner. Karflex traced the true owner and paid him for the car. This then put them in the position of being the owners of the car. The court, however, took the view that at the time they had delivered the car to Poole they were not the owners; the later acquisition of the ownership of the car did not remedy this deficiency. Poole was, therefore, entitled to the return of his deposit and since there had been a breach of the implied condition as to title, could repudiate the contract. This case concerned a hire-purchase agreement and not a sale of goods but the court applied the same principles.

In sub-section (2) there is an implied warranty that the goods are to be free of any charge or encumbrance not disclosed or known to the buyer at the time of the contract, and that the buyer will enjoy quiet possession unless disturbed by someone who has a charge or other encumbrance which was disclosed or made known to the buyer.

What this means is that if some person claims some right, which the buyer was not told of or did not know of, then there is a breach of warranty. A case which shows the application of this provision is *Niblett Ltd v Confectioners' Materials Co* 1921 where a contract to sell 3,000 tins of milk was questioned on the ground that they were labelled in such a way as to possibly infringe a trademark of a company. This company, it was accepted, could have sought to protect its trademark by obtaining an injunction to prevent the sale of the tins of milk. This meant that the seller could not sell the goods.

The matter of quiet possession was considered in the case of *Microbeads A C v Vinhurst Road Markings Ltd* 1975 where Vinhurst bought a road-marking machine. Unknown to Vinhurst, the road-marking machine infringed a patent taken out by another person. The patent was not granted until after the sale. The effect of the patent would be to make Vinhurst liable for infringement of the patent if they used the machine. For this reason Vinhurst refused to pay for the machine and the sellers Microbeads sued claiming payment. The Court of Appeal decided that there had been breach of warranty under Section 12 (2) (b) since the sub-section stated that 'The buyer will enjoy quiet possession', and this meant a continuing obligation.

The reference to sub-section (3) of Section 12 is to the situation where the buyer is made aware that the seller is transferring the title he has or some other person has, and that all charges or encumbrances known to the seller have been disclosed to the buyer. So the buyer has contracted on the basis that there is some charge or encumbrance. The implied warranty in this circumstance is that the buyer's quiet possession will only be disturbed by the charge or encumbrance made known to him before the contract was made.

Sale by description

Section 13 of the Act states: '(1) Where there is a contract for the sale of goods, by description, there is an implied condition that the goods will correspond with the description.'

A sale by description occurs when the buyer has not seen the goods but is making the contract on the basis of the description given to him by the seller. An example of this features in the case of *Varley v Whipp* 1900 where Whipp agreed to buy from Varley a second-hand reaping machine which Varley described as 'new last year and little used'. The machine was several years old and had been left in a field unprotected from the elements for some time. Whipp refused to accept the machine or pay the contact price. The court decided that there was a breach of condition since the machine did not correspond with the description.

The courts have accepted that there can be a sale by description when the goods actually exist and are on display in a shop. There has to be some aspect of description involved. For example, if a suit is sold as being of 100 per cent pure wool that is a description. If the suit does not meet that standard then there is a breach of condition.

A specified description must be satisfied in its entirety. The House of Lords indicated in the case of *Arcos Ltd v E. A. Ronaasen and Son* 1933 that if a written contract specified some matter such as weight or measurement then that must be satisfied. 'Substantial' compliance will not satisfy the requirement. A prime example of this is the House of Lords decision in *Re Moore and Co Ltd v Landauer and Co Ltd* 1921 where buyers contracted to buy 3,000 tins of canned fruit which were to be packed in cases of 30 tins. On delivery it was found that about half the cases contained 24 tins only. The correct quantity purchased, 3,000 tins, was delivered. The Court of Appeal decided that the buyer was entitled to reject the whole consignment. In the opinion of the court there had been a breach of Section 13.

This decision has been doubted by the House of Lords in a later case but has not been overruled. The decision might be justified on the ground that the buyer had a greater number of cases to transport and store because of those which held 24 tins instead of 30 tins as specified. It might also be the case that the buyer had agreed to sell to others cases of tinned fruit each containing 30 tins, and the delivery of cases with 24 tins created contractual problems for him.

The courts may interpret the word description in a less precise way if they take the view that description refers to quality rather than to identify the goods with precision. This is to be seen in the House of Lords decision *Cehave NV v Bremer Handelsgesellschaft m.b.h.* 1976 where the contract for sale was for a quantity of fruit pellets which were to be used in the manufacture of animal feed. The contract had in it a term that the goods were to be shipped in 'good condition'. The goods were damaged but only to a small degree; the damage was not such as to prevent them ultimately being used for animal feed. The buyer however, sought to reject the goods 'on the ground that there was a breach of an express term in the contract that the goods would be in "good condition" '. This, however, was not accepted by the House of Lords as a breach of Section 13.

What appears to be an authoritative ruling by the House of Lords is in the case of *Ashington Piggeries Ltd v Christopher Hill Ltd* 1972 where the contract of sale was for Norwegian herring meal and preservative. Unfortunately the preservative used made the herring meal poisonous to mink. The purchase had been made for feeding to mink. The decision was that the contract was for identifiable goods and these had been supplied.

In sub-section (2) of Section 13 it states: '(2) If the sale is by sample as well as by description it is not sufficient that the bulk of the goods corresponds with the sample if the goods do not also correspond with the description.' By this provision it is a condition that a sale by description as well as by sample must conform to the description. The fact that the bulk of the goods corresponds with the sample does not, in itself, fulfil the contract. The requirement as to description must also be met.

Section 13 finishes by providing that goods being sold by description are still sold in that way even if the buyer made the selection. For instance, if a power tool is sold by description but is displayed on a shelf and the buyer picked one from the display then the provision in Section 13 still applies.

Implied terms about quality and fitness

Section 14, which deals with merchantable quality and fitness for purpose, is probably the most important section in the Act and the one which gives the greatest difficulty to the courts in application. The definition of 'merchantable quality' in the section is generally accepted as being unsatisfactory and a new and, hopefully, clearer definition may be produced by Parliament as a result of the work of the Law Commission.

Section 14 sub-section (1) states:

> (1) Except as provided by this section and section 15 below and subject to any other enactment, there is no implied condition or warranty about the quality or fitness for any particular purpose of goods supplied under a contract of sale.

What this sub-section does is to establish that there is no implied condition or warranty about the quality or fitness for any particular purpose other than those in this section or Section 15.

Sub-section (2) states:

> (2) Where the seller sells goods in the course of a business, there is an implied condition that the goods supplied under the contract are of merchantable quality, except that there is no such condition –
> (a) as regards defects specifically drawn to the buyer's attention before the contract is made; or
> (b) if the buyer examines the goods before the contract is made, as regards defects which that examination ought to reveal.

The first point to note is that the provisions only apply if the seller sells the goods in the course of business. Goods sold by a private individual who is not selling in the course of business do not come within the provisions. This does not apply to Section 13, sale by description, where a private individual is bound. A further point to note is that Section 14 applies to second-hand goods. So the seller of second-hand vehicles or equipment is subject to the provisions in the same way as the seller of new.

The sub-section implies a condition that the goods supplied are to be of merchantable quality, subject to exceptions. Before considering the application of this provision it is necessary to examine the definition of merchantable quality.

Merchantable quality is defined in sub-section (6) as:

(6) Goods of any kind are of merchantable quality within the meaning of subsection (2) above if they are as fit for the purpose or purposes for which goods of that kind are commonly bought as it is reasonable to expect having regard to any description applied to them, the price (if relevant) and all the other relevant circumstances.

Added to this is the definition in Section 61 of the Act that 'quality', in relation to goods, includes their state or condition.

From the definition of merchantable quality it can be seen that the goods have to be fit for the purpose or purposes for which goods of that kind are commonly bought. So if a buyer uses goods for an unusual purpose then he will have difficulty in proving that they were not of merchantable quality. Furthermore, the fitness for purpose is governed by the requirement that it is to be reasonable having regard to any description applied to the goods. The price of the goods, if relevant, must be taken into account; as must all the other relevant circumstances.

Consideration of some cases may help to show the courts' approach to the interpretation of merchantable quality. In the case of *Wilson v Rickett, Cockerell and Co Ltd* 1954 the Court of Appeal decided that a consignment of Coalite, a form of solid fuel, which contained a detonator was not of merchantable quality. The detonator, the presence of which was unknown to both the seller and the buyer, exploded in the fireplace and caused serious damage to the building. The court refused to accept that the purchase was of the fuel alone and did not include the detonator. The purchase included the detonator. It was not a situation where the offending object could be excluded from the sale. The High Court decision in *Bernstein v Pamson Motors (Golders Green) Ltd* 1987 attracted both interest and criticism. Bernstein bought a new car for £8,000 on 7 December 1984. On 3 January 1985 when the car had done 140 miles only it broke down. It had to be towed away for repairs. Bernstein the next day gave notice to the sellers that he considered the car not to be of merchantable quality. The car was repaired under the manufacturer's warranty. The judge decided that, despite the owner's use over a three week period only and some 140 miles, the owner had had a reasonable period of time to examine and try out the car. This meant that he had, in the judge's opinion, lost his right under Section 35 to reject the goods. The judge accepted that the car when delivered was not of merchantable quality since it had the potential for damage and the safety consideration was not that that was needed. The judge's ruling on what constituted a reasonable period was fatal to Bernstein's wish to reject the car. In the case of *Rogers v Parish (Scarborough) Ltd and Others* 1987 the Court of Appeal dealt with the breakdown of a new Range Rover. The car was bought for £16,000 and had a 12 months manufacturer's warranty. Some six months later, with 5,500 miles of use, the car broke down with a number of defects. These were repaired under the warranty. The Court of Appeal took a very different view to the High Court judge who had come to the conclusion that the car was of merchantable quality. He took into account that the defects could be repaired and did not make the car unroadworthy, unusable or unfit for the normal purposes for which a Range Rover might be used. The Court of Appeal rejected the High Court judge's approach and decision. They took account of the price paid, above that paid for an ordinary family car, the defects in the car and the standard a buyer was entitled to expect. They took the view that the manufacturer's warranty was an additional feature which did not affect the seller's obligation. The court declined to rule on whether the buyer's rejection had been made within a reasonable period of time since that had not been pleaded or argued before the court.

In sub-section (2) there are two exceptions to the implied condition as to merchantable quality. The first, that defects have been specifically drawn to the attention of the buyer before the contract is made, covers the situation where there is a reduced price because of the defect and the buyer is told that the price is reduced for that reason and told what the defect is. In that circumstance the buyer makes his decision in the light of the information provided. The second exception covers the position of the buyer having had the opportunity to examine the goods in a way which ought to reveal defects detectable by that examination. There is no obligation on the buyer to examine the goods but if he does then this exception may prevent the implied condition applying.

Sub-section (3) states:

(3) Where the seller sells goods in the course of a business and the buyer, expressly or by implication, makes known –
   (a) to the seller, or
   (b) where the purchase price or part of it is payable by instalments and the goods were previously sold by a credit-broker to the seller, to that credit-broker,

any particular purpose for which the goods are being bought, there is an implied condition that the goods supplied under the contract are reasonably fit for that purpose, whether or not that is a purpose for which such goods are commonly supplied, except where the circumstances show that the buyer does not rely, or that it is unreasonable for him to rely, on the skill or judgment of the seller or credit-broker.

This provision, again, only applies when the seller is in business. It implies a condition that when the buyer has made known, expressly or by implication, to the seller that the goods are to meet a particular purpose, then the goods are to be reasonably fit for that purpose. This is so even if the goods are not commonly supplied for that purpose. The exception is where the buyer does not rely on the seller's skill or judgment or it would be unreasonable for him to rely on that skill or judgment.

The reference to a credit-broker covers the situation where the buyer is buying on a conditional sale agreement and the dealer introduces him to the finance company with whom he actually makes his contract.

If the sub-section is to apply there must be some reliance on the seller's skill or judgment . If that is not so then the implied condition does not apply. So if the buyer knows exactly what he wants and proceeds on that basis the sub-section does not apply. An example of this would be the buyer buying goods under a trade name, possibly protected by a patent. Where, however, the buyer makes known his need to the seller and this then involves the seller's skill or judgment the implied condition applies.

The case of *Cammell Laird and Co Ltd v Manganese Bronze and Brass Co Ltd* 1934, decided by the House of Lords, dealt with the application of this provision. Here Manganese undertook the manufacture of two propellers for two ships Cammell Laird were building. The specification provided by Cammell Laird did not deal with every feature of the manufacture and, consequently, Manganese Bronze had to use their skill and judgment as manufacturers. The propellers had a defect in them which made them unfit for their known purpose. This was a breach of the implied condition.

A simple example of the use of this provision is the case of *Priest v Last* 1903. Here the buyer purchased from a chemist's shop a hot-water bottle. The hot-water bottle shortly after purchase burst scalding the buyer. The Court of Appeal decided that it had been purchased for a particular purpose and was not fit for that purpose.

The buyer is under an obligation to pay proper regard to any warnings or instructions given with the goods. Indeed if goods are used in circumstances where their continued use would create danger the seller will probably not be liable. In the case of *Wormell v R. H. M. Agriculture (East) Ltd* 1987 a farmer bought a quantity of weed-killer. The containers carried clear warnings that the use of the chemical was not recommended at a certain stage of growth of the crops. The farmer disregarded the warning and used the weed-killer. It was ineffective and he sued for the cost of the weed-killer. The Court of Appeal decided that the claim failed. The weed-killer was fit for its purpose if applied in the right conditions. In the case of *Lambert v Lewis* 1982 a buyer of a towing coupling for a vehicle discovered that it was defective. The defect was a fault of manufacture. The buyer continued to use the coupling after it was obviously in a dangerous or unfit state. An accident occurred and the buyer had to pay damages to those injured. He then sued the seller. The House of Lords rejected the claim. The coupling when sold had not been fit for its purpose but the continued use after its dangerous and unfit state was known broke the link. What had occurred was the result of the buyer's own negligence.

Sub-section (4) states: 'An implied condition or warranty about quality or fitness for a particular purpose may be annexed to a contract of sale by usage.' This provision takes into account the fact that parties to a contract in a particular trade do so on the basis of the custom and usage of that trade.

Sub-section (5) states:

> (5) The preceding provisions of this section apply to a sale by a person who in the course of a business is acting as agent for another as they apply to a sale by a principal in the course of a business, except where that other is not selling in the course of a business and either the buyer knows that fact or reasonable steps are taken to bring it to the notice of the buyer before the contract is made.

This provision deals with an agent acting in the course of business where his principal is also acting in the course of business. In this circumstance the provisions in Section 14 apply. If, however, the principal is not acting in the course of business and the buyer is aware of this or reasonable steps are taken to bring it to his attention, then the provisions in the section do not apply. So if an agent acting in the course of business makes it known to the buyer that the principal is not in business, but a private individual, then the provisions do not apply.

Implied terms for a sale by sample

Section 15 states:

> (1) A contract of sale is a contract for sale by sample where there is an express or implied term to that effect in the contract.
> (2) In the case of a contract for sale by sample there is an implied condition –
>   (a) that the bulk will correspond with the sample in quality;
>   (b) that the buyer will have a reasonable opportunity of comparing the bulk with the sample;
>   (c) that the goods will be free from any defect, rendering them unmerchantable, which would not be apparent on reasonable examination of the sample.
> (3) In sub-section (2) (c) above 'unmerchantable' is to be construed in accordance with Section 14 (6) above.

A sale by sample arises when that is expressly stated to be the case. For instance, where an order form which is the written contract states that the purchase is made on the basis of the sample. Where this is not done it is a question of the particular facts whether the sale is by sample. It might be that a sample is available, and even inspected by the buyer, but the contract is a sale by sample only if it is intended that it shall be. The buyer might have intended to place the order even if a sample had not been available for inspection.

The requirement that the bulk shall correspond with the sample means that if only a few of the goods fail to correspond with the sample the buyer cannot reject the goods. He has to sue for damages for those which are not to sample.

The right of the buyer to have a reasonable opportunity to compare the bulk with the sample means that until this has occurred the buyer cannot be held to have accepted the goods. If, however, the buyer accepts the goods the right to reject is lost and the remedy is to sue for damages.

The requirement that the goods are to be free from defects rendering them unmerchantable, not apparent on reasonable examination of the sample, means that the implied condition will not apply if the defects were detectable on reasonable inspection. The goods are to be of merchantable quality as set out in Section 14 (6) if the seller is in business.

Performance of the contract

In Sections 27 to 37 of the Sale of Goods Act 1979 there are a number of provisions which govern the performance of a contract for the sale of goods. As these are less likely to give rise to disputes than the provisions considered earlier a general consideration should be sufficient.

The seller of the goods is under a duty to deliver the goods and the buyer to accept and pay for them in accordance with the terms of the contract. Unless otherwise agreed delivery and payment are to occur at the same time. The contract is to determine whether the buyer is to take possession of the goods or the seller to send them. Subject to the contract, the place of delivery is the seller's place of business or his residence. If the time for delivery is not fixed then the goods have to be sent within a reasonable time.

Where the seller delivers a quantity of goods less than the contract stipulates the buyer may reject them but if he keeps them he must pay the contract sum. In the case of over-delivery the buyer may reject the whole or keep the contracted amount and reject the surplus. If the over-delivery is kept the contract rate must be paid for all the goods. There is no obligation on the buyer to accept delivery in instalments unless the contract so provides.

In the case of a contract where the seller is authorised or required to send the goods to the buyer, delivery of the goods to a carrier for transmission is prima facie deemed to be delivery to the buyer. Unless authorised by the buyer the seller is to make a contract with the carrier as is reasonable in the circumstances; failure to do so allows the buyer to decline to treat delivery to the carrier as delivery to himself or he may hold the seller liable in damages.

When goods are delivered to the buyer he is to have a reasonable opportunity to inspect the goods and until then he is not deemed to have accepted them. The same right exists when the seller tenders delivery.

When the buyer has accepted the goods he loses the right to reject the goods and may only sue for damages. Acceptance occurs when the buyer intimates to the seller his acceptance; when he does any act after the delivery of the goods which is inconsistent with the seller's ownership of the goods; and when a reasonable time has elapsed and he has failed to indicate to the seller his intention to reject the goods.

When delivery has been made to the buyer and he exercises his right to refuse to accept them, he is not bound to return the goods. It is sufficient if he informs the seller of his rejection of the goods. In the case of *Kolfor Plant v Tilbury Plant* 1977 the court decided that the buyer, who had exercised his right of rejection and so informed the seller, was entitled to recover the expense he had incurred transporting the goods to a secure place and then storing them.

EXEMPTION CLAUSES

At one time it was standard practice for sellers of goods to have in their terms of business clauses which sought to exclude or limit liability. Some contracts excluded completely the provisions in the Sale of Goods Act 1893. As a form of compensation the buyers were offered some form of manufacturer's guarantee. An exclusion clause excludes liability whereas a limitation clause limits the seller's liability, usually, to a stated amount. The matter of clauses which place restrictive or onerous conditions on the buyer or otherwise seek to exclude or restrict any right or remedy available to the buyer are dealt with by Section 13 of the Unfair Contract Terms Act 1977. A requirement that when goods are delivered damaged or are insufficient in number the notification of that fact has to be made in a particular way or within a stated time may be struck down by the Act.

Until the passing of the Unfair Contract Terms Act 1977 the courts had to rely on the common law to provide some means of protecting a buyer from what would otherwise be unfair treatment. A number of the common law provisions are still applicable. The first consideration must be whether a clause is a term in a contract. To be such it must be incorporated into the contract at the time of its formation; terms cannot be added after the contract is made. Incorporation depends on full knowledge of the terms at the place where the contract is made and of their application to the contract.

The clause will be ineffective if there was misrepresentation in the formation of the contract, or if later an oral statement is made which is contrary to the clause. This was the decision by the Court of Appeal in the case of *Curtis v Chemical Cleaning and Dyeing Co Ltd* 1951 where terms in a receipt for clothes left for dry cleaning were much wider then the shop assistant explained to the customer. This amounted to misrepresentation other than for the matters explained by the shop assistant.

A measure used by the courts is one of the rules of construction. That is that a clause will be construed against the person who inserted it in the contract if some doubt arises. This was the approach of the court in the case of *Andrews Bros Ltd v Singer and Co Ltd* 1934. A contract for the sale of a 'new' Singer car excluded all implied conditions and warranties. The car in fact was not new and the buyer sought to rescind the contract. The court permitted this on the ground that the car had to be new and this was an express condition. This meant that it was not subject to the clause excluding implied conditions and warranties.

The Sale of Goods Act 1979 Section 55 allows, subject to the Unfair Contract Terms Act 1977, a right, duty or liability which would be implied under the Act to be negatived and varied by express agreement. Such matters may also be negatived or varied by the course of dealing between the parties, or by such usage as binds both parties to the contract. The Section also states that an express condition or warranty does not negative an implied condition or warranty unless inconsistent with it. This particular provision requires any express condition or warranty to be so drafted as to clearly exclude any implied condition or warranty.

Unfair Contract Terms Act 1977
This Act was introduced to control the use of terms, both in contracts or otherwise, which unfairly excluded or limited a person's legal rights. As has already been noted it was usual before this Act was passed to sell goods subject to the exclusion of all implied conditions and warranties under the Sale of Goods Act 1893. The effect of this was to remove the protection of the Act.

In controlling the use of exemption clauses in contracts the Act deals separately with consumers and non-consumers. The reason for this is that it was considered that consumers needed greater protection than non-consumers. Non-consumers are commercial organisations accustomed to negotiating contracts and prepared to accept terms as part of a commercial risk. They therefore need less protection.

Section 12 of the Act defines a consumer as:

(1) A party to a contract 'deals as consumer' in relation to another party if –

(a) he neither makes the contract in the course of a business nor holds himself out as doing so; and

(b) the other party does make the contract in the course of a business: and

(c) in the case of a contract governed by the law of sale of goods or hire-purchase, or by Section 7 of this Act, the goods passing under or in pursuance of the contract are of a type ordinarily supplied for private use or consumption.

Putting this in simple terms a consumer is a person who buys but not in the course of a business and the other party sells in the course of a business, and the goods are those normally used by a private individual. So a private individual who is selling his second-hand car does not come within the Act. The purchase of goods for or in the course of business will not be a consumer sale. In the case *R. and B. Customs Brokers Co Ltd v United Dominions Trust* 1988 the Court of Appeal decided that where a limited company had bought a car for the use of a director that was a consumer sale.

Section 12 also clarifies two points:

(2) But on a sale by auction or by competitive tender the buyer is not in any circumstances to be regarded as dealing as a consumer.

(3) Subject to this, it is for those claiming that a party does not deal as consumer to show that he does not.

The importance of showing that a contract is a consumer sale is that under Section 6 the seller cannot by contract terms exclude or restrict any of the provisions in Sections 12 to 15 of the Sale of Goods Act 1979. By this provision a private individual is given the full protection of the provisions in the sections. Any attempt to exclude or restrict the seller's liability is null and void.

In the case of a non-consumer the position is different since, as we have noted, it might be to the commercial advantage of the buyer to accept a contract with exclusion or restrictive terms. In addition commercial organisations are experienced in contract negotiations and so need less protection.

Section 6, therefore, prohibits exclusion or restriction of the seller's liability under Section 12, implied condition as to title. Other than this, the seller dealing with a person other than as a consumer can exclude or restrict by terms in the contract the provisions in Sections 13 to 15 provided the term satisfies the requirement of reasonableness.

Test of reasonableness

Section 11 states that the requirement of reasonableness is that the term shall have been a fair and reasonable one to be included having regard to the circumstances which were, or ought reasonably to have been, known to or in the contemplation of the parties when the contract was made. The section also states that in deciding whether a term satisfies the requirement of reasonableness regard is to be had to the matters in Schedule 2 of the Act.

Schedule 2 gives 'guidelines' for the application of the reasonable test. These are guidelines only and other circumstances may have to be taken into account in the determination.

The guidelines are:

(a) the strength of the bargaining positions of the parties relative to each other, taking into account (among other things) alternative means by which the customer's requirements could have been met;

(b) whether the customer received an inducement to agree to the term, or in accepting it had an opportunity of entering into a similar contract with other persons, but without having to accept a similar term;

(c) whether the customer knew or ought reasonably to have known of the existence and extent of the term (having regard, among other things, to any custom of the trade and any previous course of dealing between the parties);

(d) where the term excludes or restricts any relevant liability if some condition is not complied with, whether it was reasonable at the time of the contract to expect that compliance with that condition would be practicable;

(e) whether the goods were manufactured, processed or adapted to the special order of the customer.

The first (a) deals with the position where the seller is in a monopoly or almost monopoly position of supply with limited other means of supply. With (b) a buyer who accepted a price reduction in return for a contract with exemption clauses may find that they are held to be reasonable. With (c) the question as to the ordinary use of a term has to be considered. With (d) consideration has to be given to the use of conditions which, if not observed, could bring into operation an exemption term. With (e) an exemption clause may be reasonable if goods of any unusual nature are required to be manufactured.

Two leading cases on exemption clauses are *Mitchell (G) Chesterhall Ltd v Finney Lock Seeds Ltd* 1983 and *Rees Hough Ltd v Redland Reinforced Plastics Ltd* 1984. The first was decided on the Supply of Goods (Implied Terms) Act 1973, which contained provisions similar to those in the 1979 Act. Here a seller of seeds limited liability to the cost of the seed or replacement in the event of failure of the seed. The seed supplied was the wrong seed and the crop had to be ploughed in. When sued Finney Lock put up as defence the limitation clause. The House of Lords rejected the clause as not satisfying the requirement of reasonableness. The reasons for this were: the term was inserted by the sellers and was not the result of trade negotiations; the sellers had not used the term in the past and had paid out compensation; the supply of the wrong seed was due solely to the sellers' negligence; and the sellers could have obtained insurance to cover them for this type of claim.

In the case of *Rees Hough Ltd v Redland Reinforced Plastics Ltd* 1984 the sellers of plastic pipes had an exclusion clause which sought to avoid liability in tort and in contract for any defect in the pipes. The pipes which were to be capable of withstanding a specified load in pipe-jacking failed. The High Court judge decided that the wide exclusion clause failed to satisfy the reasonable test. His reasons for the decision were: on previous occasions Redland had compensated customers for defective goods; the term was Redland's and had not been negotiated by trade and contractors' organisations; and Redland could have insured against this type of claim.

Other exemption clauses

In addition to the use of the exemption clauses considered, sellers of goods make use of other clauses, such as that the other party has to accept contract performance which is different to that reasonably expected of him or that there is no liability if the contract is not performed at all. Section 3 states that where a contract is made with one party as consumer or on the other party's written standard terms of business then that party cannot by a term in the contract exclude or restrict any liability in respect of his breach or for substantially different performance or non-performance of the contract, unless the requirement of reasonableness is satisfied.

Two final points to note with exemption clauses are that under Section 5 the manufacturer of goods ordinarily supplied for private use or consumption cannot by a contract term or notice exclude liability in negligence for loss or damage from the defective goods he has manufactured. In the Misrepresentation Act 1967, which was amended by the Unfair Contract Terms Act 1977, any term which seeks to exclude or restrict liability for misrepresentation is of no effect unless it satisfies the requirement of reasonableness.

RESERVATION OF TITLE

Section 19 of the Sale of Goods Act 1979 allows the seller in a contract of sale of specific goods to reserve the right of disposal of the goods until certain conditions are fulfilled. In such a case, notwithstanding the delivery of the goods to the buyer, the property in the goods does not pass to the buyer until the conditions imposed by the seller are fulfilled.

By use of this provision a seller may reserve his title to goods even though they have been delivered to the buyer. Reservation of title clauses in contracts vary greatly in their particular words. What they basically set out to do is to retain ownership of the goods until the seller is paid. In addition, they may require the buyer to keep in a separate banking account the money from the sale of the goods and to mark and store the goods separately from other goods.

The use of reservation of title clauses has become standard commercial practice in the last 20 years. The matter first came before the courts in the case of *Aluminium Industrie Vaassen BV v Romalpa Aluminium Ltd* 1976, usually referred to as the Romalpa case. Aluminium Industrie (AIV) sold aluminium foil to Romalpa subject to a reservation of title clause. The clause reserved ownership of the foil until AIV were paid, claimed ownership if the foil was mixed with other material, and specified that money received from the sale of the foil was to be held to be accountable to AIV. Romalpa became insolvent and a receiver was appointed. Romalpa owed AIV over £100,000. The unused foil had a value of over £50,000 and some £35,000 was identifiable as money received from the sale of the foil. The Court of Appeal was asked to rule on the effectiveness of AIV's reservation of title clause. Their decision was that the clause was effective. The clause entitled AIV to reclaim the foil which had not been used. The receiver could not retain the foil since Romalpa did not own it. The sum of £35,000 could also be claimed by AIV since this was a sum of money which was clearly identifiable in a separate bank account as derived from the sale of the foil and from no other source.

Since this case similar clauses have been referred to as Romalpa clauses but not all have followed the same working exactly. The approach of the courts is that the particular words in the clauses determine their effectiveness and their extent in application.

The question of the effectiveness of a reservation of title clause when the goods are mixed with others to form a different object was considered by the Court of Appeal in the case of *Borden (UK) Ltd v Scottish Timber Products Ltd* 1979. Borden supplied resin to Scottish Timber for use in the manufacture of chipboard. The contract of supply contained a reservation of title clause. Borden supplied the resin on a regular basis and knew that it would be used within a few days of delivery. Scottish Timber became insolvent and over £300,000 was owed to Borden. Borden made claim under the clause to be entitled to part of the value of the chipboard for the resin used in its manufacture. This claim was rejected. The Court of Appeal rejected the claim on the ground that there was no claim to the chipboard. Borden knew that the resin would be incorporated into the chipboard shortly after delivery. When that occurred it lost its separate identity. It was then not possible to call for its return.

In addition to reservation to title clauses, there are provisions in standard forms of contract used in the construction industry which deal with the ownership of goods. Clause 16 of the JCT 1980 Edition states that when goods have been paid for by the employer in an interim certificate the ownership of the goods passes to the employer. This provision seems simple and straightforward but its application in practice may well not be so. This is to be seen from the decision of the High Court in *Dawber Williamson Roofing Ltd v Humberside County Council* 1979. Here a contract was made using the JCT 1963 Edition, which contained a clause similar to Clause 16 in the JCT 1980 Edition. The main contractor made a sub-contract with Dawber Williamson for the roofing work. The sub-contract acknowledged that the sub-contractor had knowledge of the provisions in the main contract. Dawber Williamson brought a large quantity of slates on to the site. The value of these was included in an interim certificate and paid to the main contractor. The main contractor, however, did not pay the sub-contractor and shortly afterwards became insolvent. The employer then made claim to the slates on the basis of the payment made and the clause in the contract. The High Court rejected the employer's claim. The reason for this decision was that the judge was satisfied that Dawber Williamson had not sold the slates since the sub-contract was a supply and fix contract. This being so there had not been any transfer of title to the main contractor which the employer could then acquire by the interim certificate payment. The council which had prevented Dawber Williamson from removing the slates was ordered to release them and to pay damages for their unlawful retention.

As will be appreciated, the matter of the use and effectiveness of reservation of title clauses depends on the exact wording of the clauses and the circumstances. A ruling from the House of Lords on this topic could well remove the uncertainty which exists at present.

10 EMPLOYMENT LAW

INTRODUCTION

Employment law is one of the most important branches of law the practising builder has to deal with. It is also complex and, unfortunately, changes at frequent intervals.

At one time the contract of employment was a matter almost entirely to be decided by the employer and employee. The intervention by the state was limited to legislation as a safety measure for those working in factories. Gradually the state intervened more and more to protect employees. There was an increased recognition that the employer and employee were not in an equal bargaining position in the making of a contract of employment. This meant that the contract of employment was not just a common law matter but that various statutory provisions were included.

We now have employment law where the greater part is in the form of statute law. The principal act is the Employment Protection (Consolidation) Act 1978, as amended. This provides the main form of protection for the ordinary worker. For the more senior worker the common law aspects of his contract of employment often give greater rights than the statutory provisions even though they apply to him just as they apply to the ordinary worker.

Before we examine employment law in detail it is appropriate to remember that this law applies only in a contract of employment. A contract of self-employment is one which, in the main, is not affected by employment law. In the construction industry, with its extensive use of self-employed operatives and others, the distinction between these two forms of contract is of great importance.

COMMON LAW PROVISIONS IN A CONTRACT OF EMPLOYMENT

The common law provisions which might exist in a contract of employment are: express terms, incorporated terms and implied terms. In some respects the status of the employee determines which of these will apply to the contract. The more senior employee is likely to have express terms in a written contract, whereas the operative on a site is likely to be subject to terms which are incorporated into his contract from an agreement made between his union and the employer. With both types of employee implied terms are applicable but their application will depend on the status of the employee.

Express terms

Express terms are those the parties have put in the contract. Usually they will be set out in a written document but they may be in a contract made by word of mouth. The written contract may be one which has been specially prepared for a particular employee or it may be a standard document used by the employer for all those employees whose status does not justify specially prepared contracts. A contract by word of mouth can be a less satisfactory arrangement since it may give rise to difficulty in the future from the parties' misunderstanding of what was agreed some time earlier.

The express terms usually inserted in a written contract include hours of work, responsibilities and rights to such benefits as a car, life insurance and medical insurance. The remuneration payable would be set out in some detail if bonuses and commissions were to be payable in addition to a salary.

An express term which is being used increasingly is that which restricts the employee from working for a competitor for a period of time after leaving his employment. This is known as a restrictive covenant. It is based on the House of Lords decision in *Nordenfelt v Maxim Nordenfelt Guns and Ammunition Co Ltd* 1894. In this case Nordenfelt, who was an extremely successful manufacturer of guns and ammunition, sold his business for a large sum of money. At the same time he entered into a restrictive covenant not to engage, directly or indirectly, for the next 25 years in any similar business. Despite this covenant two years later he went back into the same line of business in direct competition with the company. The House of Lords decided that the main provisions in the covenant should be upheld so as to restrict Nordenfelt. In their decision the Law Lords decided that a restrictive covenant would be void unless it satisfied the test of reasonableness. This test contains two rules:

1) That the restraint must be shown not to be unreasonable in the public interest.
2) That the restraint must be shown to be not unreasonable between the parties having regard to their interests.

The application of these rules is a matter for the courts to decide having regard to the circumstances of individual cases. From recent decisions of the courts it seems that a restraint of not more than one year will be accepted as reasonable. The area over which the restraint is to apply depends on individual circumstances. In one case concerning an estate agent in North London a restraint over an area of one mile from the employer's office was accepted as reasonable. The court, however, indicated that if the distance had been more than one mile it would probably be unreasonable.

A breach of a covenant by a former employee can be restrained by court order. This may be seen in the Court of Appeal decision in *Evening Standard Co Ltd v Henderson* 1986. In this case Henderson had been a production manager for 17 years. He was subject to a restraint in his contract not to work for other than the company and to devote his entire interests to the company. Although this was not strictly a restrictive covenant since its purpose was to restrain the employee during his employment and not when he left his employment its principle is similar. Another term in the contract was that Henderson had to give one years notice to terminate his employment. He accepted an offer from the proprietor of a new newspaper. He then gave his employers two months notice instead of the 12 months to terminate his employment. When his employers learnt of his intention to work for what would be a competitor they sought an injunction to restrain him from leaving before the period under his contract had expired. In general the courts will not grant an injunction which restrains a person and puts him in the position of either having to continue to work for his employers or not to work and then being idle or starve. In this case because the employers offered to pay Henderson his full salary and provide the other benefits under his contract until the one years notice expired the court was prepared to grant an injunction. Furthermore, the employers were willing to have him to continue to work. In all these circumstances the making of an injunction restraining him from working for a present or future competitor was appropriate.

An express term of importance to the construction industry is that requiring the employee to work where the employer may need him to work. Without such a term an employer would have difficulty in proving that it was a contractual requirement that his employees should go anywhere in the country to work for the employer. To secure this it would be necessary to prove that that was implied in the contract, which would be difficult to do.

An example of this difficulty came in the case of *O'Brien v Associated Fire Alarms Ltd* 1969 which was decided by the Court of Appeal. Here O'Brien was one of four employees who were employed at the Liverpool branch office of the company. The company was a national organisation with branches throughout the country. O'Brien had joined the company at the Liverpool office and his contract did not require him to work from any other branch. He had been employed for some years at Liverpool and although he travelled in the area immediately outside Liverpool he was always able to return home each evening. When work declined in the Liverpool area he and the other employees were asked to go and work in the Cumberland area. This would mean that O'Brien would be able to get home at weekends only. O'Brien and the others refused to move and they were dismissed. O'Brien claimed that the dismissal was for redundancy and so a redundancy payment was due. This was disputed by the company. Their view was that there was an implied term in the contract that the employees would work outside the Liverpool area. The court refused to accept this, holding that the only implied term was that they should work within an area which allowed them to return home each evening.

Incorporated terms

Employees frequently work under a contract of employment where the terms of their employment are contained in some other document. These terms are incorporated into the contract of employment by express incorporation or implied incorporation.

Express incorporation arises when there is a term in the contract of employment which states that the provisions in, say, some national agreement are to apply to the contract.

An example of this is seen in the Court of Appeal decision in *National Coal Board v Galley* 1958. Here Galley was a coal mine deputy and was a member of a trade union, the National Association of Collier Overmen and Deputies and Shotfirers. The union negotiated pay and working conditions for deputies. In 1947 the union agreed with the Board that the deputies would work reasonable overtime if so required. Galley in 1949 agreed with the Board by a written agreement that his contract of employment should be regulated by the national agreement. The agreement was amended in 1952 and this included a requirement that the deputies would be paid a fixed wage without any extra payment for weekend working. Weekend working became necessary and this resulted in the miners, who were paid hourly, earning considerably more than the deputies. Galley and other deputies refused to work weekends and the Board sued for breach of contract. The court decided that Galley's contract was regulated by the national agreement. He had worked to the terms of the national agreement and so accepted them. The agreement was meant to have a binding effect and this meant that there had been a breach of contract by Galley.

In the construction industry the terms incorporated are those in the Working Rule Agreement which is made by the National Joint Council for the Building Industry. The Agreement lays down the principles which govern the terms and conditions in the industry with provision for regional variations.

Implied incorporation arises where both the employer and the employee, without expressly agreeing to incorporation, act in such a manner that it must be taken to be the case that there has been incorporation. This may be seen to be so when the employer pays and the employee expects that the hourly rate of pay, holidays and others matters which affect the contract will be the same as in the Working Rule Agreement.

Implied terms

From the relationship which exists between an employer and employee when a contract of employment is made various duties are implied. Both employer and employee are subject to these implied duties. A breach of these duties will be treated as a breach of the contract of employment.

Duty to provide work

It is accepted as a duty on the employer's part to allow the employee to earn the expected remuneration. A less certain matter is whether the employer is under a duty to provide work. Some case law suggests that it is sufficient if the employer pays the employee his salary; there is no obligation to provide work. Some judges, however, believe that there can be a duty to provide work. The basis for this belief is that some highly skilled employees need to have full opportunity to work if their careers are not to suffer. This question arises with senior employees who have to give lengthy periods of notice. The employer does not want the employee to continue to work since this could mean that up-to-date confidential information could be made known to the employee. This would be harmful to the employer. The employer, therefore, will pay the employee not to work.

Duty to work

The employee is under several obligations implied at common law under his contract of employment. One is that his contract is one of personal service. That is, that it is the employee only who is to perform the work and no one else. The justification for this implied term is that the employer selected the employee, on a personal basis, to work for him. To have the work done by someone else is unacceptable.

The employee must be ready and willing to work. This means that the employee must turn up for work at the agreed place and at the agreed time and undertake the work his contract requires of him. If, therefore, an employee fails to turn up for work for some unacceptable reason he is in breach of his contract and the employer may treat that breach as ending the contract. Breach of this obligation arises when employees go on strike or take other industrial action such as 'go-slow'. When either of these two actions occur the employer may dismiss the employees for breach of contract, if the employer so chooses. To take this action could have the most serious of consequences to an employer since he could lose his entire labour force many of whom would be highly trained and skilled. When, therefore, an employer is faced with a strike or industrial action he may, as an attempt to get his employees back to work and working properly, serve them with notices informing them of his intention, after a stated date, of treating their actions as ending their contracts of employment. This puts the position fairly to the employees so that they can then decide whether to stop their actions and return to work or whether to continue their actions. It is also a measure which strengthens the employer's position if an employee should contest the action on the ground that the employer had broken the contract.

The House of Lords decision in *Miles v Wakefield Metropolitan District Council* 1987 gives some guidance on the matter of industrial action. Miles was a superintendent registrar of marriages, deaths and births. His duties included working on Saturday mornings. As part of a national action with regard to salary increases he refused to work on Saturday mornings. This refusal went on for more than a year despite the employer's threat to withhold payment for the time not worked on Saturday mornings. Eventually the employer deducted part of Miles' salary. Miles then brought an action claiming payment of the salary withheld. The action failed. The Law Lords decided that his failure to be ready and willing to work deprived him of his right to payment. He had refused to perform the full duties of his employment.

A further obligation is to obey all reasonable orders which come within the scope of his duties under the contract. All such orders must be ones which come within the contract. An order to commit a crime is an order which is outside the contract since no contract can lawfully require that. What constitutes an unreasonable order must depend on the individual circumstances. For example, an operative who refused to go on a scaffold because he considered it unsafe would be acting properly if the scaffold was unsafe; if not then he was refusing a reasonable order. An example of refusal of an employer's order is the decision of the National Industrial Relations Court (now the Employment Appeal Tribunal) in the case of *Morrish v Henlys (Folkestone) Ltd* 1973. Here Morrish was a stores driver who drew diesel oil for his vehicle from his employer's pumps as the need arose. Three times he drew five gallons of diesel oil and entered that on his monthly fuel invoice. He later discovered that each of these entries had been altered to seven gallons. The alterations had been made by the manager. Morrish was told that the alteratons had been made to cover a deficiency. Morrish refused to accept an entry which showed two gallons more than the true amount. He was told that if he did not accept the alterations he would be dismissed. He was dismissed. He was awarded £100 compensation by an industrial tribunal. The tribunal, however, had reduced the amount awarded because they thought that Morrish had contributed to his dismissal by not accepting the manager's assurance. The court refused to accept that the employee had acted unreasonably in refusing to obey the order to falsify the fuel record. He was fully entitled to refuse to be a party to such falsification. The tribunal had acted incorrectly. As a result of the court's decision the employers re-engaged Morrish.

Duty to co-operate

A recent development by the courts has been a willingness to accept that the relationship of employer and employee has an implied term that the parties are under a duty to co-operate. In the main this is an obligation on the employee. The duty has arisen when a company needed to change, in some respect, the nature of its business. When economic difficulties put companies at risk it may be necessary to change the nature, size and location of the businesses. The employees are, in these circumstances, expected to co-operate in the changes. In the case of *Sim v Rotherham Metropolitan Borough Council* 1986 the refusal of a teacher to cover a class for 35 minutes in the absence of another teacher led to a deduction of salary. When she sued for payment of her full salary her claim was dismissed. The court decided that the nature of her contract and professional responsibilities required her to co-operate in the running of the school. Her action failed.

The duty to co-operate is linked closely with the duty to maintain mutual confidence and trust. This last duty falls on the employer as well as the employee. The Court of Appeal in the case of *Woods v W. M. Car Services (Peterborough) Ltd* 1981 had to deal with a claim made by Mrs Woods of unfair dismissal. The company was taken over and the new employers in their staff assessment took the view that Mrs Woods' position as secretary and accounts clerk was overpaid and carried an unjustified position of seniority. They, therefore, told Mrs Woods that she would be required to accept a pay reduction and a change in status. This she refused and left claiming that she had been constructively dismissed. The court decided that she had not been dismissed. In the judgment the court indicated the importance of maintaining mutual trust and confidence between employer and employee. Persistent attempts by the employer to vary the employee's conditions under the contract would destroy or damage this trust and confidence. On the employee's part it was not acceptable for an employee to wrongfully refuse to accept a change in employment conditions so as to allow his employer to improve his business.

Duty not to harm the employer's business interests

This is an important duty which covers several topics and is of increasing importance with the employer's confidential information available to a large number of staff.

A requirement under this duty is to work only for the employer in the employer's time. Clearly to work for another when being paid by an employer is disloyal and possibly dishonest. Few would disagree that in this circumstance an employer would be justified in dismissing the employee. A less certain position is where an employee works outside his contractual hours of work. In general courts are reluctant to impose any restriction on an employee working in his own time. To restrict an employee would be an unreasonable restraint in most cases. An exception to this is where an employee when working in his own time could harm his employer's business interests. The leading case on this exception is *Hivac Ltd v Park Royal Scientific Instruments Ltd* 1946. Here employees of Hivac were engaged in highly skilled work with hearing aids. They went and worked at the weekends at a competitor, Park Royal, doing the same work. Hivac thought that this put their trade secrets at risk and sought an injunction to restrain Park Royal from employing the workers at weekends. The Court of Appeal granted an injunction even though there was no evidence of Hivac's employees misusing knowledge they had of their employer's trade secrets. The mere danger of wrongful disclosure was sufficient to justify an injunction being granted.

The most recent development in protecting the employer's business interests is the protection of the employer's confidential information. This is information which does not come within the classification of trade secrets. The case which dealt in some detail with confidential information is *Faccenda Chicken Ltd v Fowler* 1986. Fowler occupied a position as a sales manager with the company. This position meant that he knew of the company's policy of purchases, sales and pricing of the chickens they sold. He left and formed his own company in the same business. The employers sought to restrain him on the ground that he was in breach of an implied term not to use confidential information. The Court of Appeal refused to restrain Fowler since it considered that what Fowler knew was not confidential information. The court gave guidance by stating that an employee who habitually handled confidential information could be under a higher obligation than other employees; that material which required protection would be protected and that only; and where the employer had impressed on the employee the confidentiality of the material.

All employees are under a duty not to make secret profits or to take bribes. Any such sums may be recovered by the employer from the employee since the legal position is that such sums were only obtained because of the employer and employee relationship. The opportunity to make secret profits usually arises when an employee is in a position to place contracts with suppliers. Bribes would arise when payment were made in order to obtain information of a confidential nature.

Employer's duty to employees for their safety

This is a most important implied duty since it is the main ground on which an injured employee will sue the employer in order to recover damages for injuries suffered. The other ground, which is frequently used with this breach of duty of care, is the tort of breach of statutory duty. The use of this was seen in the case of *Ferguson v John Dawson and Partners (Contractors) Ltd* 1976 considered earlier.

Before considering the extent of the duty it is necessary to understand that the duty is that of the employer and that it cannot be delegated to another. This fact was emphasised by the House of Lords in the case of *McDermid v Nash Dredging and Reclamation Co Ltd* 1987 where McDermid was injured on a tugboat. The tugboat operated on two shifts, turn and turn about. On one turn there was an English master and on the other a Dutch master. Nash Dredging was a subsidiary company of a company called Stevin Baggeren. The Dutch master was an employee of Stevin and it was whilst he was in control of the boat that McDermid was injured. The defence of Nash Dredging was that at the time the accident happened the tugboat was under the control of the Dutch master who was not an employee of Nash Dredging. This, it was claimed, meant that if anyone was liable it was the Dutch master and his employer. The House of Lords rejected this, holding that the employer's duty of care was non-delegable and was a personal duty. McDermid's claim succeeded against Nash Dredging.

The decision in McDermid's case was applied by the Court of Appeal in *Morris v Breaveglen Ltd (trading as Anzac Construction Co)* 1992. The facts of the case were that Breaveglen was the employer of Morris. Under a labour only contract Morris was sent to work on a site for a main contractor, Sleeman Construction Ltd. On a previous contract Morris had been permitted by his employers to drive a dumper truck even though he had not been give proper instruction in its use. In the sub-contract with Sleeman Breaveglen bound themselves to observe and perform all safety obligations at common law and statute. They also agreed to maintain employer's liability insurance. Whilst working for Sleeman Morris offered to drive their dumper truck. Whilst doing this the truck turned over and Morris was injured. When legal proceedings started Breaveglen pleaded that when the accident happened Morris was Sleeman's employee for the work he was doing and that Sleeman was responsible for his safety. The Court of Appeal applied the reasoning in McDermid's case and held Breaveglen to be liable. Morris was their employee. That responsibility could not be delegated. They had permitted Morris to drive a dumper truck earlier without proper instruction, which was a contravention of the Contruction (General Provisions) Regulations 1961. This was a breach of their statutory duty to Morris. They also had failed to provide a safe system of work at common law.

A further example of the employer's personal responsibility is seen in the case of *Driver v William Willett (Contractors) Ltd* 1969. Here Willetts were building contractors who contracted with a firm of safety consultants for them to advise Willetts as to what was needed to comply with the law on their building sites. This made the firm safety advisers under regulations then in force, the Building (Safety, Health and Welfare) Regulations 1948. On a site where Driver worked a practice arose of using a hoist in an unsafe way when moving scaffold boards. One scaffold board fell and struck Driver, seriously injuring him. The site had been visited by the safety advisers whilst this unsafe practice was being followed, but they had not drawn Willetts' attention to the matter. Driver sued his employers and the safety advisers. The court decided that both were liable to Driver to the extent of 60 per cent by the safety consultants and 40 per cent by the employers. Willetts then were held to be entitled to recover from the safety consultants the amount they had been ordered to pay Driver. This was for breach of contract by the consultants.

Elements of the duty of care The House of Lords in the case of *Wilsons and Clyde Coal Co v English* 1938 decided that the employer's duty of care was made up of:

(1) the provision of competent staff;
(2) the provision of proper premises and plant; and
(3) the provision of a safe system of work.

In assessing the duty of care the courts use this approach.

Competent staff The simplest example of this requirement is that an employer must not appoint a person to operate machinery without proper training. To put an untrained person in charge of a crane on a construction site would be a failure by the employer. That appointment would put others at risk. Another example would be to make use of an untrained scaffolder. The extent to which the duty applies may be seen from the case of *Hudson v Ridge Manufacturing Co Ltd* 1957. Here the employers had a worker who indulged in foolish horseplay whilst at work. His fellow workers complained to their foreman who then warned the worker about his conduct. Despite this warning the worker's horseplay continued.

Hudson was undertaking his work when he was knocked down by the worker's horseplay and broke his wrist. He was successful in his claim against his employers. The employers had, by reason of the complaint to the foreman, knowledge of their employee's conduct. The warning had been inadequate and so the employers were liable.

Proper premises and plant Under this obligation the employer must ensure that the premises where his employees work are reasonably safe. This obligation applies whether or not the employer owns the premises where the employee works. Clearly the premises owned by the employer are more easily controlled with regard to safety. Other premises not so owned are still ones where the employer has responsibilities. In the case of *Wilson v Tyneside Window Cleaning Co* 1958 the Court of Appeal expressed the view that whilst it was acceptable for an employer to send an employee to a private house to carry out a work of repair without first checking the safety of the premises this was not so with other types of premises.

An example of the application of this obligation on a contractor is in the case of *Clay v A. J. Crump and Sons Ltd* 1964. The facts here were that in the course of demolition work, prior to new construction, a wall was left standing with little support. The main contractors, Crump and Sons, came on the site. A hut was erected for storage and for the operatives to take their meals. This was positioned near to the wall. A few days later the wall fell on the hut whilst Clay and two others were taking a meal. Clay was seriously injured and the two others killed. Clay sued the architect, the demolition contractor and his employers. His claim against his employers was based on their failure to provide proper premises. The premises were not reasonably safe for the employees. Clay's claim was successful against all he sued.

In the case of equipment the employer must provide equipment that is appropriate in the circumstances. We saw earlier in the case of *Paris v Stepney Borough Council* 1951 that an employer was held to be liable to an employee who lost the sight of his one good eye because of the failure to provide him with protective goggles. The fact that goggles were not normally provided for such work was no defence since the employer knew of the employee's disability. The employer is not required to do more than is reasonable in order to comply with the common law; with statutory provisions the position may be different. In the case of *Davie v New Merton Board Mills Ltd* 1959 an employer was held not to be liable when a tool provided for an employee broke and injured him. The tool, which was brittle from excessive hardening, had no readily detectable signs of being unsafe. Moreover it has been purchased from a reputable supplier. As a result of this decision, which deprived the injured employee of any common law damages for his injury, Parliament passed the

Employer's Liability (Defective Equipment) Act 1969. This Act provides that if a piece of equipment provided by an employer for the use of an employee has a defect which was not the fault of the employer then, if an employee is injured, the employer is liable. This is so even though the defect cannot be detected by any reasonable examination. An employer who is held to be liable under the Act may be able to recover the amount the court has awarded from the manufacturer or supplier.

Safe system of work   This obligation imposes on an employer a duty to so arrange the work that it can be done safely. This obligation can take various forms. Basically it is not sufficient to provide proper premises and plant and staff. The premises and plant with the staff must work together so as to carry out the work safely.

The leading case on this duty is the House of Lords decision in *General Cleaning Contractors Ltd v Christmas* 1953 where an experienced window cleaner made a claim against his employers for the injuries he suffered when he fell from a window-sill. Christmas was sent to work at some premises where his employers had a contract to clean the windows. At one position it was not possible for him to use a ladder and there was no provision for using a safety belt. Christmas, therefore, stood on a narrow sill holding with one hand a sash of the window. This moved unexpectedly causing Christmas to lose his balance and fall some distance. In answer to Christmas's claim for damages the employers contended that they were entitled to rely on an experienced worker to take appropriate steps to look to his own safety, and as it was not a building they owned they had no right to fix securing bolts so that safety belts could be used. The House of Lords accepted that the employers had no right to fix securing belts but nevertheless held them to be liable to Christmas. The employers were not entitled to leave to an employee, no matter how skilled and experienced the employee might be, the responsibility for arranging adequate and safe methods for carrying out the work. It was the employers' responsibility to provide a safe system of work and this they had failed to do. Christmas was successful with his claim.

A further House of Lords decision of interest is that of *Boyle v Kodak Ltd* 1969. Boyle was a skilled experienced painter who was used to working from ladders. He was sent to paint an oil storage tank. Under regulations then in force both Boyle and his employers were under a statutory duty to see that the ladder was safely lashed at the top before working from it. Although Boyle could have secured the top of the ladder by making use of an external metal staircase on the tank, he climbed the ladder instead. He fell when the ladder moved and suffered injuries for which he sued his employers. His claim was rejected by the High Court and the Court of Appeal but was successful before the House of Lords. The employers' defence was that they were entitled to assume that a skilled and experienced man would have knowledge of and comply with the statutory requirements. The Law Lords accepted that Boyle believed that what he was doing was normal procedure. Although he was aware of the regulations he either had not studied them or had failed to understand them. The employers ought to have realised that there was a substantial risk that a skilled man might not know of the regulations sufficiently to prevent a breach. It was the duty of employers to instruct employees with regard to the regulations so as to prevent a breach. Boyle's claim was successful but he was held to be 50 per cent contributorily negligent.

The House of Lords decision in *McWilliams v Sir William Arrol and Co Ltd and Another* 1962 shows that because an accident happens from what appears to be a breach of duty it does not necessarily follow that a successful claim may be made against the employer. The facts in the case were that McWilliams, an experienced steel erector, was fixing a staging on the tower of a tower crane from which others were to work. Without anyone witnessing the accident he fell to the ground killing himself. Part of the staging he was erecting was found on the ground suggesting that part of the staging had collapsed. McWilliams had not been wearing a safety belt and no belt was available for him to have used if in fact he had chosen to wear one. McWilliams' past work practice was that he had very seldom been known to use a safety belt. When his widow sued, the House of Lords treated the practice of McWilliams' not wearing a safety belt as being of the utmost importance. They were satisfied that even if there had been a breach of duty of care by the employers that was not the cause of the accident. McWilliams would not have worn a safety belt even if one had been available. That fact defeated his widow's claim.

Making a claim for damages

An injured employee may sue his employer for either breach of duty of care under his contract or breach of statutory duty or both. The great advantage of suing for breach of statutory duty is that once it can be shown that the statutory provision applies to the employee it is easier to prove the case. In the case of a breach of duty under the contract, as we have seen, the question of reasonable care is a matter which may defeat the claim.

In an action by an injured employee the defences considered earlier may be used by the employer. It must not be forgotten that in such a claim the burden of proof lies on the employee. He has to prove his claim and if he fails to do so the employer has won. The two usual defences used by employers are contributory negligence and *volenti non fit injuria*. As we saw earlier, if it is that the plaintiff in some way contributed to the accident which caused him the injuries for which he is making his claim then the provisions in the Law Reform (Contributory Negligence) Act 1945 apply. The court, therefore, will reduce the amount awarded by the percentage which is attributable to the fault of the plaintiff. The percentage is fixed by the judge having heard the evidence. In claims for industrial accidents, especially when the employee is an experienced worker, deduction of 50 per cent is not unusual. *Volenti non fit injuria* is a defence which is seldom successful in a claim by an employee against his employer. The courts are reluctant to accept that an employee volunteered to run a risk. If the circumstances are similar to those in *Imperial Chemical Industries Ltd v Shatwell* 1965, considered earlier, then the defence may succeed. Otherwise the defence will fail.

In making a claim for personal injuries the Limitation Act 1980 requires that the action shall be started within three years of the date of the accident. This means that the writ must be issued before the three years has expired.

Since the passing by Parliament of the Courts and Legal Services Act 1990 the jurisdiction of the county courts has been extended to allow claims for personal injuries to be made up to £50,000. Above this amount the claim must be made in the High Court.

The Employers' Liability (Compulsory Insurance) Act 1969 requires that employers shall have insurance cover for not less than £2 million to meet any claim made against them. The insurance must be with approved British insurers. The Act requires that terms and conditions which would normally apply in insurance policies, which would allow the insurers to avoid liability, shall not deprive employees of the protection of the insurance cover. It is a criminal offence not to have the required insurance cover.

STATUTORY TERMS IN A CONTRACT OF EMPLOYMENT

The Employment Protection (Consolidation) Act 1978, as amended, includes a number of provisions which protect those employees to whom the Act applies. These provisions provide rights for the employee at the beginning of the employment, during it and at its end if the question of unfair dismissal arises.

Written particulars of terms of employment

Sections 1 to 5 deal with the duty of the employer to provide stated information to the employee. This duty arises at once with an employee working more than 16 hours a week. In the case of an employee who works less than 16 hours but more than 8 hours a week the employee has to satisfy a qualifying period of five years before he becomes entitled to the information.

The employer is required, not later than 13 weeks after the beginning of the employee's employment, to provide the employee with a written statement. The statement has to:

(a) identify the parties;
(b) specify the date when the employment began;
(c) specify the date on which the employee's period of continuous employment began (taking into account any employment with a previous employer which counts towards that period).

The purpose of these provisions is to indicate the parties to a contract (in the past there were difficulties with employees of groups of companies); specify the stating date of employing, which determines the start of qualifying periods under the Act; and specify the start of employment taking into account a change in employer, this covers a 'take-over' of a company.

The employer must also provide the following information which is to be based on the position not more than one week before the information is given. The purpose of this provision is to ensure that the employee is provided with up-to-date information. The information required is:

(a) the scale or rate of remuneration, or the method of calculating remuneration;
(b) the intervals at which remuneration is paid (that is, whether weekly or monthly or by some other period);
(c) any terms and conditions relating to hours of work (including any terms and conditions relating to normal working hours);
(d) any terms and conditions relating to –
  (i) entitlement to holidays, including public holidays, and holiday pay (the particulars given being sufficient to enable the holiday pay, on the termination of employment, to be precisely calculated);
  (ii) incapacity for work due to sickness or injury, including any provision for sick pay;
  (iii) pensions and pension schemes;
(e) the length of notice which the employee is obliged to give and entitled to receive to determine his contract of employment; and
(f) the title of the job which the employee is employed to do.

Requirements (a) and (b) inform the employee of the essential matters concerning payment for his services. Under (a) the employee is to be told of the arrangements, if any, as to payment by bonuses or commission. Under (c) the employee is to be told of the hours of work, including whether or not overtime is required and, if so, any limitation of the overtime an employee may be called upon to work. Under (d) the requirement as to holidays includes the provision that entitlement is to be capable of precise calculation; this allows an employee who leaves his employment to receive payment for holiday he is entitled to but has not taken. The provision as to sick pay does not place an obligation to have a sick pay scheme but if there is one details must be provided. The same comment applies to a pension scheme. Under (e) the period of notice has to be specified. In practice this depends on the seniority of the employee. A senior employee might have to give and be entitled to three months notice or more to end the contract of employment. Under (f) the requirement as to the title of the job seeks to avoid difficulties by clarifying what the employee is employed to do.

The statement must also specify the disciplinary rules applying to employees. The person must be specified to whom an employee can apply to question disciplinary action taken against him or to whom he may apply to have any grievance redressed. Any further actions are to be explained and if that information is in a document it is to be reasonably accessible. Health and safety matters are not to be included in disciplinary decisions, grievances or procedures.

Where there are no particulars to be entered then this fact has to be stated. So if there is no pension scheme this fact must be stated. It is not sufficient to make no comment on that matter.

The Act allows these requirements to be satisfied by reference to some other document which the employee can read in the course of his employment or have reasonable access to.

If there should be a change in the terms of employment, then the employee is to be informed of the change not later than one month after the change. This provision does not have to be observed if in the original statement it was stated that any change would be entered in another document. This covers changes agreed in working rules agreements.

If an employer does not provide a written statement which complies with the requirements, the employee may require that the matter be referred to an industrial tribunal. The tribunal may issue a statement as if it had been made by the employer or remedy a statement issued but found to be inadequate.

Guarantee payment

A number of industries have systems of guarantee payments to employees. One such is that in the NJC for the Building Industry in the Working Rules Agreement. Where the employee does not have this protection the Employment Protection (Consolidation) Act 1978 provisions apply. In brief, these entitle an employee to a guarantee payment provided the absence of work for the employee to do is by reason of a reduction in the need for work the employee is employed to do, or some other occurrence which affects the normal working of the employer's business in relation to the employee's work. No claim can be made for days which would be holidays or days on which work would not normally be done. There is an obligation on the employee to accept alternative work, provided it is suitable in all the circumstances.

The amount of guarantee payment is fixed in the Act as, at present, for each day not exceeding £14.10. This amount can be amended by the Secretary of State. The number of days an employee can claim under the provision, in general, is five. This number may not be exceeded in any period of three months. The right to this payment does not affect the employee's right to payment under his contract of employment. If, however, any guarantee payment is made that goes towards meeting any contractual requirement. An employee who believes that his employer has failed to pay the whole or part of a guarantee payment to which he is entitled may complain to an industrial tribunal. The complaint must be made within three months of the day when the payment was due but not paid.

Time off rights

The law recognizes that there are certain circumstances where it would be right for an employee to take time off his work and in limited cases be paid for the time away from his work. Under the Trade Union and Labour Relations (Consolidation) Act 1992 officials of recognised trade unions are entitled to time off from their work, without loss of pay, so as to allow them to carry out their duties and to receive relevant training. The trade union official's duties must be ones which concern the employer on matters which could be a trade dispute. The time off for training must also be for matters associated with the employer's business. There are also some circumstances where a trade union official may take time off from his work but without payment. An example of this would be the official's attendance at a national or regional meeting of his union. An official who believes that he has wrongly been refused time off may make a complaint to an industrial tribunal. The tribunal may order payment to be made.

Under the Employment Protection (Consolidation) Act 1978 employees are entitled to reasonable time off, without pay, for carrying out a number of specified public duties. The usual public duties which require employees to be absent are membership of a local council and acting as a magistrate. Again a complaint may be made within three months to an industrial tribunal.

Also under the 1978 Act an employee who has been dismissed is entitled to time off to look for work or to make arrangements for training. The employee must have had two years employment continuously with the employer. The time off, which is with pay, is to be a reasonable period. Unreasonable refusal to allow the employee to have time off or to pay him may be dealt with by an industrial tribunal. A complaint must be made within three months of the day when time off should have been allowed.

Notice to terminate the employment
At common law either party to a contract of employment may give the other that period of notice the contract stipulates. The period of notice is that that the parties agreed when forming the contract of employment. The period fixed is usually related to the importance and seniority of the employee. As we saw in the case of *Evening Standard Co Ltd v Henderson* 1986 a senior manager in a highly competitive business had a 12 month period of notice in his contract. For most employees one months notice in writing is the usual period in the contract.

Where there is no express provision in a contract of employment then the period of notice has to be that that is reasonable in the circumstances. Guidance on this is to be had from the decision of the Court of Appeal in the case of *Hill v C. A. Parsons and Co Ltd* 1971 where a senior engineer with over 30 years service with his employers and within two years of his retirement was dismissed for the sole reason that he refused to leave his trade union and join the union his employers had recognised as the union with which it would deal to the exclusion of all others. The employers who were entirely satisfied with his services had been threatened with a strike unless he was dismissed. Hill was given one months notice. His contract did not contain any express term as to notice. The Court of Appeal held one months notice to be inadequate taking into account Hill's age, seniority and length of service. They said notice in his circumstances had to be at least six months and possibly as long as 12 months. Hill, therefore, obtained an injunction to restrain his employers from dismissing him on the one month notice.

It is important to note with this decision that, at common law, the employers were not acting incorrectly in dismissing Hill. Their mistake was in giving him notice which was too short in his own particular circumstances. His dismissal was wrongful in this respect only.

Unlike the statutory provisions in the Employment Protection (Consolidation) Act 1978 the common law allows either party to end the contract of employment provided what is done is within the contract. Not to do so is wrongful dismissal for which the dismissed employee may bring a claim for damages for breach of contract in the civil court.

It is permissible for either party to end the contract without giving notice if that is justified. The right to so act depends on one of the parties committing a fundamental breach of contract. So an employer can dismiss an employee without notice if the employee has committed an act of gross misconduct; that dismissal is not wrongful. What is gross misconduct depends on the circumstances. Actions such as dishonesty, disregard of safety requirements, putting others at risk and fighting have all been accepted as being of gross misconduct. In addition, an employer may indicate that a certain act will be considered to be gross misconduct and dealt with as such by the employer. A series of minor acts of misconduct could eventually lead to the employer being able to dismiss the employee without notice. This was the case in *Pepper v Webb* 1969 when a gardener had been inefficient over a period of time and, finally, spoke in an extremely insolent and offensive way to his employer and walked off. The employer was held by the Court of Appeal to have been justified in dismissing the employee without notice.

The problems associated with the ending of contracts of employment and the injustice of long-serving employees having no right to a longer period of notice than those with much shorter periods of service led Parliament to legislate to provide remedies. This was first done in the Contracts of Employment Act 1963 and now found in the Employment Protection (Consolidation) Act 1978, as amended.

Section 49 states:

(1) The notice required to be given by an employer to terminate the contract of employment of a person who has been continuously employed for one month or more –
   (a) shall be not less than one weeks notice if his period of continuous employment is less than two years;
   (b) shall be not less than one weeks notice for each year of continuous employment if his period of continuous employment is two years or more but less than 12 months; and
   (c) shall be not less than 12 weeks notice if his period of continuous employment is 12 years or more.
(2) The notice required to be given by an employee who has been continuously employed for one month or more to terminate his contract of employment shall be not less than one week.

As can be seen, the provisions entitle a dismissed employee to a period of notice which varies according to his length of service subject to a maximum of 12 weeks notice. The requirement that an employee need only give one weeks notice indicates that the provisions are to protect the employee and not the employer. The section also provides that if a person has been continuously employed for three months or more on contracts for one month or less then the provisions in the section apply. This prevents an employer getting round the requirements of the section by employing the employee on contracts of one month or less. If, however, the employee is employed for the performance of a specific task which is not expected to last for more than three months then the provisions do not apply, unless the employee has been continuously employed for more than three months.

The section also states that the provisions are not to affect the rights of either party to the contract to treat the contract as ended without notice by reason of the conduct of the other party. This allows either party to treat the gross misconduct of the other as justification of dismissal without notice or ending the contract without notice. It would otherwise be contrary to common sense and good employment practice to have to give, say, ten weeks notice or pay in lieu to an employee who has been discovered to have been dishonest to his employer for some time.

The final point to note with regard to these statutory provisions is that they are minimum periods of notice. If an employee is entitled under his contract of employment to a greater period of notice then that is what is to apply.

An employee who has been dismissed by his employer either with or without notice or by reason of his fixed term contract not being renewed under the same contract is entitled to a written statement giving the reasons for his dismissal. The written statement is to be provided within 14 days of the employee's request. In order to be entitled to this written statement the employee must have not less than two years continuous employment. An employee refused a statement or who believes the reasons given to be untrue or inadequate may make complaint to an industrial tribunal. The tribunal may then make a declaration as to what the reasons were for the dismissal and order the employer to pay the employees two weeks pay.

Unfair dismissal
The concept of unfair dismissal was introduced by Parliament in the Industrial Relations Act 1971. Before that Act the provisions with regard to dismissal were in the common law only. This meant that an employer could dismiss an employee however long his service for any reason at all or, indeed, for no reason. The unfairness of this and the belief that the relationship of employer and employee ought to be on a better basis caused Parliament to introduce the concept of unfair dismissal. The present provisions are in the Employment Protection (Consolidation) Act 1978, as amended.

Not all employees are qualified to make a claim for unfair dismissal. There is a qualifying period of two years for full-time employees and five years for part-time employees, that is those who work between eight and 16 hours a week. Also excluded are employees who are past the normal retiring age for employees in that position or, if there is no such normal retiring age, the age of 65 for both sexes; employees who ordinarily work outside Great Britain; share fishermen; the police; members of the armed forces and certain Crown servants.

Section 54 of the Act states that in every employment to which the Act applies every employee has the right not to be unfairly dismissed by his employer. This is the starting point of the unfair dismissal procedure in the Act. If an employee is excluded then these statutory provisions are not of assistance to him if he is dismissed. His remedy, if any, is at common law for wrongful dismissal.

Dismissal

In order to bring a claim for unfair dismissal it is necessary for the employee to show that he has been dismissed in one of the ways set out in Section 55 of the Act.

The relevant provisions in the section are:

(2) Subject to sub-section (3), an employee shall be treated as dismissed by his employer if, but only if, –
  (a) the contract under which he is employed by the employer is terminated by the employer, whether it is so terminated by notice or without notice, or
  (b) where under that contract he is employed for a fixed term, that term expires without being renewed under the same contract, or
  (c) the employee terminates that contract, with or without notice by reason of the employer's conduct.
(3) Where an employer gives notice to an employee to terminate his contract of employment and, at a time within the period of that notice, the employee gives notice to the employer to terminate the contract of employment on a date earlier than the date on which the employer's notice is due to expire, the employee shall for the purposes of this Part be taken to be dismissed by his employer, and the reasons for the dismissal shall be taken to be the reasons for which the employer's notice is given.

Under (a) no problem arises if the employer gives the employee proper notice of the termination of employment and this may be in writing or by word of mouth. Problems do arise, however, if the words used are not ones of clear dismissal. To be told to 'get your tool bag packed and get off the site' would leave a worker in no doubt that he had been dismissed. The main difficulty arises when strong and possibly obscene words are used in a heated argument between employee and employer.

Under (b) an employee is dismissed when his fixed term contract ends without renewal under that contract. The inclusion of this is to prevent employers having employees working for them on short fixed term contracts. When these end the employers could renew them. This practice could continue for years and, without the inclusion of (b), such employees would not be treated as dismissed. It is, however, permissible for an employee with a fixed term contract of one year or more to agree in writing to forego any rights to unfair dismissal.

Under (c) it is the employee who terminates the contract whether with or without notice by reason of the employer's conduct. This is known as 'constructive dismissal'. Parliament included this provision in order to prevent an employer in effect 'driving out' an employee by the employer's conduct. Without this provision the employee would be ending the employment and no question of unfair dismissal could arise. In the case of *Western Excavating (E.C.C) Ltd v Sharp* 1978 the Court of Appeal ruled that for there to be a 'constructive dismissal' the employee has to show that the employer's conduct has to amount to fundamental breach of contract. Cases in which constructive dismissals have been accepted include unjustified allegation of criminal conduct, using obscene language in inappropriate circumstances and belittling conduct to an employee in front of less senior members of staff. The employer's conduct does not have to be a single serious event. It may be a series of minor matters which breach the mutual trust and confidence which is considered to be essential to a contract of employment. This amounts to fundamental breach of contract.

Sub-section (3) has the effect of preserving the dismissal of an employee even though the employee, after his dismissal, gives notice during the period of termination of employment that he intends to leave earlier. By this provision the employee can still claim unfair dismissal even though it was his notice which actually ended the contract. So if an employee dismissed by his employer has an opportunity of another job but this requires an early start he may end his work earlier and leave to take up his new job.

Whilst not actual dismissal the question of the frustration of a contract of employment has been considered by the courts. It is accepted that a long illness or a sentence of imprisonment may frustrate a contract. In the case of *F. C. Shepherd and Co Ltd v Jerrom* 1986 an apprentice plumber was sent to Borstal for between six months and two years. The sentence of the court was held by the Court of Appeal to have frustrated the contract of apprenticeship. When Jerrom was released the employers refused to have him back and this was held not to be dismissal since his sentence had terminated the contract by frustration.

Grounds for fair dismissal

Section 57 deals with these grounds by stating:

(1) In determining for the purposes of this Part whether the dismissal of an employee was fair or unfair, it shall be for the employer to show –

   (a) what was the reason (or, if there was more than one, the principal reason) for the dismissal, and

   (b) that it was a reason falling within sub-section (2) or some other substantial reason of a kind such as to justify the dismissal of an employee holding the position which that employee held.

(2) In sub-section (1)(b) the reference to a reason falling within this sub-section is a reference to a reason which –

   (a) related to the capability or qualifications of the employee for performing work of the kind which he was employed by the employer to do, or

   (b) related to the conduct of the employee, or

   (c) was that the employee was redundant, or

   (d) was that the employee could not continue to work in the position which he held without contravention (either on his part or on that of his employer) of a duty or restriction imposed by or under an enactment.

   (a) 'capability' means capability assessed by reference to skill, aptitude, health or any other physical or mental quality;

   (b) 'qualifications' means any degree, diploma or other academic, technical or professional qualification relevant to the position which the employee held.

An important point to note is that it is for the employer to show what the reason was for the dismissal and that it was a reason which is one within the section as being a fair reason justifying dismissal. This requirement reverses the normal rule that the person bringing a case must prove his case if he is to succeed. Here a dismissed employee can make a complaint of unfair dismissal and it is then the duty of the employer to show that the dismissal was fair.

The provision that an employee may be dismissed for a substantial reason of a kind such as to justify the dismissal of an employee holding the position the employee held, has been used to meet the needs of a business. If a business needs to reorganize itself because of economic pressure and this means adjusting staff conditions which a member of staff refuses to accept then the dismissal of that employee would be fair. This is to be seen in the case of *Hollister v National Farmers' Union* 1979 where the union had to reorganize the insurance section. This changed the position of the staff who sold the insurance. Hollister objected to this change. He was dismissed and his claim for unfair dismissal was rejected. The Court of Appeal said that if a reorganization was the only sensible way to deal with a business problem then it was fair to dismiss an employee who refused to agree to the new arrangement.

As can be seen, the words 'capability' and 'qualifications' are given particular meanings. In the case of capability it should be kept in mind that the period of two years continuous employment before a complaint of unfair dismissal can be made should allow an employee's capability to be assessed. Capability, however, is defined in such a way as to cover an employee who has been employed for some time before his lack of capability becomes apparent. This is to be seen in the case of *Hindle v Percival Boats Ltd* 1969. Here the employer had for many years built wood boats. The economic situation in boat building was such that the company had to change to building fibreglass boats. All the employees including Hindle were re-trained. Hindle, however, was unable to work at an acceptable rate and he was dismissed. This was accepted by the Court of Appeal as being a fair dismissal since Hindle's work was uneconomic in the new situation. He was not redundant since there was no reduction in the need for employees for this work. Another example of capability in the case of *Dunning (A.J.) and Sons, (Shop fitters) Ltd v Jacomb* 1973. Here Jacomb was a contracts manager whose manner was described as 'unco-operative and unbending'. On a number of occasions his actions led to difficulties with large and important regular clients. The clients told the employers that they did not want Jacomb on their sites. He was dismissed. This dismissal was held not to be unfair since Jacomb did not have the capability to discharge the responsibility of the job.

The matter of qualifications arises if an employer requires an employee to possess a particular qualification and it is discovered that in fact the employee does not possess that qualification; in these circumstances his subsequent dismissal is not unfair.

Conduct of an employee is a common reason for the dismissal of employees. Most employees are provided with statements as to what are to be considered disciplinary matters and how the employer will deal with a breach of discipline. Most employers base their disciplinary procedures on the Code of Practice 1 Disciplinary Practice and Procedures in Employment which is produced by the Advisory Conciliation and Arbitration Services (ACAS). Under this code it is suggested that, except where there has been an act of gross misconduct, no employee should be dismissed until the system of warnings has been used. The code suggests that there should be an informal oral warning, a formal oral warning, a written warning and a final written warning. In appropriate circumstances it may be right to omit the earlier warnings and to give an employee a written warning. If the system of warnings is used correctly any further act of misconduct, such as coming to work late, can lead to instant dismissal and that is a fair dismissal.

Redundancy is an acceptable reason for dismissal. As it is a topic with its own particular features it is considered in more detail later.

The last reason, that an employee could no longer work in the position he held without contravention, either by himself or his employer, of some duty or restriction imposed by or under an Act of Parliament covers the situation where an employee lorry driver is disqualified from driving. To allow that employee to continue his work would be a criminal offence both by the employee and his employer.

Remedies for unfair dismissal

A complaint of unfair dismissal by an employee will be heard by an industrial tribunal. The remedies available to a tribunal when satisfied that an employee has been dismissed unfairly are: reinstatement, re-engagement and compensation.

Before making an order for reinstatement or re-engagement the tribunal have first to see whether this is something the dismissed employee desires, and whether it is practicable for the employer to comply with the order. The employee's own conduct must also be taken into account. The order for reinstatement is intended to put the employee back in the position the employee previously occupied. If this is not considered practicable then re-engagement may be ordered. Re-engagement intends to put the employee back with his employer in a position somewhat similar to that he previously occupied with not less favourable terms.

In practice tribunals seldom order reinstatement or re-engagement since the orders have little chance of success. Despite the use of the word order the tribunal cannot make an employer obey an order. Most employers are reluctant to take back employees who have been dismissed.

Compensation is the usual remedy granted by an industrial tribunal. The amounts of compensation are fixed by the Secretary of State for Employment and are varied from time to time, usually annually. The forms of compensation are: basic award; compensatory award; additional award; and a special award.

The basic award is compensation for the dismissal and follows the pattern of redundancy payments. The maximum award is at present £6,150, based on £205 per week. The basic award may be reduced by a percentage if it appears just and equitable having regard to the employee's own conduct. This reduction may take into account that the employee's misconduct is discovered after his dismissal.

The compensatory award is the amount the tribunal considers just and equitable in the circumstances having regard to the loss suffered by the dismissed employee. The amount at present has an upper limit of £10,000. The award takes into account the employee's loss of a company car, medical insurance and other benefits. The employee's prospects of obtaining new employment are also relevant.

The additional award only arises when a tribunal's order for reinstatement or re-engagement has not been observed. In this circumstance the tribunal may award between 13 and 26 weeks pay based on the maximum figure of £205 per week. So the maximum for this award is £5,330.

A special award is payable only when an employee has been dismissed for a reason relating to membership or non-membership of a trade union. The tribunal has to have made an order for re-employment and that has not been observed, in which case the minimum is £20,100 with no limit to the maximum. If no such order is made then the award is a minimum of £13,400 and a maximum of £26,800.

Redundancy

Until the passing by Parliament of the Redundancy Payments Act 1965 there was no statutory obligation on an employer to make a payment to an employee dismissed for redundancy. The concept of the payment is that the dismissed employee should be rewarded for past service taking into account the employee's age and length of service. It also acts as a financial cushion to help the older worker tide himself over the period of getting another job, if in fact he can.

The redundancy payment is tax free and does not affect a dismissed employee's right to unemployment benefit. The payment is a minimum payment and many employers, particularly when seeking volunteers for redundancy, will offer much larger amounts to redundant employees.

In order to qualify for a redundancy payment a dismissed employee must show that he is not excluded, the grounds for which are the same as unfair dismissal considered earlier, and has at least two years continuous employment if full-time and five years if part-time. Under Section 91 the burden of proof is on the employer to disprove that the dismissal was not for redundancy.

Redundancy arises in two situations. Under the provisions in Section 81 these are:

(a) that the employer has ceased, or intends to cease, to carry on the business for the purposes of which the employee was employed by him, or has ceased, or intends to cease, to carry on that business in the place where the employee was so employed.

(b) the fact that the requirements of that business for employees to carry out work of a particular kind have ceased or diminished or are expected to cease or diminish.

With regard to (a) it covers the situation where the complete business closes down, or intends to, or where, say, a branch business of a national organization closes down, or intends to. In the second situation it is simply a matter of a reduced need for employees undertaking a particular type of work. If a company has a reduced need for estimators then to dismiss a number of those is a redundancy situation even if the business is successful and extra staff are being recruited in other sections of the business.

Parliament recognized that an employer might seek to avoid a redundancy situation, which would put him to expense, by laying off workers or putting them on short-time working. By acting in this way an employer might induce a number of his employees to leave and find work elsewhere. This would correct his difficulty by his employees ending their employment by them giving notice. In order to prevent this 'driving out' of employees Section 87 contains provisions designed to deal with the situation.

An employee is laid off if the employer does not provide him with work in any week and does not pay him for his absence. Short-time working is where an employee earns less than half a week's pay. Where an employee is laid off or put on short-time working for four or more consecutive weeks or for six weeks within a 13 week period the employee may give notice and treat the ending of the employment as redundancy. The employer may contest this claim by serving a counter-notice that there will be no further lay-offs or short-time workings in the next 13 weeks.

If an employee dismissed for redundancy is offered, before his contract ends, a new contract which is the same work or is employment of a suitable alternative he must accept that unless he has reasonable grounds for refusal. Refusal without reasonable grounds deprives the employee of any right to a redundancy payment. As the new job may not be suitable there is provision for a four week trial period. If within this period the employee decides, on reasonable grounds, that the alternative employment is not suitable he may leave and still receive the redundancy payment.

When a business is taken over at common law the employees have had their contracts of employment ended because these contracts are of a personal nature. Theoretically the employees are redundant and entitled to redundancy payments. In order to deal with this situation both the Employment Protection (Consolidation) Act 1978 and the Transfer of Undertakings (Protection of Employment) Regulations 1981 contain provisions to continue the contracts of employment. In brief, if the new owners offer to continue the contracts on the same terms or suitable alternative terms the employees are not entitled to any redundancy payments.

In making selections for redundancy an employer must consult with a recognized trade union. The greater the number to be dismissed the greater the period of notice to be given to the union and also to the Department of Employment. Whatever method of selection is adopted by an employer it must be fair in the circumstances. There is no legal compulsion to have a 'last in first out' system.

Claims for redundancy payment must be made in writing to the employer within six months of the employment ending. The amount of payment is determined by the employee's age and service. The period of service has a maximum of 20 years reckoned backwards from the date of dismissal. Under the age of 18 no service counts. From 18 to 21 each year of service counts for half a week's pay. From 22 to 41 it is one week and from 42 to 65 it is one and a half week's pay. The week's pay is, as with unfair dismissal, limited to a maximum of £205 per week. So the total maximum is £6,150. Employees over the age of 65 or their normal retirement age, if lower, are not entitled to a redundancy payment. In the case of an employee in the year leading up to the 65th birthday there is a reduction of one-twelfth for each month of that year.

If an employer's business becomes insolvent then, clearly, there is no money or insufficient to pay the employees their redundancy payments. In this circumstance the Department of Employment pays the sums due to the employees and then recovers what can be recovered in the liquidation.

INDUSTRIAL TRIBUNALS AND PROCEDURE

Industrial tribunals were first set up by the Industrial Training Act 1964 with the purpose of hearing appeals from the imposition of levies by training boards. Since then their jurisdiction has been extended so that employment disputes, such as complaints of unfair dismissal and of redundancies, occupy much of their time. It is possible that their jurisdiction will be extended to cover contract disputes between employer and employee.

Tribunals are situated throughout the whole of the country and meet as frequently as the volume of work requires. A tribunal has three members. The chairman, who may be full-time or part-time, is qualified as either a solicitor or barrister. The two other members are not legally qualified and are selected from the employers' side and the trade union side of industry. They provide the industrial experience which the chairman does not possess. All the members have equal voting power.

The justificaton for the use of industrial tribunals instead of courts is that the system is cheaper, speedier and the informality of the procedure is felt to be better for complainants. Legal representation whilst permitted is not essential since the aim of the procedure is to allow a claim to be considered without the use of a lawyer. For this reason, and to avoid employees being reluctant to bring claims, an unsuccessful claimant will only be ordered to pay costs in unusual circumstances. That is when the claim is frivolous, vexatious or otherwise unreasonable.

As most of the matters that come before industrial tribunals are factual rather than legal there is a limited right of appeal from their decisions. The appeal goes to the Employment Appeal Tribunal which has the standing of a division of the High Court. It is presided over by a High Court judge and two lay members selected from both side of industry. From the Employment Appeal Tribunal an appeal lies to the Court of Appeal and then to the House of Lords. Appeals from the Employment Appeal Tribunal are, however, not all that frequent.

When a dismissed employee makes a complaint of unfair dismissal the complaint must be made on the appropriate form and made within three months of termination of employment. There is a right for the tribunal to accept a claim later than this provided they are satisfied that it was not reasonably practicable for the complaint to have been made within the three month period.

When the complaint has been made the employer is sent a copy and has to reply within 14 days. After this the Advisory Conciliation and Arbitration Service's conciliation officer is sent the papers. He may use his services, which are free and confidential, in an attempt to resolve the dispute. As a rule these are not successful since by this time both the employer and the employee are in fixed positions and unwilling to compromise.

The tribunal may examine the papers and conduct a pre-hearing assessment. If as a result of this it appears that the complainant has a weak case that view is given to the complainant. To then proceed puts that party at risk of being called upon to pay costs.

The hearing itself, whilst informal, is conducted in the manner of a court. The employer's representative makes an opening statement so that the tribunal is aware of the employer's case. His witnesses are then called to give evidence. After this the employee's representative, who frequently is a trade union official, makes a statement to the tribunal and calls his witnesses. Both representatives then address the tribunal, after which the tribunal makes its decision. This decision has to be sent in writing to both the parties.

In reaching its decision the tribunal has to apply the law and reach a decision by following any directions it is required to observe. With unfair dismissal Section 57 requires that in the determination of the question as to whether the dismissal was fair or unfair regard has to be had to the reason shown by the employer, and to whether in the circumstances the employer acted reasonably or unreasonably in treating the reason as sufficient for dismissal of the employee. In reaching its decision the tribunal has to take into account the size and administrative resources of the employer's undertaking and the substantial merits of the case, with the decision based on the equity of the case.

What this means in simple terms is that the tribunal has to decide whether the employer acted reasonably, applying good industrial practice, in deciding to dismiss the employee. The size and resources of the employer are relevant. A large organization would be expected to be more able to put an employee in another position rather than dismiss him. A smaller organization would find this more difficult, if not impossible. The decision reached has to be equitable in the circumstances and consistent with the merits of the case.

11 HEALTH AND SAFETY AT WORK ETC ACT 1974

INTRODUCTION

Before the Health and Safety at Work etc Act 1974 was passed by Parliament the law regarding safety was mainly found in the Factories Act 1961. This Act was the latest in a series of similar acts which had started in the nineteenth century. In the late 1960s a review of the Factories Act 1961 was being considered. The trade unions were of the opinion that a more fundamental change was needed than a revised Factories Act would produce. There was a strong belief that the provisions in the Factories Act 1961, and the subordinate legislation, was inadequate both in form and content. The administration of the Act was also considered to be unsatisfactory. The government decided that there was a need to have an inquiry made of the existing provisions and to obtain the views of all interested parties.

In 1970 the Committee of Inquiry on Safety and Health at Work was set up under the chairmanship of Lord Robens. In 1972 the committee made its report. The report was critical of the existing legal provisions and their administration and made a number of recommendations. A particular feature of the report was that there were some five million people who had been found to be engaged in work activites but were not covered by the existing health and safety legislation.

A number of other inadequacies were noted by the committee including that management appeared to be solely responisble for matters of health and safety at work; the workers were often not involved. In addition the economic loss to the country from the absence of workers due to accidents and the need to pay them social security benefits was a matter, the committee believed, requiring attention.

The Robens Report contained many recommendations, a number of which were not adopted when Parliament passed the Health and Safety at Work etc Act 1974. The Act was brought into force in stages. One purpose of the Act is, over a period of time, to replaced existing legislation with new regulations and codes of practice.

The purpose of the Act may be said to be a new approach to health and safety with protection being provided for persons at work generally and not for instance as in the Factories Act 1961 where the protection was only for those who worked in factories.

ADMINISTRATION OF THE ACT

A serious criticism made by the Robens Report was that the administration of the previous legislation was unsatisfactory. There were no powers to conduct research, carry out investigations or conduct inquiries, and the general administration was poor.

The 1974 Act set out to remedy these deficiencies by creating the Health and Safety Commission and the Health and Safety Executive. The Commission, which is under the control of the Secretary of State, is concerned with policy and those things associated with policy, whereas the Executive is concerned with the application of the Act.

The Commission has six to nine members and a chairman. All of these appointments are made by the Secretary of State for Employment. In making the appointments the Secretary of State is required to consult with organizations representing employers and employees, and organizations representing local authorities, professional bodies and others. The responsibilities of the Commission are wide. They may instruct the executive to discharge obligations of the Commission. They may carry out research or encourage others to carry out research, provide information, to make regulations and generally to further the purposes of the Act. The Commission has to give effect to any directions given by the Secretary of State, and from time to time submit reports to the Secretary of State. An importance function is to direct investigations and inquiries.

The Health and Safety Executive consists of three persons one of whom is the director. The responsibilities of the Executive are the administration of the provisions of the Act and subordinate legislation, to give effect to directions of the Commission and to exercise on behalf of the Commission such of the Commission's functions as the Executive are directed to exercise.

When the 1974 Act was passed by Parliament it was realized that the Executive would not be able to administer the provisions of the Act in all the premises where people work. There is a long history of duties being given to local authorities which require the inspection of premises in order to ensure that some statutory provisions are being observed. It was, therefore, considered appropriate to have the local authorities involved in the administration of the provisions of the Act.

The Health and Safety (Enforcing Authority) Regulations 1977, which were amended in 1985, allocate the responsibilities between the Executive and local authorities. The regulations are detailed but the division is basically that offices, shops and similar premises where the work activities are less hazardous are the responsibility of local authorities. Other premises with more hazardous activities are the responsibility of the Executive. So far as the construction industry is concerned the effect of this division is that the provisions of the Act are administered by the Executive on sites, whilst in builders' offices the local authority is the administering authority. The provisions of the Act are enforced in exactly the same way by both the Executive and the local authority.

It is not possible for inspectors of enforcing authorities to discharge their functions properly unless they are informed of events which might require their attention and use their powers. The Reporting of Injuries, Diseases and Dangerous Occurrences Regulations 1985 require that the employer or person having control of the premises shall forthwith notify the enforcing authority by the quickest possible means and within seven days send a report to the enforcing authority of any matter coming within the regulations. The regulations require notification of death or serious injuries, certain diseases and the occurrence of certain events. Dangerous occurrences may be events where no one is killed or injured but something has happened which could have caused death or injury. The events which are classed as dangerous occurrences are set out in a schedule to the regulations. Two examples of dangerous occurrences are the collapse, overturning or failure of any load-bearing part of a lift, crane, hoist, excavator or pile-driving frame; and the collapse or partial collapse of any scaffold which is more than five metres high.

MEANS TO ACHIEVE THE AIMS OF THE ACT

The 1974 Act is laid out in a substantially different way to most enforcing acts. This was necessary to give effect to a number of the recommendations in the Robens Report. The main means are:

1) General duties;
2) Regulations;
3) Codes of practice;
4) Improvement and prohibition notices;
5) Safety policies;
6) Safety committees;
7) Safety representatives.

General duties, as will be seen, are duties imposed which are not so specified as to be applicable in limited circumstances only. Previous legislation has been so detailed that on occasion a clear wrongdoing could not be dealt with because it did not fit precisely within a statutory provision. To have a general duty, therefore, gives a flexibility which allows action to be taken over a wide range of matters.

Regulations are detailed statutory provisions which are considered necessary in particular circumstances. The Reporting of Injuries, Diseases and Dangerous Occurrences Regulations 1985 is an example of regulations made under the Act.

Codes of practice are one of the new features in the Act. They are not statutory provisions in the sense of a failure to observe a code being a criminal offence. They are intended to prevent accidents by indicating the most suitable method of carrying out a work activity.

Improvement and prohibition notices have provided powers which did not exist in earlier legislation. For instance, under the Factories Act 1961 there were no provisions for inspectors to serve notices requiring infringements to be put right within a prescribed time. The inspector had either to prosecute or have the infringement corrected by persuasion. Now infringements can be dealt with, according to their seriousness, by the service of improvement or prohibition notices. Failure to comply with the notices is a criminal offence.

Safety policies are policies prepared by employers showing how the health and safety of employees is to be safeguarded. There is an obligation to keep the policy under review and to revise it from time to time. The requirement to have a policy made employers give thought to safety and health of employees which they might not have done previously.

Safety committees comprise management and employees who meet at intervals to consider health and safety matters. The requirement to have a safety committee means that there is a recognized means for employees to raise questions about their health and safety.

Safety representatives are employees appointed as such by trade unions. They are empowered under regulations to be involved in matters concerning the employees' health and safety. They negotiate with employers on these matters and have powers to inspect and investigate work activities.

Because the Act did not immediately repeal earlier safety legislation, so that legislation continues in force, it has been necessary to give a description to cover both the new legislation and the previous legislation. The term used in the Act for this purpose is 'relevant statutory provisions'.

General duties

The main provisions in the Act are contained in the sections dealing with general duties. What is probably the most important section is that dealing with the general duties of employers to their employees. This is Section 2 and states:

(1) It shall be the duty of every employer to ensure, so far as is reasonably practicable, the health, safety and welfare at work of all his employees.

(2) Without prejudice to the generality of an employer's duty under the preceding sub-section, the matters to which that duty extends include in particular –

    (a) the provision and maintenance of plant and systems of work that are, so far as is reasonably practicable, safe and without risks to health;

    (b) arrangements for ensuring, so far as is reasonably practicable, safety and absence of risks to health in connection with the use, handling, storage and transport of articles and substances;

    (c) the provision of such information, instruction, training and supervision as is necessary to ensure, so far as is reasonably practicable, the health and safety at work of his employees;

    (d) so far as is reasonably practicable, as regards any place of work under the employer's control, the maintenance of it in a condition that is safe and without risks to health and the provision and maintenance of means of access to the egress from it that are safe and without such risks;

    (e) the provision and maintenance of a working environment for his employees that is, so far as is reasonably practicable, safe, without risks to health, and adequate as regards facilities and arrangements for their welfare at work.

(3) Except in such cases as may be prescribed, it shall be the duty of every employer to prepare and as often as may be appropriate revise a written statement of his general policy with respect to the health and safety at work of his employees and the organisation and arrangements for the time being in force for carrying out that policy and to bring the statement and any revision of it to the notice of all of his employees.

(4) Regulations made by the Secretary of State may provide for the appointment in prescribed cases by recognised trade unions (within the meaning of the regulations) of safety representatives from amongst the employees, and those representatives shall represent the employees in consultations with the employers under sub-section (6) below and shall have such other functions as may be prescribed.

(5) [. . .]

(6) It shall be the duty of every employer to consult any such representatives with a view to making and maintenance of arrangements which will enable him and his employees to co-operate effectively in promoting and developing measures to ensure the health and safety at work of the

employees, and in checking the effectiveness of such measures.

(7) In such cases as may be prescribed it shall be the duty of every employer. If required to do so by the safety representatives mentioned (sub-section 4) above, to establish, in accordance with regulations made by the Secretary of State, a safety committee having the function of keeping under view the measures taken to ensure the health and safety at work of his employees and such other functions as may be presecribed.

Sub-section (1) imposes on an employer, in the widest possible way, a duty to ensure the health and safety of his employees. This duty is qualified by the words 'so far as is reasonably practicable'. The provision does not, therefore, impose an absolute duty on an employer. He is not under a duty to guarantee his employees' safety.

The expression 'so far as is reasonably practicable' is not defined in the Act but from cases decided under earlier legislation where the same term was used some guidance may be obtained. First the word 'practicable' means that it must be something which is physically possible. The use of the word 'reasonably' means that the degree of risk involved must be balanced against the expense of guarding against that risk. So a risk which is high should be guarded against even if this means heavy expenditure. Whereas if the risk is low then great expenditure cannot be justified. An employer, therefore, has to take those precautions which are reasonable in the circumstances; if he does so he has discharged his obligation. It was decided in the case of *Martin v Boulton Paul (Steel Construction) Ltd* 1982 that the fact that something was done in the same way in an industry did not in itself mean that the employer had done all that was reasonable.

Sub-section (2), without affecting the duty under sub-section (1), sets out in some detail matters to which the duty of the employer extends. This means that if some matter comes within anything set out in the paragraphs action would be taken in that respect. Otherwise action would be taken under sub-section (1).

With regard to paragraph (a) it should be noted that it is not sufficient just to provide plant and systems of work. Their maintenance, whatever it might be, must also be carried out if the employer's duty is to be discharged.

Paragraph (b) requires proper arrangements for the use, handling, storage and transport of articles and substances. There are a number of regulations supporting ths general duty.

With paragraph (c) the duty extends over a range of matters. An employer may discharge his duty by simply providing his employee with a leaflet which explains some activity. He may, however, have to give supervision to discharge his duty. The age and experience of an employee is relevant here. The young inexperienced employee will require more from the employer than the older experienced employee who undertakes the same task.

Paragraph (d) is of particular importance to an employer in the construction industry. As can be seen, the provisions are of relevance to a construction site. A site which is littered with materials and rubbish would be a place of work which did not satisfy the requirements in the paragraph.

With paragraph (e) there is a requirement that the working environment shall be safe and without risks to health as well as adequate as regards the provision of welfare facilities and arrangements. Premises where employees had to work in unpleasant atmospheres from fumes or steam would make the employer liable under this paragraph.

All of these provisions are subject to the qualification 'so far as is reasonably practicable'. Where, therefore, the employer has done that there is no liability.

The leading case on Section 2 is that of *R v Swan Hunter Shipbuilders Ltd and Another* 1982. The facts in the case were that a ship was being constructed with the shipbuilders' employees and sub-contractors' employees working on it when it was being fitted out. The layout of the ship was such that two decks were not well ventilated. This was a matter of importance since if oxygen accumulated in those decks there was a serious danger of a fierce fire breaking out. This was a known risk because of the use of oxygen for welding operations on the ship. The oxygen supply was brought by pipes on to the ship from plant on the quayside. The safety officer of Swan Hunter was sufficiently concerned about the fire risk in an oxygen enriched atmosphere that he prepared a booklet explaining how this could come about and the danger. Copies of this booklet were distributed to all the employees of the shipbuilders. In addition to the warning in the booklet of the danger of leakages from oxygen supply pipes there was a system of shutting down all valves at meal breaks and at the end of shifts. The night patrols on the ship were also to check that valves were closed and there were no leakages. The sub-contractors' employees were not given copies of the booklet or otherwise warned of the danger.

Despite the warning to the shipbuilders' employees a serious leakage occurred during one night with the result that when work was about to start next morning there was an oxygen enriched atmosphere. As oxygen is colourless and tasteless there was no indication of its presence in great quantity. An employee of a sub-contractor struck an arc to start welding and a serious fire broke out. The fire caused the death of eight workers.

The shipbuilders were prosecuted under Sections 2 and 3 of the Act. The Court of Appeal accepted that there had been a failure to observe the duty on the employers in that by their failure to warn the sub-contractor's employees of the fire risk they thereby put their own employees at risk. This had to be so since the shipbuilders' employees were working by the side of the sub-contractors' employees. One lot of workers knew of the danger and what was needed to guard against it and the other workers were ignorant of those matters. Both lots of workers, however, were subject to the same danger. Swan Hunter were convicted and fined. The sub-contractors pleaded guilty and they too were fined.

Another case on Section 2 was *Tesco Stores Ltd v Seabridge* 1988. Here three of the four securing screws to the protective plate to the control panel for a lift had been removed. This had been done by some unknown wrongdoer. An employee of Tesco put his hand to the panel and received a severe burn. Tesco Stores were prosecuted and convicted. Their defence that they had done all that was reasonably practicable in that they had a system of safety inspection was rejected. The court was of the opinion that the failure to detect the fault was clear evidence that the inspection system had failed. Tesco Stores were convicted and fined.

Safety policy

Sub-section (3) of Section 2 places a duty on employers to prepare a written statement of their general policy with respect to the health and safety at work of their employees. The statements and any revisions, which are to be made as appropriate, are to be brought to the notice of all their employees. An exception to this obligation is found in the Employers' Health and Safety Statements (Exceptions) Regulations 1975. The regulations except any employer who has fewer than five employees from the obligation.

The purpose of an employer's safety policy is to make the employer give thought to health and safety in his undertaking and, having identified the hazards, specify how they are to be dealt with and those persons who are to have responsibilities in the matters.

Safety representatives

Sub-section (4) to (7) of Section 2 deal with safety representatives. A point of importance is that safety representatives are appointed by recognized trade unions from amongst employees. A recognized trade union is a trade union which has been certified as being independent and is recognized by the employer for negotiating purposes. The appointment by the trade union ensures that the safety representatives will not be employees who would not do anything which could upset the employer.

The representatives have the duty of representing the employees in consultations with the employer. It is the duty of the employer to consult with the representatives for making arrangements to enable him and his employees to co-operate effectively in promoting and developing measures to ensure the health and safety at work of the employees. By this provision the employer is required to work with the representatives in order to achieve good standards of health and safety. Without the provision some employers would not co-operate with the safety representatives and the purpose of their appointment would be largely lost.

The appointment, power and functions of safety representatives are set out in the Safety Representatives and Safety Committees Regulations 1977. The regulations were amended by the Management of Health and Safety at Work Regulations 1992. Safety representatives are given wide powers to make inspections of work places at regular intervals; to stop work and to investigate accidents; to represent employees with the employer; to investigate complaints; to receive information from inspectors; to take time off work with pay to perform their functions and to undergo training.

Sub-section (5), which was repealed by the Employment Protection Act 1975, had provisions which dealt with the appointment of safety representatives when there was not a recognized trade union. In other words a non-union work place.

Safety committee
Sub-section (7) of Section 2 requires an employer, if requested by safety representatives, to establish a safety committee. The safety committee is to keep under review measures taken to ensure the health and safety at work of the employees. Under Regulation 9 of the Safety Representatives and Safety Committees Regulation 1977 a safety committee is to be set up if at least two safety representatives request the employer, in writing, to do so. The committee is to be established within three months of the request and notice of its establishment, stating the composition of the committee, posted in the work place where it may be read by the employees.

General duties of employers and the self-employed to persons other than their employees
A substantial change in the 1974 Act from the previous legislation is the recognition of the number of workers who are self-employed and the acknowledgement that it is appropriate, in certain circumstances, that duties should be owed to those who are not employees. In the past the system has been that the employer owed duties to employees and to no one else, certainly not to the public. The 1974 Act has changed all this and placed duties on employers and self-employed workers to those who are not employees.

Section 3 states:

(1) It shall be the duty of every employer to conduct his undertaking in such a way as to ensure, so far as is reasonably practicable, that persons not in his employment who may be affected thereby are not thereby exposed to risks to their health or safety.

(2) It shall be the duty of every self-employed person to conduct his undertaking in such a way as to ensure, so far as is reasonably practicable, that he and other persons (not being his employees) who may be affected thereby are not thereby exposed to risks to their health or safety.

(3) In such cases as may be prescribed, it shall be the duty of every employer and every self-employed person, in the prescribed circumstances and in the prescribed manner, to give to persons (not being his employees) who may be affected by the way in which he conducts his undertaking the prescribed information about such aspects of the way in which he conducts his undertaking as might affect their health or safety.

In the case of *R v Swan Hunter Shipbuilders Ltd and Another* 1982, apart from the duty under Section 2, Swan Hunter were held to be in breach of their duty under sub-section (1) of Section 3. As will be seen, the duty was owed to those persons not in their employment who might be affected by the way the employers conducted their undertaking. By their failure to prevent the escape of the oxygen and to organize a safe system of work Swan Hunter put the sub-contractors' employees at risk. This was a breach of Section 3 and they were convicted for that offence.

The requirement that an employer shall conduct his undertaking in such a way as to ensure that persons who are not his employees are not thereby exposed to risks to their health or safety was considered in the case of *R v Mara* 1987. In this case Mara was a director in a small industrial cleaning company. The company obtained a contract to clean a supermarket. Most of the work was done early morning with the use of various cleaning machines. Part of the work involved the loading bay for the store. This created some difficulty in the delivery of goods. It was therefore agreed that this part of the cleaning operation would be left to the store's own staff so that the cleaning could be done at a convenient time. To assist in this the cleaning company made available a floor polishing machine.

This machine, which was used by the cleaning company in the store, had an electric cable which had become damaged. The cable had been repaired by wrapping with insulating tape. Mr Mara had been responsible for some of this repair work. He, therefore, had full knowledge of the state of the machine and possible danger to a user of the machine. An employee of the stores was using the machine in the loading bay in wet conditions when he was electrocuted. Mara, as the main director of the cleaning company and as a person who had been involved with the machine, was prosecuted and convicted. He was in breach of the duty to non-employees by the way in which he had conducted his undertaking.

There are a number of circumstances on construction sites where similar happenings could occur. The hire of plant or equipment or their loan could result in a breach of this provision.

In sub-section (2) there is the recognition of self-employed workers being involved in all aspects of work. It was necessary, therefore, to place a duty on that class of person in just the same way as an employer. The duty is to conduct his undertaking, so far as is reasonably practicable, so that he and other persons, who are not his employees, are not put at risk with regard to their health and safety. As can be seen there is a personal duty to himself not to put himself at risk. This duty also extends to others provided they are not his employees. If the self-employed person has employees then his duty to them is as an employer under Section 2, considered earlier.

The application of this provision on a construction site could be in the use of a self-employed bricklayer. He is under a duty to look to his own health and safety; if he does not do so he has committed a criminal offence. He is also under a duty to those who are not his employees. So if the bricklayer is doing his work in such a way that others on the site are at risk to their health or safety the duty has been breached and a criminal offence committed. This duty also would be breached if someone outside the site, a member of the public, was put at risk. Finally if the self-employed bricklayer employs others he owes them the duty under Section 2.

Under sub-section (3) there is a duty to provide information to certain people in prescribed circumstances and in a prescribed manner. So far the Secretary of State has not prescribed these matters so the sub-section is not fully operative.

General duties of persons concerned with premises to persons other than their employees

Section 4 is broad in its application but has particular importance where a builder sends his employees to work at premises which are not under his control. This differs from the usual situation where a builder is given full control of a site in order to erect a building.

(1) This section has effect for imposing on persons duties in relation to those who –
    (a) are not their employees; but
    (b) use non-domestic premises made available to them as a place of work or as a place where they may use plant or substances provided for their use there,

and applies to premises so made available and other non-domestic premises used in connection with them.

(2) It shall be the duty of each person who has, to any extent, control of premises to which this section applies or of the means of access thereto or egress therefrom or of any plant or substance in such premises to take such measures as it is reasonable for a person in his position to take to ensure, so far as is reasonably practicable, that the premises, all means of access thereto or egress therefrom available for use by persons using the premises, and any plant or substance in the premises or, as the case may be, provided for use there, is or are safe and without risks to health.

(3) Where a person has, by virtue of any contract or tenancy, an obligation of any extent in relation to –

(a) the maintenance or repair of any premises to which this section applies or any means of access thereto or egress therefrom; or

(b) the safety of or the absence of risks to health arising from plant or substances in any such premises;

that person shall be treated, for the purposes of sub-section (2) above, as being a person who has control of the matters to which his obligation extends.

(4) Any reference in this section to a person having control of any premises or matter is a reference to a person having control of the premises or matter in connection with the carrying on by him of a trade, business or other undertaking (whether for profit or not).

The first point to note is that in sub-section (1) the duties are to be to those who are not their employees but who use non-domestic premises as a place of work or a place where plant or substances are provided for their use. Sub-section (1), therefore, does not apply to the employees of the person under the duty nor does it apply to domestic premises. So the section is applicable to workers who go and work at non-domestic premises which are under the control of a person who is not their employer. Therefore, employees of a builder who are sent to work at an industrial or commercial premises under the control of someone else are owed the duties under the section. These duties also fall on a builder who has control of a site when others, such as sub-contractors' operatives, come and work on the site.

The breadth of sub-section (1) can be seen from the fact that it imposes duties on a person who has control of a launderette or dry cleaner where members of the public use the plant and substances. The members of the public are not employees and the premises are non-domestic.

Sub-section (2) specifies the duties owed by the person having control of the premises. The duties relate to the premises, plant or substances and the means of access to and egress from the premises. The duty is to ensure that persons using the premises are, so far as is reasonably practicable, to be safe and without risks to health. To take the example of the main contractor who has control of a site, failure on his part to control the site and access to it and egress from it so that there is no risk to the safety or health of sub-contractors' employees is a breach of the duty.

Sub-section (3) deals with the situation where because of a contract or tenancy some person other than the occupier has responsibility for maintenance or repair of the premises, the access to and egress from the premises or seeing to the safety and risks to health from the plant or substances. So a landlord who, under the tenancy agreement, has responsibility for maintenance or repair of the premises is the person under the duties. This is also the case where under a contract a manufacturer leases washing machines to a launderette and is responsible for their maintenance; the duty is his.

Sub-section (4) defines the premises to which the section applies. A point of importance is that the business does not have to be profit making.

The House of Lords considered the provisions in Section 4 in the case of *Mailer v Austin Rover Group PLC* 1989. The facts in the case were that Austin Rover made a contract with a cleaning company for cleaning to be done to one of their factories. Part of the work involved cleaning a paint spraying booth. Beneath the booth there was a large sump for the collection of excess paint and thinners during the operations. There was also a piped supply of thinners to the booth for the spraying. Thinners were also used for cleaning the booth. Austin Rover engaged the cleaning contractor to clean the booth when production was stopped. The contractor was required not to use Austin Rover's thinners and to ensure that no one was down the sump when another person was working above. Furthermore, if a person entered the sump a safety lamp had to be used to guard against the danger associated with the use of an ordinary extension lead lamp.

When the contractor's employees started to clean the booth the control valve on the pipe supplying the thinners was turned off and the ventilating system to the booth closed down. Despite the warnings an employee went down the sump without a safety lamp and made use of the thinners in the piped supply. An explosion occurred and the employee down the sump lost his life. The cleaning contractor was prosecuted and pleaded guilty. Austin Rover were also prosecuted under Section 4.

The basis of the case against Austin Rover was that they had failed to take such measures as were reasonable for them to take to ensure, so far as was reasonably practicable, that the sump and piped thinners were safe and without risks to health. They were convicted in the magistrates court but appealed to the Divisional Court of the High Court and were successful in the appeal. The inspector then appealed to the House of Lords.

In the magistrates court, where Austin Rover had been convicted, it had been decided that they were at fault in not capping off the thinners' supply pipe and failing to provide effective ventilation. All these things were under the control of Austin Rover and, it was claimed, could have been achieved at modest cost.

The Law Lords considered Section 4 and expressed the view that if the premises were not a reasonably foreseeable cause of danger to persons using the premises in a manner or in circumstances which might reasonably be expected to occur, it was not reasonable to require any further measures to be taken to guard against unknown and unexpected events which might imperil their safety. In the circumstances it was not reasonable for Austin Rover to take steps to make the paint spraying booth and sump safe against misuse by the cleaning contractor's employee which could not be anticipated.

This finding by the Law Lords confirmed that even though the premises were under their control Austin Rover were not liable. To put the finding in simple terms, it was not reasonable to expect Austin Rover to guard against conduct by contractor's employees which was totally unexpected. The employees had been warned of the dangers and there was no reason to suspect that those warnings would be disregarded.

This decision does not cover the circumstances where there is a dangerous activity on the premises and it would be insufficient to warn contractors' employees. More active steps would be required by the person in control. One of the Law Lords gave as an example a floor of a warehouse which has a known safety load, and that knowledge is made known to a contractor. If the contractor exceeded the safety load then the person having control is not liable. Where he would be liable would be if he failed to guard large holes in the floor or allowed work to be done near to unstable walls.

Duties of employees and others

The statutory provisions in force before the Health and Safety at Work etc Act 1974 was introduced did not place duties on employees. There was, however, a recognition that employees should be subject to some requirements concerning health and safety. The 1974 Act has done that. Section 7 states:

It shall be the duty of every employee while at work–
  (a) to take reasonable care for the health and safety of himself and of other persons who may be affected by his acts or omissions at work; and
  (b) as regards any duty or requirement imposed on his employer

or any other person by or under any of the relevant statutory provisions, to co-operate with him so far as is necessary to enable that duty or requirement to be performed or complied with.

Paragraph (a) places a clear duty on every employee while at work to take reasonable care for himself and for others who may be affected by his acts or omissions. An employee who fails to fulfil this duty has committed a criminal offence. A number of prosecutions have been brought for a breach of this provision. An early prosecution was for a worker in a factory smoking in an area where petrol was stored and warning signs clearly stated that smoking was prohibited. A builder would contravene this provision, apart from any other, if he worked on a scaffold which he knew to be improperly erected or if he worked in an unsupported trench which he knew ought to have supports.

The duty of the employee also extends to co-operating with his employer so that the employer can satisfy any duty or requirement which is imposed on him.

Section 8 states: 'No person shall intentionally or recklessly interfere with or misuse anything provided in the interests of health, safety or welfare in pursuance of any of the relevant statutory provisions.'

Before any offence arises under this section it is necessary to prove that what occurred was done intentionally or recklessly. The fact that a person was careless is not sufficient to constitute a breach of the provision. It should also be noted that the provision applies to any person and not just an employee. So a member of the public could be guilty of an offence under the section.

Section 9 states: 'No employer shall levy or permit to be levied on any employee of his any charge in respect of anything done or provided in pursuance of any specific requirement of the relevant statutory provisions.'

This provision prohibits an employer from charging any employee for anything done or provided in order to comply with some safety provision. If, therefore, an employee was to remove asbestos from a building he must be provided with the specified protective clothing and equipment. No charge can be made against him for any item so provided. A problem that arises not infrequently is that an employee is provided with something specified by a statutory provision and by his carelessness loses it. That has to be replaced but the employee cannot be charged for the replacement. The only course of action open to the employer is to treat the loss as an employment disciplinary matter.

Codes of practice
The Robens Committee Report drew attention to the need to avoid

accidents. One way, which the Act provides, is for a person to be given guidance as to the most suitable and safe way to do something. This method is by codes of practice. Sections 16 and 17 deal with codes of practice. The Commission has the power to approve and issue codes of practice whether or not prepared by the Commission. The Commission may also approve codes of practice issued or intended to be issued by some other body. Examples of codes of practice are those issued by the Commission with regard to safety representatives and safety committees, and some British Standards not issued by the Commission but approved by the Commission.

An approved code of practice does not create a criminal liability. It may, however, be used in evidence to show that some other breach of safety law occurred. For instance, if an employee is injured because his employer failed to establish a safe system of work, and that accident would not have happened if an approved code of practice had been followed, then the failure to follow the code is evidence of the employer's failure to provide a safe system of work.

Improvement and prohibition notices

As was mentioned earlier, before the 1974 Act there were no provisions for inspectors to serve notices to require contravention to be remedied. The 1974 Act remedied this deficiency.

Section 21 deals with improvement notices and states:

If an inspector is of the opinion that a person
(a) is contravening one or more of the relevant statutory provisions; or
(b) has contravened one or more of those provisions in circumstances that make it likely that the contravention will continue or be repeated.

he may serve on him a notice (in this Part referred to as 'an improvement notice') stating that he is of that opinion, specifying the provision or provisions as to which he is of that opinion, giving particulars of the reasons why he is of that opinion, and requiring that person to remedy the contravention or, as the case may be, the matters occasioning it within such period (ending not earlier than the period within which an appeal against the notice can be brought under Section 24) as may be specified in the notice.

The first comment to make about the provisions in the section is that it is the inspector himself who makes the decision. There is no obligation for him to report back to his enforcing authority and obtain approval of his action. The next comment is that the contravention may be one occurring at the time the inspector detects it or it may have occurred and is likely to continue to be repeated. This last matter deals with the situation where an activity is carried on at intermittent intervals and is not occurring when the inspector visits. If, however, he is of the opinion that when the activity is being carried out there will be a contravention he may serve an improvement notice.

As can be seen from the section the inspector when he decides to serve an improvement notice must satisfy a number of requirements. These are intended to give the recipient of the notice the full details of the contravention, what is needed to remedy it and the period of time within which that must be done. The period of time within which an appeal may be made to an industrial tribunal is 21 days. The time allowed for the notice to be complied with must not be less than 21 days and must be sufficient to allow the execution of any necessary works.

Section 22 deals with prohibition notices and states:

(1) This section applies to any activities which are being or are likely to be carried out by or under the control of any person, being activities to or in relation to which any of the relevant statutory provisions apply or will, if the activities are so carried on, apply.

(2) If as regards any activities to which this section applies an inspector is of the opinion that, as carried on or likely to be carried on by or under the control of the person in question, the activities involve or, as the case may be, will involve a risk of serious personal injury, the inspector may serve on that person a notice (in this Part referred to as 'a prohibition notice').

(3) A prohibition notice shall –
    (a) state that the inspector is of the said opinion;
    (b) specify the matters which in his opinion give or, as the case may be, will give rise to the said risk;
    (c) Where in his opinion any of those matters involves or, as the case may be, will involve a contravention of any of the relevant statutory provisions, state that he is of that opinion, specify the provision or provisions as to which he is of that opinion, and give particulars of the reasons why he is of that opinion; and
    (d) direct that the activities to which the notice relates shall not be carried on by or under the control of the person on whom the notice is served unless the matters specified in the notice in pursuance of paragraph (b) above and any associated contravention of provisions so specified in pursuance of paragraph (c) above have been remedied.

(4) A direction contained in a prohibition notice in pursuance of sub-section (3)(d) above shall take effect –
    (a) at the end of the period specified in the notice; or
    (b) if the notice so declares, immediately.

Sub-section (1) defines the application of the section. The section applies to activities which are being or are likely to be carried on, and those activities are or will be subject to relevant statutory provisions. The fact that the provisions in the section can be used when activities are likely to be carried out means that a prohibition notice may be served before any activity begins at all.

Sub-section (2) contains the most important part of the whole section. This part is the requirement that there has to be a risk of serious personal injury. If there is a risk of serious personal injury, and this is for the inspector to decide, then a prohibition notice can be served. If, however, there is not a risk of serious personal injury then the provisions in the section cannot be used.

Sub-section (3) sets out the details the inspector is required to provide so that the recipient of the prohibition notice is fully informed of all the relevant matters. The notice is also to direct that the activities are not to be carried out until matters specified in the notice have been remedied.

Sub-section (4) indicates clearly the strength and importance of a prohibition notice. The notice may direct that the activities shall stop either at the end of a specified period or immediately. The effect of service of a prohibition notice with an immediate effect on a building contractor can be substantial. Difficulties are caused to completion of the contract, to the client and, possibly, lead to a claim for liquidated damages.

Sections 23 and 24 contain provisions which supplement improvement and prohibition notices. In the service of a notice the inspector may give directions as to the measures to be taken to remedy any contravention. In doing this the inspector may use an approved code of practice and a choice of different ways to remedy the contravention. If a notice is served which is not to take immediate effect, the inspector may withdraw the notice or extend the time specified in the notice.

An appeal may be made against the service of either an improvement or a prohibition notice, within 21 days of its service, to an industrial tribunal. If an appeal is made against an improvement notice the making of that appeal automatically suspends the operation of the notice until the appeal is finally disposed of or the appeal is withdrawn. In the case of a prohibition notice the notice will only be suspended if the industrial tribunal so directs. The person making the appeal must apply to the tribunal for that direction.

In dealing with an appeal the tribunal may either cancel or affirm the notice. If the notice is affirmed the tribunal may modify it as the tribunal thinks fit. In order to assist the tribunal in dealing with matters which could be highly technical assessors may be appointed.

Enforcement

In order to allow an inspector of an enforcing authority to discharge properly the functions of the 1974 Act and relevant provisions it is necessary to provide the inspector with wide powers. There are, therefore, a number of provisions, mainly in Section 20, which provide these powers. An inspector has power to enter premises, taking with him others if necessary, and to make inspections and take samples. He may make investigations and question staff. He may inspect and make copies of entries in books and other documents which have to be kept by law. He can require any person to afford him facilities and give him assistance for any matter within that person's control and for which that person has responsibilities.

All the matters we have considered constitute criminal offences if they are not observed. Under Section 33 the various offences are listed. In general it may be said that the more serious offences can be tried in the Crown Court on indictment. The less serious offences are dealt with by summary trial in the magistrates court. The difference between the two is that on conviction in the Crown Court the offender may be sent to prison for not more than two years, or a fine imposed, or both be imposed. In the magistrates court the fine may not exceed £5,000.

In prosecuting for offences companies are frequently charged. As a company is a separate legal entity this means that in the ordinary course of events officers of the company are not prosecuted as individuals. This can mean that the true offenders escape prosecution and punishment. In order to prevent this happening with safety offences Section 37 sets out the circumstances whereby officers of corporate bodies may be prosecuted. If an offence has been committed by a corporate body which was committed with the consent or connivance of, or to have been attributable to any neglect on the part of any director, manager, secretary or similar office of the corporate body, then that person is guilty of an offence as well as the corporate body. Any such person may be prosecuted and punished in the same way as the company.

Regulations

There are a number of regulations made under both the Factories Act 1961 and the Health and Safety at Work etc Act 1974 which affect the construction industry. Some of these regulations, mainly those made under the Factories Act 1961, apply solely to the construction industry, other apply generally to industries including the construction industry.

All these regulations are detailed and therefore it is not possible to do more than consider their general provisions. For fuller detail the individual regulations will have to be consulted.

The Construction (General Provisions) Regulations 1961

These regulations apply to building operations and works of engineering construction when undertaken by way of trade or business or for any industrial or commercial undertaking or by any public body. The regulations are to be discharged by every contractor and employer of workmen.

Every contractor and employer who normally employs more than 20 persons is to appoint a person who is suitably experienced and qualified to act as a safety supervisor. That person may act for two or more contractors and employers.

There are detailed provisions regarding the guarding of excavations and the timbering of excavations. The timbering has to be adequate according to the nature of the ground. All such work shall be done under the direction of a competent person. With cofferdams and caissons there must be supervision in their construction, alteration or dismantling. There must also be daily inspection by a competent person. In the demolition of a building the work must be under the supervision of a competent person and specified precautions taken. Any infringement of a regulation is a criminal offence.

The Construction (Working Places) Regulations 1966

These regulations apply in exactly the same way as the regulations just considered. The regulations are mainly concerned with scaffolds. There is, however, a requirement that there be suitable and sufficient safe access to and egress from every place at which people work and that access and egress shall be maintained. So far as scaffolds are concerned they are not to be erected, altered or dismantled except under the immediate supervision of a competent person and where possible by competent workmen possessing adequate experience in such work. Materials to be used in scaffolds are to be inspected by a competent person on each occasion before being used. All materials used in scaffolds are to be of good construction, sound and of adequate strength.

Every scaffold is to be properly maintained and so fixed, secured or placed as to prevent accidental displacement. No scaffold is to be partly erected or dismantled and remain in a condition that it is capable of being used unless there is a prominent warning notice that it is not to be used and access to the scaffold is, so far as is reasonably practicable, blocked off.

The regulations contain detailed provisions as to how a scaffold shall be erected so as to be stable and secure. Those scaffolds which are to be used as working platforms, and from which a person might fall more than two metres, have to be of minimum width with toe boards and guard rails. Provisions regarding ladders are that they are to be of suitable material, of adequate strength and proper attention paid to their safe use. In order that the regulations are observed properly the regulations require that reports be made and a prescribed record kept of inspections made. The record is to be available to inspection.

The Construction (Health and Welfare) Regulations 1966

These regulations, some of which have been repealed, apply in the same circumstances as those just considered. A contractor is to provide at or in the immediate vicinity of every site, for the use of persons employed and conveniently accessible to them, adequate and suitable accommodation for shelter in bad weather and for depositing clothing not worn at work. Other requirements, which depend on the number employed on the site, are that there shall be facilities to dry clothing and warm the worker, for taking meals and for heating food if heated food is not provided. Drinking water, clearly marked as such, has to be available at suitable points. Washing facilities, the type of which have to vary with the number of workers, are to be provided. The contractor has to provide sanitary accommodation, the number of conveniences varying with the number of employees.

The Health and Safety (First Aid) Regulations 1981

These regulations, which apply generally and not just to the construction industry, replaced the regulations dealing with first aid in the Construction (Health and Welfare) Regulations 1966. The regulations require that an employer shall provide or ensure the provision of such equipment and facilities as are adequate and appropriate in the circumstances for rendering first aid to his employees. An employer shall provide or ensure the provision of a sufficient number of persons suitably trained in first aid. In certain circumstances the employer may, instead of having a trained first-aider, put another person in charge of the equipment and facilities and to be responsible for securing help from a doctor or nurse. The employees are to be informed of the first-aid facilities. A self-employed person is to provide or ensure the provision of equipment as is adequate and appropriate in the circumstances to enable him to render first aid to himself.

Construction (Head Protection) Regulations 1989

These regulations require an employer to provide for his employee suitable head protection to provide protection, so far as is reasonably practicable, against foreseeable risks of injury to the head. A suitable head protection would be one which conformed to a proper standard, such as British Standard BS5240. The regulations apply to building operations and engineering construction. The employer has to ensure, so far as is reasonably practicable, that his employees wear the head protection unless there is no foreseeable risk of injury to his head other than by his falling. This same duty applies on every employer, self-employed person or employee to persons over whom they have control. The person in control of a site may make rules regarding the wearing of head protection. There is a duty on every employee who has been provided with head protection to wear the head protection where the rules require. Employees also have to take reasonable care of the head protection and report any loss or obvious defects. The self-employed are subject to the same duties as employers.

Under the provisions in Sections 11 and 12 of the Employment Act 1989 a Sikh who wears a turban does not have to wear head protection. His failure to do so is not a contravention of the regulations.

Control of Substances Hazardous to Health Regulations 1988

These regulations were amended by the Control of Substances Hazardous to Health (Amendment) Regulations 1992. The regulations specify certain chemicals which are not to be imported, supplied or used. The main provisions in the regulations are that no employer is to carry out work liable to expose any employee to any substance hazardous to health unless he has made a suitable and sufficient assessment of the risks to their health from such work. The assessment is to be reviewed if it is no longer valid or if there has been a significant change in the work to which the assessment relates. As a result of that assessment the employer has to ensure that dangers from substances hazardous to health are either prevented or controlled. The control is, so far as is reasonably practicable, to be secured by measures other than personal protective equipment. Where, however, control is not possible without personal protective equipment then that must be provided. In certain circumstances employees must be subject to health surveillance, and where that is done records must be kept for a prescribed number of years. Information, instruction and training must be given, as appropriate, to persons exposed to substances hazardous to health. For certain prescribed substances there are occupational exposure standards and maximum exposure limits. By the use of these employees are to be protected from undue exposure over both short and long periods of time.

The Management of Health and Safety at Work Regulations 1992

These regulations follow the pattern of those just considered in that they require a risk assessment to be made. In these regulations the assessment is to be suitable and sufficient to assess the risks to the health and safety of his employees to which they are exposed at work, and the same risks to persons who are not his employees which arise out of or in connection with the conduct by him of his undertaking. The purpose of the assessment is to identify what measures are required to comply with requirements and prohibitions under the relevant statutory provisions. The same duty is imposed on a self-employed person. Assessments are to be reviewed if they are no longer valid or there has been a substantial change in the matters to which they relate. If an employer has five or more employees the significant findings of the assessment and the employees especially at risk are to be recorded. Every employer is required to make appropriate arrangements, having regard to the nature of his activities and the size of his undertaking, and to record the arrangements if he employs five or more employees. Employees are to be provided with health surveillance if appropriate. Every employer is to appoint one or more competent persons to assist him in the measures needed to comply with the requirements and prohibitions placed on him. To be a competent person a person must have sufficient training, experience, knowledge and other qualities. Every employer shall establish and give effect to an appropriate procedure where there is a serious and imminent danger to persons at work. Adequate information is to be provided for all employees as to risks to health and safety revealed by the assessment, the preventative and protective measures, the appropriate procedures and the persons in control.

A matter of importance to the construction industry is the requirement that an employer who has another employer's employees come to work in his undertaking is to provide them with comprehensible information as to risks to health or safety from working in his undertaking and the measures taken to comply with the requirements and prohibitions imposed on him under the relevant statutory provisions. The same provision applies to a self-employed person.

The regulations require every employer to have regard to his employees' capabilities as regards health and safety. The employees must also be given adequate health and safety training when they are recruited, when exposed to new or increased risks to health or safety and when changes are made with machinery and equipment. Employees are to use machinery and equipment in accordance with their training. They must also inform the employer or other person with the specific responsibility of any serious and immediate danger to health and safety and of any shortcoming in the employer's health and safety arrangements.

INDEX